T0291364

Agents of Innovation

Agents of Innovation: Entrepreneurs, Facilitators and Intrapreneurs

BY

LOUIS JACQUES FILION

HEC Montréal, Canada

United Kingdom – North America – Japan – India – Malaysia – China

Emerald Publishing Limited
Emerald Publishing, Floor 5, Northspring, 21-23 Wellington Street, Leeds LS1 4DL

First edition 2024

British Library Cataloguing in Publication Data
A catalogue record for this book is available from the British Library

ISBN: 978-1-83797-013-1 (Print)
ISBN: 978-1-83797-012-4 (Online)
ISBN: 978-1-83797-014-8 (Epub)

To Christine, with love. Many thanks for your endless support.

Table of Contents

About the Author

Louis Jacques Filion, MA, MBA, PhD, DHC, is an Emeritus Professor in the Department of Entrepreneurship and Innovation at HEC Montréal, where he managed the Rogers-J.-A.-Bombardier Chair of Entrepreneurship for more than 20 years. He is frequently invited as a guest professor by numerous universities including the Fribourg School of Management (HEG-FR) in Switzerland. He has published more than 20 books, 100 papers and 100 case studies. His research is concerned mainly with the activity systems and imaginative mindsets of entrepreneurs and other agents of innovation. He is a Fellow of the ICSB.

About the Contributors

Prof PhD Rico J. Baldegger is a Professor of Strategy, Innovation and Entrepreneurship and Dean of the Fribourg School of Management (HEG-FR), Switzerland. He studied at the Universities of St Gallen and Fribourg in Switzerland. His research focuses on innovative start-ups, the entrepreneurial behaviour of individuals and organizations, and the phenomenon of rapid-growth companies. He has published 16 books and numerous papers. Since the early 1990s, he has also managed a business development support company. He is what can be described a 'serial entrepreneur', having created many companies. He is a fellow of the ICSB.

Cândido Borges is a Professor of Entrepreneurship and Innovation at the Universidade Federal de Goiás, Goiânia, Brazil, where he is also Director of the Entrepreneurship and Innovation Research Laboratory. He obtained his PhD at HEC Montréal. His current research focuses on entrepreneurship, new ventures and entrepreneurship policy.

Fernando Dolabela is a prolific author. One of his books, 'O segredo de Luísa', was a best seller and is still a long seller 20 years later. Dolabela designed one of the most popular entrepreneurship teaching programs in Brazil, for universities and basic education (ages 4–17 years). He has delivered workshops to more than 5,000 university teachers, preparing them for entrepreneurship education. His experience with youth education is exceptional and his 'Pedagogia Empreendedora' methodology has been implemented by institutions in more than 150 cities in numerous countries including Brazil, Argentina, Chile, Peru and several African countries (through UNO-UNIDO).

Joëlle Hafsi earned her Bachelor's and Master's degrees from the Sorbonne in Paris and her PhD from Boston University. Specializing in case writing, she has published numerous cases in Business Policy, Leadership and Entrepreneurship.

Francine Richer, MA (Andragogy), Université de Montréal, is a specialist in andragogy and a professional writer, and was an associate member of the SME Development and Succession Chair at HEC Montreal for 20 years. She has conducted research and published several case studies as well as two books on strategies for women entrepreneurs wishing to start their own firms or take over family businesses.

Foreword

A well-known entrepreneur recently tweeted: 'You have to be an entrepreneur to understand an entrepreneur'. At first glance, it seems like a reasonable thing to say. If you've never launched a business, how can you possibly understand the passions, the struggles, the failures, the suffering, the doubts, the successes and the satisfactions experienced by these 'agents of innovation?'

But Louis Jacques Filion doesn't agree, and you'll quickly understand why as you read the stories of the entrepreneurs, facilitators and intrapreneurs that this specialist has presented with such finesse in his book. These six very different life histories, unfolding at different times and on different continents, gradually lift the veil on what it means to innovate in business. The author and his co-authors have clearly mastered the art of unravelling the mysteries of the entrepreneurial mindset. They do an outstanding job of telling the stories of these six inspiring people!

They uncover, recount and share their secrets:

The name of Coco Chanel evokes fashion, perfume and jewellery – but what do we really know about the tumultuous life, the creativity and the entrepreneurial qualities of one of the first women ever to build a business empire?

Quebecers are familiar with Couche-Tard, but did you know that Alain Bouchard built his Circle K empire by becoming a master of acquisitions, leveraging a single corner store into a network of nearly 15,000 stores in more than 30 countries?

The devil is in the details, or so the saying goes. It's not enough to have a vision; as with most other things in life, execution is key. Without Réal Plourde's organizational skills and his flair for staff recruitment and talent management, who knows if Alain Bouchard would have achieved the same level of success?

When Pierre Nelis first joined Softimage, who would have guessed that he would play such a major role in the firm's spectacular success, and go on to create the Inno-Centre network as a way of putting his facilitation skills to work for other entrepreneurs?

Do you remember the slogan 'You don't wear the same tie every day, so why wear the same watch?' And do you know who really invented the Swatch? You might be surprised to learn that it was the same person who later went on to launch Creaholic, a veritable nursery of Swiss innovation, with its own innovative organizational model, 'capitalist kholkhoz'. The riveting story of Elmar Mock illustrates his many facets as an inventor, intrapreneur and entrepreneur and reveals his love of metaphors as vehicles for his ideas, dreams and passions.

If ever there was an archetypal uninventive environment, it would be the business school (well, perhaps I'm exaggerating a bit here). It's difficult to imagine how someone could shake up the academic world and revolutionize its teaching methods sufficiently to create one of the most innovative institutions in the world, and then transform it into a global phenomenon in just a few short years. Emerson De Almeida, with his tremendous powers of persuasion, energy and organizational strength, did all this and more!

Louis Jacques and his co-authors look at these stories from different angles and answer many questions in the process.

The life histories of these six people who changed the world will move you, stir you to dream and – who knows – may even ignite your own innovative or entrepreneurial fire. I encourage you to immerse yourself in their stories, enjoy their adventures and appreciate the many subtleties presented so skillfully by Louis Jacques and his team.

Yves Pigneur
Professor, University of Lausanne
Inventor, with Alex Osterwalder, of the 'Business Model Canvas'

Preface

We live in a world of innovation, where new elements add value and help to improve our lives. As a result, the subject of innovation is becoming increasingly popular as time goes by. People are keener than ever before to understand innovation and the innovative process. Of course, not all of them will become innovators. Many will go on to work with people involved in the practice of innovation, such as entrepreneurs. But even in a supporting role, they will need to understand who these people are, how they think, what they do and how they do it.

Because of their genuine interest in innovation, they all earn the title of *innovationist.* Their understanding of innovation makes their relationships with people who practice it much easier. It also helps them to understand the world they live in. Others may use this first step to build their own culture of innovation and become more creative in what they do. Those who take this additional step are called *agents of innovation.*

The case histories in this book are outstanding examples that will inspire anyone who wants to become an innovationist or an agent of innovation. Practical exercises have also been included to help structure their innovative potential and prepare to become involved in innovation-related activities. Innovation requires a particular pattern of thinking that includes a mix of imagination and learning about specific subjects, along with continuous learning.

As a reader, whether you are an artist or an engineer, or anything in between, you will find something in these cases to interest you and make you learn. The stories chosen for this book illustrate some of the many different configurations that exist in the world of innovation. They will help you to understand the progression of different types of *agents of innovation* and the processes they design in order to generate and implement innovations. Combined with the exercises suggested at the end of the book, they form a learning tool that is both structural and practical.

The stories in this book focus on six *agents of innovation*: two entrepreneurs, two entrepreneurial facilitators and two intrapreneurs.[1] Regardless of whether you decide to become an *innovationist* or an *agent of innovation*, by working as an entrepreneur, a facilitator or an intrapreneur, you will at least be aware and have a better understanding of what is involved in the practice of innovation. This is

[1]For the sake of simplicity, 'entrepreneurial facilitators' will be referred to as 'facilitators'.

something that you can apply in your personal and professional life, whatever your job and whatever the context.

This book was designed to provide a proactive learning experience. It transmits knowledge through stories of real-life experience and will encourage you as a reader to think creatively about what it means to build your own culture of innovation.

I hope you enjoy the stories and are inspired by them. The suggested exercises at the end should sharpen your desire to become more creative and help you to feel more comfortable in our world of innovation.

Louis Jacques Filion

Acknowledgements

I am very grateful to the subjects of these cases. They were generous with their time and patient enough to answer questions during numerous interviews over a period of many years: Alain Bouchard and his assistant Martine Coutu, Réal Plourde, Pierre Nelis, Elmar Mock and his wife Helene and Emerson de Almeida. Additional materials were added regularly, until the final versions of the cases were produced. These case studies have been used extensively in MBA programs in Asia, Europe and North America. They are very popular among students.

Many thanks also to my co-authors, especially to Joëlle Hafsi, a case writing specialist who co-wrote three of the case studies in this book (Alain Bouchard, Réal Plourde and Pierre Nelis). Special appreciation goes to Francine Richer who undertook the gigantic task of reviewing the available documentation on Coco Chanel. She and I read and analyzed more than a dozen books and countless other documents, including films, over a period of several years. I am grateful to Rico Baldegger for his contributions and thank him sincerely for organizing numerous meetings with Elmar Mock. I also thank Candido Borges and Fernando Dolabela who were involved in arranging and attending my interviews and meetings with Emerson de Almeida, and in co-writing the case.

Thanks to the HEC Montréal Case Centre (http://www.hec.ca/en/case_centre). The catalogue includes more than 2,000 case studies and other teaching aids (mostly in French) for management courses. To see other case studies on the same topic and order them for use in the classroom, please visit www.evalorix.com.

My heartfelt thanks go to my colleagues Franck Bares, Luis Cisneros and Mai Thai, and to Brigitte Campeau and Rachel Bonnier, from HEC Montréal's Department of Entrepreneurship and Innovation, for their unflagging support over the years. Leo-Paul Dana, Ayman ElTarabishy, Mark Freel, Dafna Kariv, Ken O'Neil and George Solomon were also kind enough to offer comments and support, and I am grateful to them.

Note: In the case studies, references may not be provided for some of the quotes. These quotes are excerpts from interviews conducted by the author with the subject of the case.

Louis Jacques Filion

Introduction

The Age of Innovation and the Emergence of Innovationism

Thousands of products and services are created every year throughout the world, but many of them fail. Why? There are many reasons for this. For example, the people who create and launch an innovation may never have had contact with or learnt from someone who has innovated successfully. It is useful to start by understanding how innovations are generated and learning about the people who generate them: why and how do they go about doing this? Whatever you do in life, whatever your craft or profession, the basic process is always the same: learn gradually, step by step. The same applies to innovation. The good news is that it can be learnt.

As a teacher of entrepreneurship and innovation, I am often asked about how to deal with agents of innovation or how to become more innovative. My students, at all levels including experienced MBAs, want to know how they should prepare and what they need to learn. 'Would it help to work for an entrepreneur or other agent of innovation? What do I need to know about innovative thinking and practice? What if I simply want to be more creative in my own personal life? Where can I find examples on which to model my own future self and activities?' And what if they do not want to become agents of innovation themselves, but prefer to work in a service sector with entrepreneurs or small business owner-managers as their customers or subcontractors? The life stories in this book will provide some answers to many of their questions. They show that each person involved in innovation has to find their own way.

We live in an ever-changing world where we often need to innovate in order to survive.

Colleges, universities and business schools have traditionally focused on preparing people to become managers. Nowadays, however, managers and others who work in organizations need to learn not only how to adapt to change, but also how to *generate* it. This is a process known as innovation: the contribution of new products, services and/or processes that add value. The number of people wanting to become agents of innovation is growing steadily. Entrepreneurs are seen as the ultimate examples, but facilitators and intrapreneurs, many of whom are inventors of new processes, add value to the enterprises that employ them. And people who work with agents of innovation in all kinds of service sectors, including lawyers, consultants, psychologists, subcontractors and so on, need to understand how these agents of innovation think and how they work.

'An image is worth a thousand words', or so the saying goes. Conventional wisdom suggests that real-life examples are worth dozens of theories. This book presents the life stories of six agents of innovation who had to overcome difficulties and be highly creative and tenacious in their respective fields of activity. Becoming a successful agent of innovation, whether as an entrepreneur, a facilitator or an intrapreneur, involves facing the challenges that often stand in the way of the creative process. The people whose life stories you will read in this book were able to do that. They serve as powerful role models for anyone who wants to improve their understanding of the fascinating world of self-actualization through innovation.

The Terms Used in This Book

The terms used in this book are known but have sometimes been defined differently by different authors, depending on the context in which they are used. The following paragraphs explain their meanings as they are used in this book.

The main theme of this book is *innovation*. An innovation is something new that adds value. An *innovator* is the person who designs and/or creates it. *Entrepreneurs* not only design innovations but also create and implement them, usually in the form of new products or services, and set up an enterprise to produce and sell them. The innovations they generate will occupy new spaces in the market. *Facilitators* devise process innovations that help entrepreneurs to succeed and realize their visions and projects. They are commonly seen in finance, technology, law, marketing and other support sectors. Their role is to help the products or services created by entrepreneurs to win a space in the market. *Intrapreneurs* play a similar role to entrepreneurs or facilitators, but as creative employees within the organizations that employ them.

There are two terms that are used extensively in this book. The first, *innovationist*, is used to refer to people who develop an interest in innovation. The second, *agent of innovation*, is used to refer to entrepreneurs, facilitators and intrapreneurs. Many entrepreneurs maintain their interest in innovation and their creative ability to generate innovations throughout their lives. Innovation becomes part of their way of thinking. It is what motivates and energizes them.

Innovation From Different Perspectives

Organizations today need *innovationists* with the potential to become *agents of innovation*. Societies need entrepreneurs to improve living conditions and facilitators who understand innovation, innovation processes and their entrepreneur's vision, and can support its application. Organizations need intrapreneurs, not only to support, improve, develop and implement value-added projects but also to redefine and re-energize those that already exist. All these agents of innovation must be able to think outside the box and constantly improve or renew what already exists. Agents of innovation make a difference in the quality of life of the societies in which they live.

There are steps in whatever we do. Many people start out as innovationists, developing an interest in the process of innovation. Innovationists are much more likely to support change in an organization and become instrumental in making it happen. They tend to become part of the forward movement instead of a weight that pulls the organization to a standstill or even backwards.

There are, of course, many different levels of innovation, from the 'incremental' innovations that help to improve and facilitate a company's operations, to the more 'radical' innovations that revolutionize entire sectors, such as Elmar Mock's invention of the Swatch and Pierre Nelis' transformation of Softimage's marketing approach. In some cases, an innovation can be a creative adaptation of something that already exists.

To understand the activity systems of organizational actors, it is useful to study not only the main actor but also the supporting cast. If we take the technological or manufacturing field as an example, it is impossible to understand how an enterprise works unless we consider not only its engineers and technology experts, but also the people who support them, in every area of the enterprise's activity.

The same applies to most other fields: architecture, information systems, law, accounting, consulting and the different areas of management, such as marketing, finance, operations and so on. Organizations in all these fields rely on trained technicians to carry out the support activities that are essential to their operations. People specialized in other areas such as human behaviour, technology and law are also often required.

There are currently not enough people who are educated to become *innovationists*. Innovation and entrepreneurial activity require inputs from a variety of people, each with their own complementary expertise, in both the technology sector and in other aspects of organizational life. Organizations benefit greatly from people who have become *innovationists* and can understand how agents of innovation think and act.

Entrepreneurs may create the groundswell and lead the process of designing and implementing innovations, but they need to be surrounded by people who understand what designing and implementing innovation is all about. Entrepreneurship involves living with the uncertainty of creating something that does not exist. By understanding and becoming familiar with the specifics of innovation and entrepreneurship, the entrepreneur's supporting cast becomes more creative and more efficient in their own spheres and lives.

Cultivating an Attitude Conducive to Innovation

The life stories that follow provide answers to many of the questions asked not only by would-be agents of innovation, but also by would-be innovationists, people who are curious about innovation and/or the entrepreneurial world or who simply want to become more innovative in what they do.

Twenty or 30 years ago, entrepreneurship education was aimed at people who wanted to create a business. They were a minority. If 15 people enroled in an optional venture creation course, it was a good year. Nowadays, thousands of students in colleges, universities and business schools enrol in dozens of optional courses on entrepreneurship, venture creation, innovation, small business development, creativity, intrapreneurship and so on, every year. Innovation is becoming increasingly popular across most sectors, and more people than ever before are interested in the different aspects of venture creation. More than 75% of firms are created by teams in which several partners act as facilitators. They come from many different specialties, such as finance, law, technology, marketing and others. A basic knowledge of innovation and entrepreneurial activity helps them to become more effective in supporting the entrepreneur who leads the innovation process. This is now a concern for almost all students, regardless of their fields of study.

Many entrepreneurs and some intrapreneurs are also inventors of products. Sometimes they not only invent the products, they also contribute creatively to some or all the steps needed to take those products to the market. Sometimes, facilitators are needed to design imaginative marketing processes that will make the product or service more successful. Amazon was created to sell books online. However, the ingenuity of the entrepreneur and his facilitators made it possible to expand the service to all kinds of additional products. Facilitators have become extremely creative and instrumental in all kinds of activities, such as finance, especially for new venture creation, development and acquisition processes, technology use, human resource expertise, creative approaches to international markets and so on.

Inspiring Life Stories

The six chapters that follow present two life stories from each of the three main categories of agents of innovation mentioned above. The stories show how these agents of innovation grew and evolved from their early interest in innovation. They describe the circumstances, steps and contexts that led these protagonists to become creative and innovative, and to build or help build successful enterprises. They will certainly serve as inspiration to readers who are thinking of becoming innovationists and would like to improve their understanding of how the innovative process works.

Section 1: Entrepreneurs

The stories begin with two outstanding entrepreneurs. **Coco Chanel** is generally considered to be the first female global entrepreneur. Her story is colourful and provides information about many aspects of the creative process. **Alain Bouchard** began with a single convenience store and grew it into an empire of more than 15,000 stores employing more than 125,000 people in 30 countries.

Section 2: Facilitators

The two facilitators both made major contributions to the firms that employed them. **Réal Plourde** and **Pierre Nelis** spent their lives facilitating the success of the entrepreneurs who were wise enough to hire them. **Réal Plourde** played a major role as Alain Bouchard's partner in the development of Couche-Tard/Circle K. As for **Pierre Nelis**, he was a key player in the development of Softimage and continued in his role as a facilitator after Microsoft took over the business. As an intrapreneur, he eventually went on to develop an impressive network of entrepreneurs, CEOs and top managers who act as part-time small business consultants and external facilitators at Inno-Centre, a non-profit organization that supports new venture creators and small business owner-managers focused on growth.

Section 3: Intrapreneurs

The two intrapreneurs, **Elmar Mock** and **Emerson de Almeida**, each created movements that ultimately transformed the firms that employed them, by inventing, re-energizing and innovating. Like many intrapreneurs, they also went through periods in which they became entrepreneurs launching their own firms. Later in their lives, they both became external facilitators, supporting innovative initiatives in a wide range of organizations.

Being Innovative: Learning, Succeeding and Excelling Continually

The stories presented in this book suggest that the field of entrepreneurship may benefit from being broadened to include *innovationists* and *agents of innovation*: not just entrepreneurs, but also facilitators and intrapreneurs, and eventually other categories of organizational actors who contribute different forms of innovations or provide support for innovation. They all serve as learning models for aspiring innovationists and agents of innovation.

The six life stories were written to be read by anyone with an interest in organizational life, regardless of their background and context. There are no specific analysis grids because these cases can be used in many fields of study. Instead, readers are invited to develop their own grids relevant to their own fields and subjects of interest, whatever they may be.

If you want to be innovative, you need to learn how to understand and approach contexts. This is clear from the stories of the imaginative, tenacious people described in this book. Choosing to be innovative is an important step on the path to self-transformation and self-fulfilment – in other words, to becoming better users of ourselves and our potential.

A list of questions is proposed at the end of each case study. There are no absolute answers to these questions; it all depends on your perspective as an individual. For example, if you are a student of psychology, you may not have the same perspective as a student of law, marketing or engineering. The same applies to the exercises suggested at the end of this book. They were designed, as far as possible, to be relevant to readers from different specialty areas.

Section 4: Lessons for Innovationists and Aspiring Agents of Innovation

This section discusses similarities and differences of the three categories of agents of innovation whose examples are presented in this book. A table shows characteristics of each category. Reflections suggest some food for thought about which category could suit better the reader.

Appendix: The Seven Exercises

From Innovationist to Agent of Innovation

Exercise 1 Preliminary Self-Assessment
Exercise 2 Defining your Own Creative Model for Innovation
Exercise 3 Identifying a Need, Creating an Opportunity, Contributing an Innovation
Exercise 4 Defining a Vision
Exercise 5 Internal Ecosystem – Building an Internal Relations System to Support Innovation
Exercise 6 External Ecosystem – Building an External Relations System to Support Innovation
Exercise 7 Becoming Innovative – Acting as an Agent of Innovation

Section 1
Life Stories of Entrepreneurs

The life stories of entrepreneurs are fascinating because they pull back the curtain on the innovative process. As is often the case, the people with whom entrepreneurs are in contact during their childhood leave a profound impression. Chance meetings and events can also change the course of a person's life.

Entrepreneurs are people who design and create something that did not exist before. They are usually optimistic about themselves and about what they do, but they risk humiliation because they work by trial and error. For some, social networks provide support. For others, the opposite is true. Naturally, there are different levels in both creation and innovation. Entrepreneurs must learn to cope with uncertainty and manage the risks that are inherent in any kind of innovation.

To do this, they must maintain a balance between their perception of what is happening in the outside environment and what they themselves can do to add value to it. They must then develop internal and external relations systems composed of people who understand them and will support them at every phase of the process, but especially during the exploration phase.

When you read the life stories of these two intrepid people who helped to change the world, try to identify the aspects that are relevant to you. While the stories focus on the protagonists' professional lives, they also mention elements of their private lives. This is especially true for Coco Chanel, who emerged as a fashion designer and an entrepreneur in the 'Roaring Twenties' after the difficult years of the First World War.

Coco Chanel

Gabrielle 'Coco' Chanel (1883–1971) led a turbulent life, and, even today, questions remain and certain aspects of her life are still controversial. She was always very careful about the information she released to the media and to the many biographers who wrote books about her.

This case study is probably the first publication to offer a condensed summary of her life. There are countless books, magazine articles, documentaries, videos, films and texts that present different versions of her life, depending on when and by whom they were written or produced. Over the decades, Chanel often changed elements of her story. For example, she fantasized a lot about her father, who abandoned his children after the death of his wife when Coco was just 12-years old. She never saw him again, and often claimed that he had immigrated to the United States and made a fortune.

There are claims that one of her sisters committed suicide, although the reason and circumstances of her death are unknown. Coco Chanel was very discreet and managed to keep most of her personal life secret, including her close relationship with her sisters and with the person she referred to as her nephew.

She revolutionized the world of fashion, not only with the 'look' she created, but by providing women with comfortable clothes. Throughout that period, she developed close personal relationships with artists and entrepreneurs alike. The periods following wars or pandemics tend to be intense, and people tend to take full advantage of their new freedoms. Coco Chanel was no exception.

Her relationships with the Germans during the Second World War have been a source of controversy and remain enigmatic. When the war broke out, she was in her late 50s, living at the Ritz Hotel in Paris, where the German military staff were billeted. She wanted to obtain the release of her nephew who was a prisoner of war in Germany. Indeed, she visited that country on several occasions.

She spent time in Hollywood, where she revolutionized women's clothing in the nascent cinema industry. One of the last major achievements of her life was to design outfits for Jackie Bouvier-Kennedy, who visited Paris in 1961 with her husband, American President John F. Kennedy. Back in Washington, journalists asked the President what he thought of his trip to France. 'I'm the man who accompanied Jackie Kennedy to Paris', he said. The clothing Chanel (78-years old) designed for the First Lady had a tremendous impact on global women's fashion, in terms of shape, texture and colour (American Experience PBS, 2013).

Chanel died in 1971, aged 88. She remained active and creative to the end. The evening before her death, a friend drove her home to her Ritz apartment. 'I'll see you tomorrow at my office', said Chanel. These were fitting last words for a woman known for her vitality and energy.

Alain Bouchard

What more can be said about a man who started out as a convenience store owner and ended his career as the CEO of a business empire employing more than 125,000 people? As you read this story, you will discover a man who developed a passion for small neighbourhood stores very early in life and never lost it. As he launched his empire, he was also wise enough to surround himself with facilitators who were both supportive and innovative.

When Alain Bouchard was still a child, his family would sometimes go for a drive on Sunday afternoons to see what kinds of businesses were in their local area. They had just moved to a new region after a bankruptcy, and Alain's father was thinking of launching a new business. He had no money, but he still liked to identify possibilities, assess their potential and talk about buying them. These family outings would have a tremendous impact on the entire family. All the Bouchard children went on to become entrepreneurs at some level.

Alain Bouchard began to make acquisitions quite soon after starting his first business. He quickly became familiar with the concept of making acquisitions instead of starting new businesses from scratch. He had learnt the importance of acquisitions from someone he trusted; his father. Alain went on to complete more business acquisitions than almost any other entrepreneur in history – dozens of them, sometimes involving chains worth hundreds of millions, if not billions of dollars.

Even now that he is retired, he still likes to talk about the acquisitions he is considering. Examples include his offer of US $5.6 billion for Caltex in Australia in 2020 and his offer of 20 billion euros for the major French food chain Carrefour in 2021 (105,000 employees, annual sales of 81 billion Euros in 2019). These bids did not lead to transactions, for a variety of reasons outside Bouchard's control, including the French Minister of the Economy's 'polite but firm' refusal to permit the sale of an asset considered to be 'strategic' by the French government. But many of his other acquisitions were successful and contributed to the growth of his company.

Alain Bouchard has always loved to share his enthusiasm for convenience stores. Every year, he would spend several months meeting on a daily basis with store managers, some of whom were newcomers to the organization as a result of acquisitions. He communicated both his passion and his expertise to convince his managers that they should run their stores as he himself would do. The process, referred to as 'Bouchardism' (training managers to run stores as if they owned them) helped to create an innovative culture in a giant multinational organization operating thousands of units. 'Local stores have to adjust to their markets. Their management may be much more complex than most people think', he says.

The interviews conducted with Alain Bouchard over a period of decades reveal a visionary thinker who never stopped reflecting on his organization's market of the future. For example, over the years he considered many different ways of entering the 'ready to eat' market, and even after officially retiring in 2014, he continues to be a builder who thrives while encouraging others to keep improving and 'doing better'.

Point of View, Interpretation and Understanding

I am often asked about the type of analysis grid that should be used to understand and make the most of these life stories. The answer is simple. Read them as if you were reading a novel. Enjoy them. Identify the aspects that interest you and look at how the protagonist deals with them. Becoming an innovationist means learning how to understand contexts. Becoming an agent of innovation means learning how to define and implement innovations and how to create innovative processes.

Look at the 'whys' and the 'hows' of what the person does. For example, a psychologist, a product developer or a financial specialist may all focus on different aspects of why, what and how an agent of innovation acts. Analysis grids can be developed from many perspectives, in different disciplines and emerging fields of study. Undergraduate students will not look at the cases from the same perspective as experienced MBAs or doctoral students.

Some teachers use specific analysis grids for the courses they are teaching, and the case studies they use are written with this grid in mind. This approach can be helpful when exploring a particular aspect in depth. In this book, however, the life stories focus on the protagonists' general innovation activity systems. As a reader, you should experience and enjoy the story first, and then choose the aspects on which to focus in more depth – for example, the person's innovative context and ability to generate innovations. Use the web extensively with as many key words you wish to explore with the different aspects of each case study.

When reading Coco Chanel's story, for example you may wish to think about what caused her to remain creative. What are the contexts and circumstances that led her to keep creating brand new fashion trends?

Like many entrepreneurs, Alain Bouchard was self-taught and continued to learn throughout his life. He has often said that entrepreneurs must reinvent themselves constantly. He himself did this, as he transformed from a convenience store owner-manager to the CEO of a giant multinational corporation.

We live in an era of venture creation, but more than 90% of all new ventures are micro businesses employing fewer than 10 people. Many of the entrepreneurs I study do not want to grow and are happy with a smaller business. Only a handful goes on to become giants. Regardless of the size of their firms, the entrepreneurs and other agents of innovation whose stories are presented in this book were selected because they offer perspectives that should inspire readers to become entrepreneurial and innovative and succeed in their own right, regardless of the type and size of the venture they may wish to create or become involved with.

Discussions

At the end of each case study, questions are proposed to trigger discussions about the case. Other questions can of course be added, depending on the learning context or field of study concerned. There are no absolute answers; participants' views may differ and they may offer up a variety of opinions and possible answers to the questions. The goal is to understand the elements of complexity that characterize the innovative process. When these case studies are used for teaching or as course content, it may be useful to ask the participants to work in pairs before undertaking a group discussion.

References

About Caltex in Australia. https://www.reuters.com/article/us-caltex-australia-m-a-alim-couche-tard-idUSKBN2210XT; https://financialpost.com/news/retail-marketing/couche-tard-drops-caltex-australia-bid-covid-19-fallout

About Carrefour in France, Et Carrefour. https://www.reuters.com/world/americas/exclusive-canadas-couche-tard-drops-20-bln-carrefour-takeover-plan-after-french-2021-01-15/; https://financialpost.com/news/retail-marketing/canadas-couche-tard-said-to-explore-purchase-of-carrefour

American Experience PBS. (2013). JFK in Paris [Video]. YouTube. https://www.youtube.com/watch?v=yXBBUc6tAzw

Chapter 1

Coco Chanel: Building an Empire – Chanel in Three Acts

Francine Richer and Louis Jacques Filion

Abstract

Shortly before the Second World War, a woman who had never accepted her orphan status, Gabrielle Bonheur Chanel, nicknamed 'Little Coco' by her father and known as 'Coco' to her relatives, became the first women in history to build a world-class industrial empire. By 1935, Coco, a fashion designer and industry captain, was employing more than 4,000 workers and had sold more than 28,000 dresses, tailored jackets and women's suits. Born into a poor family and raised in an orphanage, she enjoyed an intense social life in Paris in the 1920s, rubbing shoulders with artists, creators and the rising stars of her time.

Thanks to her entrepreneurial skills, she was able to innovate in her methods and in her trendsetting approach to fashion design and promotion. Coco Chanel was committed and creative, had the soul of an entrepreneur and went on to become a world leader in a brand new sector combining fashion, accessories and perfumes that she would help shape. By the end of her life, she had redefined French elegance and revolutionized the way people dressed.

Keywords: Entrepreneur; new venture creation; fashion; clothing; Twenties (Roaring Twenties); perfume

Agents of Innovation, 5–48

Published under exclusive licence by Emerald Publishing Limited
doi:10.1108/978-1-83797-012-420231001

Case

Coco Chanel: Building an Empire – Chanel in Three Acts[1]

Act One: The Strange Little Hat-Maker[2] (1883–1918)

> If I think about the person I have become, I see that my need for independence developed when I was still a child. I can't say I was unhappy or not cared for. I heard a lot of talk about money from my aunts' servants. They said they'd go to live in the city as soon as they had enough money ... I learned early in life that independence was something you had to earn. Money has always meant just one thing to me: freedom.
>
> – Coco Chanel[3]

Shortly before the Second World War, a woman who had never accepted her orphan status, Gabrielle Bonheur Chanel, nicknamed 'Little Coco' by her father and known as 'Coco' to her relatives, became the first women in history to build a world-class industrial empire. By 1935, Coco, a fashion designer and industry captain, was employing more than 4,000 workers and had sold more than 28,000 dresses, tailored jackets and women's suits. Born into a poor family and raised in an orphanage, she enjoyed an intense social life in Paris in the 1920s, rubbing shoulders with artists, creators and the rising stars of her time.

Thanks to her entrepreneurial skills, she was able to innovate in her methods and in her trendsetting approach to fashion design and promotion. Coco Chanel was committed and creative, had the soul of an entrepreneur, and went on to become a world leader in a brand new sector combining fashion, accessories and perfumes that she would help shape. By the end of her life, she had redefined French elegance and revolutionized the way people dressed.

Unlike other fashion designers, Coco Chanel did not sketch or draw her designs, but sculpted them directly onto the model's body, draping and pinning the fabric. She worked with a cigarette between her lips, her scissors hanging around her neck on a white ribbon. When a garment – a jacket, for example – was finished, and even if it had already been worn by a client, she would, if she felt it was not up to her standards, grab it and rip out the offending element. She said she could only work if she was angry. Karl Lagerfeld, who went on to become the House of Chanel's creative director after Coco's death, confirmed her intensity: 'When she works, she turns into a different person, and is much more serious than the task requires'.

---

[1]Case written by Francine Richer and Louis J. Filion.

[2]This was how Gabrielle Dorziat first heard of Coco Chanel. Cited by Haedrich, Marcel (2008) *Op.cit.* p. 80.

[3]Haedrich, Marcel. *Op.cit.,* p. 31. Free translation from the original French. The people Coco Chanel refers to as her 'aunts' are the nuns at the orphanage where she was raised.

Her sewing skills, learned from her mother and from the nuns at the orphanage where she grew up, were limited and she was by no means a skilled seamstress. Her fashion house became known for its exciting, unusual and even revolutionary designs, and also for the professionalism of its dressmakers and seamstresses.

In Coco Chanel's mind, garments were made to serve women; they had to allow the body to move, and to be free and expressive. She was responsible for innovations such as pants made specifically for women, the 'little black dress' (originally a straight, loose-fitting, almost tube-like garment with three-quarter length sleeves), women's suits, false jewellery, five-string pearl necklaces, silk and satin pyjamas (which she loved to wear), and male-inspired garments and accessories. And, of course, for Chanel No. 5, the perfume *par excellence* for women. Today, Chanel is not just fashion: it is a style, an attitude based on difference, and the ability to invent or reinvent.

Her outstanding success as the founder of an industrial empire and one of the largest fortunes ever to be amassed by a woman was due in large part to her innovative approach and willingness to go beyond the social conventions of her time. From 'fashionista', she went on to become an intense and rigorous designer with entrepreneurial and business management skills that ultimately allowed the House of Chanel to become a synonym of French style and elegance.

Jean Leymarie, who traced her creative and entrepreneurial path through history, wrote this:

> Her success derived from a combination of her own talent, her ability to seize the moment with great flair, and the energy with which she shaped her destiny, managed her business and asserted her taste. Her decisive achievements in her own field and related fields – jewellery, perfume, interior design, show-business and cinema – were also influenced more broadly by the famous people she met and her personal reputation as a hostess and philanthropist.[4]

And yet, the relationship between Coco Chanel and her workers was always characterized by tension and confrontation, and history lost count of the number of times she fired her personal secretary, Lilou.[5] Her relationships with her models were even more intense; she treated them harshly and inconsiderately. During one fitting session, she ran her hand over the model's chest, exclaiming: 'This girl is supposed to be flat-chested, but look at her! She has no breasts, but the dress makes it seem as though she has!'[6]

---

[4]Leymarie, Jean (2010, p.7) Free translation from the original French.

[5]Artuso, Anthony. W. and A. Zalesnik (1987). Case study written by Anthony W. Artuso under the supervision of Professor Abraham Zalesnik.

[6]Gallante, Pierre (1973, p. 213). Free translation from the original French.

The Daughter of Albert Chanel, a Travelling Salesman

> I don't know anything more terrifying than the family.
>
> You're born in it, not of it.
>
> – Coco Chanel[7]

Gabrielle Bonheur Chanel was born in the Poor Hospital in Saumur, on 19 August 1883, the daughter of 28-year-old Albert Chanel and 20-year-old Eugénie Jeanne Devolle.[8] Albert Chanel was not present for the birth; as a travelling salesman, he was on the road, selling 'all types of hosiery and white items', according to the sign on his carriage. He was part of a long family tradition of tradesmen who had made a living harvesting chestnuts, managing nightclubs, producing home-made wine, doing carpentry (signed with the double-C logo that Coco Chanel would later make famous), and peddling various items door-to-door.

Albert Chanel learned the trade of peddling from his father. He was a good salesman with the 'gift of the gab', who stunned potential customers into submission with his charm and loquaciousness. A shameless skirt-chaser, he was often away from home. Gabrielle was the couple's second daughter; they married a year after she was born, in November 1884. There were three subsequent children, a girl and two boys. Eugénie Jeanne Devolle, Coco's mother, was worried and jealous, and she and her children often went with Albert on his sales trips. So Coco Chanel quickly became used to life on the road, spending part of her childhood in the world of textiles and sales.

Eugénie Jeanne's health was fragile, and her children had to take care not only of themselves but also of her. The family lived a miserable life, one that ended for Eugénie Jeanne on 16 February 1895, when she was just 32 years old. Worn out by successive pregnancies, long hours spent sewing and darning, cleaning houses and doing other menial tasks to keep herself and her children, she died as she lived – alone, with her husband away working at the time of her death.[9]

When Coco Chanel spoke of her parents, she described them as an 'ordinary' couple, but blamed her mother's unhappiness and ruin on her intense love for and jealousy of her husband.

Surviving Life in the Orphanage

When his wife died, Albert Chanel sent his three daughters to the orphanage at Aubazine, run by the Holy Heart of Mary congregation of nuns in an ancient

[7]Coco Chanel cited in Picardie, Justine (2011, p. 352).

[8]Saumur is a small town along the Loire river in western France. It is known for its riding school, castle, history and wines.

[9]Artuso, Anthony. W. and A. Zalesnik (1992), *Op. cit.*, p. 323.

Cistercian abbey founded in 1135.[10] At the time, Gabrielle was 11 years old, her sister Julie-Berthe was nearly 12 and the youngest, Antoinette, was just 8. The Chanel boys, Alphonse (10 years old) and Lucien (6 years old), were placed with farmers who used 'hospice children' as labourers. Augustin, born in 1891, died young. His death affected his sister Coco for many years.

After ridding himself of his children, Albert Chanel made a new life for himself and never saw them again. In Coco's imagination, he went to America and made his fortune. She sometimes spoke about how she and her sisters competed for their father's love, and described her relationship with her father as being better before her youngest sister was born.

Coco left the austerity of the orphanage behind her in 1901, when she was 18 years old, and moved to the Notre-Dame boarding house in Moulins to learn a trade. The nuns who kept the boarding house taught their tenants the rudiments of sewing and housekeeping.[11] Coco stayed there for two years, during which time she developed an interest in sewing. Her mother had probably already introduced her to the activity, but with the nuns, the rigour and standard of perfection were at an entirely different level. Coco Chanel told Marcel Haedrich that the nuns had given her a taste 'for order, for comfort, for having things done right, and for chests filled with linens that smell good'.[12]

Adrienne Chanel, her young aunt, friend and confidant, was born in 1882, the youngest of Albert Chanel's 18 brothers and sisters. She also lived at the Notre-Dame boarding house, but as a 'paying student', while Coco was there as a 'charity case'. Coco spent the summer at her Chanel grandparents' home. Her Aunt Louise and husband Paul Costier, who lived at Varennes-sur-Allier (located between Vichy and Moulins), had no children of their own and often had their nieces to visit. Louise taught the girls to make hats, collars and cuffs to decorate their convent uniforms. They read serials and romantic novels cut from the newspapers.

The 'charity cases', without family or money, were educated by the nuns alongside girls from good families, and were treated as second-class citizens. They were not 'socially acceptable' and had no hope of improving their lot. Coco knew she had only herself to rely on. She was stubborn and vowed never to become someone who followed the rules.

When their education was complete, the nuns found jobs for Adrienne and Coco, one as an office clerk and the other as a seamstress, at Sainte-Marie, a former Grampayre house where bourgeois customers went to buy bridal, baby and mourning clothes.

---

[10]Aubazine Orphanage: http://fr.wikipedia.org/wiki/Abbaye_d%27Aubazine.

[11]Moulins is a small town in Auvergne, in the centre of France.

[12]Picardie, Justine (2011) *Op. cit.*, p. 37.

A Citizen of the World

Adrienne and Coco worked at Sainte-Marie from 1903 to 1906. In the early days they lived in an improvised apartment in the attic, but in the spring of 1904 they moved into a very modest room on Rue du Pont-Guinguet, which they decorated nicely, with their own handmade curtains, tablecloths and bed linens. They earned additional money to make ends meet by sewing for bourgeois families and mending officers' uniforms for a local tailor.

They were keen to socialize with the patrons of Moulins many cafés. Most were cavalry officers from the nearby garrison. Coco, a timid but determined and hard-working young woman, was usually reserved and distant, but would occasionally take the microphone to sing one of the only two songs in her repertoire.[13]

Although her given name was Gabrielle, she encouraged the café customers to call her Coco, a nickname given to her by her father because he was afraid people would start calling her Gabby.[14] She would tell people that her father brought her gifts, and that she was his favourite. According to her, Albert Chanel wanted his children to be clean, properly washed with soap from Marseille, with scented hair.

Gabrielle Chanel always seemed somewhat embarrassed about her singing days at La Rotonde, and even more so when Étienne Balsan's name was mentioned.

Étienne Balsan, the Initiator

When she became famous, Coco Chanel would often complicate the lives of her biographers by changing the dates, places, facts and people in her stories. Her stories about her past differed according to the circumstances and her audience, and most owed more to her imagination than to autobiographical truth. This was especially the case for her meeting with Étienne Balsan, because it most probably took place at La Rotonde, during her singing days, in 1904.[15] Balsan was the heir

---

[13]Historians do not agree on the origins of her nickname, Coco. Some suggest, as Gabrielle Chanel herself claimed, that it was coined by her father. Others think it may have been given to her by soldiers who heard her singing the popular song *Qui qu'a vu Coco dans le Trocadero* at a café in Moulins, after she left the orphanage.

[14]Picardie, Justine. *Op. cit.*, p. 20.

[15]Coco Chanel sometimes said she had met Étienne Balsan in Vichy, in 1906, in a more elegant spa setting. There is also a story to the effect that a child was born at the convent in Moulins on 29 November 1904. Was the child really the son of Coco's sister Julia-Berthe, who subsequently married a certain Mr Palasse, who agreed to accept the child as his own, but subsequently abandoned both the boy and his mother? And was it because of Mr Palasse that Julia-Berthe committed suicide? The child, André Palasse, became an orphan when he was just 6 years old, and was known as Coco's nephew. But Isabelle Fiemeyer, who became a close friend of Gabrielle Palasse-Labrunie (André's daughter and Coco's goddaughter) and Justine Picardie, both of them biographers, thought Coco's relationship with her nephew and his daughter was more like that of a mother with her son and granddaughter.

to one of France's largest textile factories. The Balsan family had made their fortune supplying uniforms for the French and British armies.

Étienne Balsan was probably Coco Chanel's first lover. Lucien François, a very well-known Paris fashion writer, described Coco as follows: 'Coco Chanel . . . a ravishing, imperious young woman, with wild ways and a stubborn, youthful face that betrays her doe-like eyes, to such an extent that she seems genderless.'[16]

Étienne Balsan, charmed and amused by his 'wild young woman', gradually became her protector, mentor and financial angel.

In her favourite version of how she met Étienne Balsan, Coco said she was invited to tea by a young man who owned a stable and racehorses. She was 16 years old at the time. The young man kidnapped her and took her to his castle. The story seems more like the desperate dreams of a very young girl. As she herself admitted, throughout her childhood, she just wanted to be loved. Every day, she thought of ways to kill herself.[17]

When they first met in 1904, Étienne Balsan was completing his military service at Moulins. While at school in England, he had developed an interest in horses and hunting. He began his military service in Algeria, in a cavalry regiment. Arrested for sleeping on the job, he was able to have his sentence lifted by successfully treating some of the army horses that had developed an unusual skin disease, using a technique he had learned in England. He was subsequently transferred to Moulins. His love of horses lasted throughout his life.

Étienne Balsan had told his older brothers, Jacques and Robert, that he was not interested in the family business. The least that can be said about him at the time he first met Coco is that he lived well and was accountable to no-one. Whether at his bachelor pad situated at 160 Boulevard Malesherbes in Paris, at his estate in La-Croix-Saint-Ouen or at the old Royallieu monastery near Compiègne, which he converted into a training centre for his horses, he hosted the kind of parties to which everyone wanted to be invited – actors, sports personalities, well-known courtesans, dandies and their mistresses. For some, these were truly the 'good old days'.

In Coco Chanel's turn-of-the-century world, marriage was usually a decision made with the head, not the heart, and the main criterion was generally social status. Love was just for fun, and sexual orientation did not matter.

Étienne Balsan would become Coco's saviour and lover. He invited her to the Grand Café in Place d'Allier. He gave her chocolate – 'les Palets d'or' – which would become a symbol of luxury for her.

In 1906, Coco and Adrienne went to live in Vichy for several months, serving spring water to curists in exchange for tips. For the first time in her life, Coco came into contact with a group of elegant and refined women who were very different from those she had so often made fun of in Moulins. She described Vichy as a fairy-tale world – an unpleasant fairy tale, but a wonderful one when seen

---

[16]François, Lucien (1961). Remarks reported by Haedrich, Marcel, *Op. cit.*, p. 157. Free translation from the original French.
[17]Picardie, Justine. *Op. cit.*, p. 42.

through a new set of eyes. Vichy, she said, was her first-ever trip away, and would teach her about life.[18] Coco began to dream of a different life for herself, one furnished with tearooms and good company. She even attended a race meeting.

When Coco returned to Moulins later in 1906, Étienne Balsan invited her to stay at his home, in La-Croix-Saint-Ouen and Royallieu. Coco had told him quite a story about her awful childhood, and she had to confess that it was not true. According to her, she cried for a year afterwards. The only time she was happy, she said, was when she was on horseback in the forest. She learned to ride; until then, she did not have the faintest idea of what equitation was.[19]

Choosing Audacity!

At Étienne Balsan's home, Coco was by no means an esteemed guest. In fact, she was often excluded from dinners attended by the family's rich and famous friends. She ate mostly in the kitchen, with the staff, but she was free to ride around the estate on horseback.

Courtesan Émilienne d'Alençon was Étienne Balsan's acknowledged but non-exclusive mistress. She was 14 years older than Coco, who had no problem commenting on the fact: 'Étienne Balsan liked old women (...) He adored Émilienne d'Alençon. He wasn't concerned with beauty or youth. He adored tarts, and lived with her even though his family was scandalized'.

Actress Gabrielle Dorziat was another of Étienne's regular guests. Singer Marthe Davelli became Coco's confidant. All three were among Coco's first customers. Coco lived at Royallieu for 6 years, observing the courtesans and learning how to seduce men, take advantage of their influence and financial status, make friends with them and maintain those friendships over time. She also learned to like the courtesans themselves, describing them as clean, sensual, attractive, interesting and eccentric.

Coco, realizing that she could not compete with the elegant women of society or with the courtesans, chose instead to thumb her nose at tradition, in the way she lived, in what she did, in how she behaved, and in how she dressed. For example, one day she attended an elegant gathering wearing a simple dress decorated with a white collar that was reminiscent of her convent uniform.

She also borrowed shirts and ties from her protector's wardrobe. She was comfortable wearing men's clothing, and it is clear where her inspiration came from to 'feminize men's clothes' and 'masculinize women's clothes'. When out riding, she sat astride the horse like a man, wearing men's jodhpurs. At a masked ball on the theme of 'country wedding', she dressed androgynously as a male attendant. Étienne Balsan opened the doors to Paris for her: 'People saw Coco when they looked at Balsan'.

---

[18]Picardie, Justine. *Op. cit.*, p. 41.
[19]Picardie, Justine. *Op. cit.*, p. 46.

A Good Idea Triggered by Boredom

Coco eventually became bored at Royallieu. Because her outfits and hats had attracted interest and triggered curiosity, she decided to turn them into a business. Étienne Balsan offered her a studio in his bachelor pad at 160, Boulevard Malesherbes, in Paris, and she moved there in 1909. She was 26 years old.

Étienne Balsan financed the whole enterprise, amused by Coco's continued ability to surprise him. He opened a line of credit for her at the bank. Coco began by buying dummies from major department stores, including the Galeries Lafayette, and decorated them soberly, so that they stood out from the eccentric, overworked fashions of the time. Her hats quickly attracted a customer base of artists and the wives and mistresses of Balsam's friends, who were tired of the ridiculous styles sold elsewhere, which they were forced to wear because it was not socially acceptable, at the time, for women to be seen in public without a hat.

Coco's customers proved to be her most effective advertisements. She was soon overwhelmed by the demand for her creations, especially her simple boater hats, and asked her younger sister, Antoinette, to come and work for her as a saleswoman.

Arthur Capel: An Experienced and Creative Entrepreneur and Businessman

In some respects, Étienne Balsan laid the foundations for his own downfall when he introduced Coco to his British friend Arthur Capel in 1908, at a foxhunt. Capel, nicknamed 'Boy', had a bachelor pad next door to Balsan's on Boulevard Malesherbes in Paris. A good-natured rivalry for Coco's affections developed between the two friends, and they each supported her in their own way:

> I started making hats because two men were fighting over little old me. Neither wanted to give way.[20]

According to Coco, the two men decided to give her a place to make her hats in the same way they would have given a child a toy, so she could have some fun. She blamed them for not understanding how important it was for her.[21]

Arthur Capel went on to become the great love of her life – an unfaithful and tragic love, with no hope of marriage. Even more than Étienne Balsan, he believed in his mistress's dreams. 'I thought I was giving you a plaything. What I gave you instead was freedom', he said.

---

[20]Fiemeyer, Isabelle. *Op. cit.*, p. 56. Free translation from the original French.
[21]Picardie, Justine. *Op. cit.*, p. 91.

> He had a very strong personality, and was both ardent and focused. He moulded me, and he was able to develop the unique side of me, at the expense of all the rest.[22]

He had what Coco described as the kind of 'gentle authority' common in men who know and love women. He always said what he thought of her, and had no hesitation in confronting her when she was wrong, when she lied or when she behaved badly.[23]

Capel was an experienced and entrepreneurial businessman. His father had made a fortune from coal-mining in Northern England. After attending the élite Beaumont College in Old Windsor (Berkshire), run by the Jesuits, he went on to Downside College in Somerset, run by the Benedictines. Both were frequented by Britain's aristocracy and upper classes.

He took over from Étienne Balsan as Coco's financial angel, and became even more involved as a mentor, offering advice and working alongside her to understand and evaluate her intuitions. Coco certainly had plenty of ideas, and Capel would soon encourage her to leave her workshop in the Malesherbes apartment and open a store.

Chanel Fashion opened its doors on 1 January 1910, at 21 Rue Cambon, in the heart of Paris, close to the elegant Place Vendôme where the elite went shopping for luxury goods. It was not long before all the famous magazines began to feature her creations. Coco herself was photographed in the issue of *Comœdia* published on 1 October 1910, wearing a wide-brimmed hat made of black velvet and decorated with a simple long feather. The hat emphasized her characteristic long, thin neck. Her sister Antoinette and her aunt Adrienne came to help her. The workshop was invaded by customers, some of whom came simply out of curiosity, to see her. 'I was a strange animal', she said, 'a small woman with a boater hat pinned firmly to her head, and a head placed firmly on her shoulders'.

The True Launch: Deauville, Summer 1913

In the summer of 1913, Coco Chanel was 30 years old. On vacation with Capel in Deauville, a popular seaside resort in Normandy, she opened her second store, *Gabrielle Chanel*, between the Normandy Hotel and the casino, in a renovated street-front store with lots of passers-by. The couple became famous thanks to caricaturist Sem, who drew Capel as a centaur and Coco as a seductive, submissive woman.

The store was always full of customers, and Coco began to offer a line of loose-fitting garments suitable for the beach, including comfortable shirts and sailor blouses. 'All I had with me were milliners; I turned them into seamstresses. We didn't have enough fabric. I cut shirts for them out of stable boys' sweaters,

---

[22]Coco Chanel, cited by Leymarie, Jean. *Op. cit.*, p. 46. Free translation from the original French.

[23]Picardie, Justine. *Op. cit.*, p. 88.

the kinds of knitted garments I wore myself'. Adrienne and Antoinette walked along the beach and through the streets of Deauville, wearing the new clothes and cloche hats designed by Coco.

As war loomed on the horizon, Chanel's sober style quickly became what the elegant ladies of Paris wanted to wear. The Deauville store attracted a rich customer base, including Baron Henri de Rothschild. Coco estimated that she had earned 200,000 francs by the summer of 1914. It was a major turning point for her, the true launch of her business activities.

Her First Fashion House: Biarritz, 1915

In 1915, Coco Chanel opened a third store, this one in Biarritz, when Capel was home on leave. He had advised her to take refuge in Biarritz because of the war. Her target customers were Spanish, and Coco quickly became the 'queen of the beaches'.

According to Leymarie, Biarritz attracted profiteers and wealthy people from throughout the world, who came to enjoy the pleasures of its ocean and its strange beauty. Coco opened her first true fashion house in the city, hiring qualified staff and presenting her first collections. The house remained in business until the 1930s.

In the summer of 1915, dresses became shorter and corsets gradually disappeared, liberating the waistline. Lines became straight and fluid. France was at war and the textile factories were unable to deliver. Jersey, 'the fabric of the poor', woven on single-thread machines and used to make garments for the Normandy coast fishermen, was about the only thing available. Coco bought every metre she could from her supplier, Rodier. The fabric was difficult to work with, and clearly unsuited to couture. It was both a challenge and a revolution. 'When I invented jersey', she said, 'I liberated the body, abandoned the waistline and drew a brand new silhouette ... To the indignation of the couture designers, I also made dresses shorter'.

Her loose, relaxed garments that left women's ankles uncovered were first regarded as scandalous, until it became clear that everyone wanted them. In 1916, Chanel introduced another fashion innovation, in the shape of the v-necked shirt dress, which quickly conquered her French and American customers. The garment was featured on the covers of Vogue and Harper's Bazaar.

During the war many women went out to work, replacing men in factories and government services, and serving as volunteers and nurses. Coco Chanel, however, chose to remain with her own company, continuing to conquer the market with her innovative designs. She explained her position as follows: 'One world came to an end, another was born. I was there. I was the same age as the new century, and it was to me that people came for their clothes. True success is fatal'.

Fashion, a Rapidly Changing Field: A Revolution on the Horizon

Clearly, Coco Chanel had already tasted success, and plenty of it. Confirmation came 10 years after she opened her first store. She had learned to fulfil the need of women to show, through their clothing, the 'other' life that society now allowed them to live. It was a time when the feminist movement was taking its first, hesitant steps.

There was nothing to bind her to the past. The male businessmen with whom she surrounded herself kept encouraging her to do something different and move away from the beaten track. She became incredibly intense, giving a sheen of newness and avant-gardism to everything she touched. After the 'Great War' of 1914–1918, attitudes changed. Society – and Coco Chanel with it – rushed headlong into the Roaring Twenties. Thanks to her flair, she was able to grasp the opportunities that arose and remain true to herself. According to Hal Vaughan, she took an apartment overlooking the Seine and the Trocadero during the Great War and began to amass her fortune. Before long, she was employing 300 people to make her line of jersey dresses. However, as the company prospered she began to seek out better quality fabrics, and created her own fabric company to produce them (Vaughan, 2011, p. 8).

She seemed surprised by her own success and celebrity:

> All of a sudden, I was famous without knowing it. I didn't know what celebrity was. I'd never sought it out – it came to me. And you see, I launched a fashion for that too. Fashion designers had become fashionable, and that wasn't the case before I came along. Nobody knew anything about Mr. Doucet, even though he was a remarkable man. Go and see his library – you'll understand what he did for artists. Nobody knew about him because he was a fashion designer. His customers wouldn't have recognized him if they'd met him in the street. It's strange, but true. Life changed completely between 1914 and 1919.
>
> The war helped me. People show their true colours in difficult times. I woke up famous in 1919. If I'd have understood what it meant, I'd have crawled under a table to cry. I was stupid, sensitive and ignorant.[24]

Her relationship with Arthur Capel (Boy) never gave her the stability she obtained from her fashion house. She and Capel were never bound by contract, or by a marriage certificate, or even by a business connection. She acknowledged that he had taught her everything, even how to sign a cheque. It was on this latter subject that she once lost her temper with Capel, when he told her the bank had called him with concerns about the pace and size of the transactions on the account he had opened in her name.

It was a conversation that made Coco realize that, however much she may think her success was her own, she was still dependent on Capel. It was because of him that she was welcomed and treated as an esteemed customer by the bank. 'It was he who paid for everything! I was essentially living off him! (...) I began to

---

[24]Haedrich, Marcel (2008) *Op. cit.*, p.67. Free translation from the original French.

hate this well brought-up man who was paying for me. I threw my handbag straight at his face and ran off'. The following day, she rushed in to see her senior seamstress, and told her: 'Angèle, I'm not here to have fun or to spend money like water. I'm here to make a fortune'.

The following year, Coco repaid every cent advanced by Capel. Not only was she then debt-free, but in 1918 she was able to pay cash (300,000 francs) for a luxury villa in Biarritz, near the beach. Financially independent, she was no longer a 'kept woman'. She rode around in a chauffeur-driven limousine, a Rolls Royce. Her Biarritz workshops, employing 60 people, were overseen by her sister Antoinette and became her headquarters in the South of France. Her customers would pay a high price for a dress that looked like a high school uniform. In the fall of 1919, she made her final move, to the address that would become famous, at 31 Rue Cambon in Paris.

'Fashion Should Be the Expression of Place and Time'[25]

The fashions she launched fuelled her own existence. However, there are conflicting versions of some events in her life, such as the time she cut her hair short and started a new trend. Coco originally said a lamp had exploded and damaged her long hair, which she had to cut short as a result. Later, she would amend the story, saying she decided to cut her hair short before going out to the Opera, when she realized that Arthur Capel would never marry her, and that he was in fact about to marry the daughter of a lord.[26] In reality, she borrowed the idea of short hair from a famous dancer, Caryathis, who had appeared with short hair in a Stravinsky ballet three years earlier, in 1913. One of her biographers, commenting on Coco's exploding lamp story, suggested that the haircut, far from being an accident, had probably been a deliberate and calculated decision by the 'cold-blooded businesswoman' she had become.[27]

Regardless of how it came about, short hair became the rage among actresses and women of the world thanks to Coco Chanel.

Coco Chanel chose to live her life intensely, and firmly believed she was destined to be more than a wife and mother. She left Capel's bachelor pad and rented a house on the outskirts of Paris. She did not seem to miss him at all, which intrigued him greatly and brought him back to her, at least for a short time.

However, Capel became involved in politics and was also busy with his own business contacts, including French Head of State Clémenceau. His visits to Coco became rare. In the end, thanks to his relationship with the country's political leader, his companies began to supply the French government, and some were able to take advantage of the lucrative army market.

---

[25]Coco Chanel to Paul Morand, cited by Picardie, Justine. *Op. cit.*, p. 98.

[26]Despite his marriage to aristocratic Diana Lister and the birth of his first daughter, Capel would continue to visit Coco on a regular basis. When he died, his wife was pregnant with their second child.

[27]Artuso, Anthony. W. and A. Zalesnik (1987). See also: Haedrich, Marcel (1971, p. 199).

Inheritance and Betrayal

Then tragedy struck, in the form of an accident on 22 December 1919, that killed Arthur Capel. After his death, Coco never wore a watch again.[28]

Coco became a recluse after Capel's death. She cried for her lover, and also for his betrayal. He had left behind a young daughter, an unborn child and a widow who inherited the vast majority of his fortune, estimated at 700,000 pounds. He also left legacies of 40,000 pounds to Coco, his French mistress, and to an Italian countess whom Coco did not know existed.[29]

Coco used her inheritance to extend her premises at 31, Rue Cambon and she also bought *Bel Respiro*, a villa located in Garches, a suburb of Paris. She painted its façade beige and installed black shutters as a sign of mourning. She also had her Saint-Cloud house painted black, but changed her mind overnight and asked the painter, the following day, to paint it pink, 'to get me out of the coffin I've made for myself'.

Coco transformed black into the epitome of chic, and it became the colour of both her brand and her independence. Now alone, she took refuge in her company, and devoted all her energies to her business.

Coco Chanel: Building an Empire – Chanel in Three Acts Act Two: Mademoiselle's Flair (1918–1939)

> I did not invent the sports suit because women were doing sports, but because I was. I did not go out because I felt the need to make fashion; I made fashion because I went out, because I, first and foremost, was living the life of the century.
>
> – Coco Chanel[30]

In the years following the First World War, Coco's premises at 31, Rue Cambon became the seat of an authentic and well-known high fashion house, *the House of Chanel*. The woman who came to Paris to make her fortune was on the right path. Many of her friends from the arts community, some of whom would leave their mark on the 20th century, gradually formed a new circle around Coco Chanel. Thanks to them, she was immersed in art and culture. She discovered three facets of wealth that were previously out of her reach: power, influence and patronage.

---

[28]Fiemeyer, Isabelle. *Op. cit.*, p. 62.

[29]100 British pounds in 1919 had a value equivalent to 6, 606.17 British pounds or US$ 8, 215.33 in 2023 (one BP = US$ 1.2436).

[30]Coco Chanel, cited by Leymarie, Jean (2010, p. 7). Free translation from the original French.

Her main asset was her flair, a remarkably useful skill for Coco the entrepreneur and Coco the artist. She discovered and developed it through her relationship with Misia Sert, an exuberant woman with the ability to uncover and promote talent, who became both her friend and her rival:[31]

> She was the only friend I ever had (...) She appeared in my life at the saddest time; other people's sadness attracted her, like some perfumes attract bees. (...)
>
> We only love people for their faults, and Misia gave me plenty of reasons to love her. She only became attached to people she did not understand, and she understood almost everyone – except me. I always remained a mystery to her. It earned sporadic loyalty, a loyalty that was often taken away but always given back.[32]

A Chance Meeting

On 28 May 1917, at a dinner given by Cécile Sorel, Coco Chanel met Marie Sophie Olga Zénaïde Godebska, better known as Misia Sert, the muse of several artists. Misia was a talented pianist who shared her life with José Maria Sert, a decorative painter known for his immense fresco paintings at the United Nations headquarters in Geneva, the Waldorf Astoria and the Rockefeller Center in New York. His reputation extended to America, Italy, Brazil and Iraq. The couple travelled extensively and were frequent theatre-goers, rarely missing a première.

Misia the Friend

Misia had heard of the young fashion designer who was becoming a fixture in Parisian life even though she seemed to know little of the workings and intrigues of the city's culturally and socially exuberant society.

As they were leaving Cécile Sorel's home after the dinner, Misia complimented Coco on her red velvet coat. Coco slipped the coat from her shoulders and offered it to Misia. While Misia refused the gift, she was charmed by the spontaneity and

---

[31]Misia Sert: Born Marie Sophie Olga Zénaïde Godebska on March 30, 1872, in St. Petersburg. She was the daughter of Polish sculptor Cyprian Godebski and Sophie Servais, whose father was Adrien-François Servais, a Belgian cellist. Her mother died while giving birth to her, and she was raised by her maternal grandmother, whose circle of friends included Franz Liszt. She began by marrying her cousin, Thadée Natanson. In 1904, Renoir immortalized her as Madame Natanson. See: http://www.nationalgallery.org.uk/paintings/pierre-auguste-renoir-misia-sert Toulouse Lautrec also painted her at the piano. Pushed into the arms of Alfred Edwards by her husband Thadée Natanson, in exchange for payment of his debts, she eventually married him to save her honour. In 1908, she moved to Paris with José Maria Sert, whom she married in 1920.

[32]Coco Chanel to Paul Morand, cited in Picardie, Justine. *Op. cit.*, p. 119 and 120.

simplicity of the gesture, and by Coco's independent personality and the freedom she had earned for herself. She decided it would become her mission to introduce her new friend, 11 years her junior, to the artistic community of Paris.

In her memoires, Misia wrote that she went to Rue Cambon the day after the dinner, to see Coco. Her store, she said, was full of knitted garments, hats and all kinds of accessories for women. Two customers were there when Misia entered, and they referred to Chanel as 'Coco'. The use of the nickname upset Misia, who felt they were insulting her idol. She was very indignant.[33]

Misia and Coco had both lived in orphanages in their youth, and they developed a closeness that made Misia's partner, José-Maria Sert, jealous. Justine Picardie notes that, while Misia was Coco's closest friend, their relationship was not always good, and was too passionate to be fuelled solely by friendship. Jealousy and even hatred played a role, and the air sometimes became charged with sexual electricity. Misia herself likened their first meeting to 'love at first sight'.[34]

After Capel's death, Coco Chanel entered a period of depression that worried her closest friends. Seeing her in such a pitiful state, Misia and José-Maria Sert invited her to go with them on their honeymoon to Venice. Misia was 48 years old at the time, and José-Maria was 45. Misia's beauty and influence were at their peak. The friendship between the three of them would continue well after the trip to Venice, and would also survive the Serts' separation.

Coco would say later that the trip to Venice, and her contact with the city's art, brought her back to life. Sert took her to museums, explained the Byzantine style, and taught her to appreciate woodwork, velvet and gastronomy. She was interested in everything, and it became the fuel for what she described as her craft.

When Misia died in 1950, Coco came back from Switzerland, where she was in self-imposed exile, to dress the body. Locked in the bedroom with her deceased friend, she dressed her, did her hair, put on her makeup and made her beautiful for her final appearance. Misia's body was exposed in a canopy bed, on white sheets, and those who saw her were amazed at the beauty and youth Coco had created.

Misia and Coco, Patrons

Misia Sert was considered one of the queens of Paris. Jean Cocteau said this about her: 'You have to admire these profound and fiery women who live in the shadow of their men and work their magic quietly on the artists they meet, simply by emitting an energy that is more beautiful than the necklaces they wear'.[35,36]

---

[33]Misia Sert, cited by Picardie, Justine. *Op. cit.*, p. 116.

[34]Picardie, Justine. *Op. cit.*, p. 115.

[35]Famous French writer.

[36]Jean Cocteau, cited by Laty, Dominique (2009, p. 15). Free translation from the original French.

Dominique Laty described Misia Sert as follows: '... a woman whose sing-song accent, queen-like bearing, authoritarian assurance and seductive skills have brought so many men to their knees. This woman, of Polish origin, is anti-conformist, musical, and a supporter of the arts in general. She has a foul character'.[37]

The main source of rivalry between Coco and Misia was their influence over the artistic community. In her own way, Coco had always wanted to be part of this community. Since she could not achieve this through her own literary talent or her singing and dancing skills, she used another facet of her creative spirit: patronage. Like Misia, she had the ability to recognize, promote and associate herself with talent and beauty.

At *Bel Respiro,* her villa in Garches, on the outskirts of Paris, Coco Chanel welcomed the great artists of the 20th century: Picasso, Igor Stravinsky, his wife Catherine and their four children, and even Dali. She influenced editors to ensure that Pierre Reverdy's poems were published. For Cocteau, whose plays were presented at the Comédie française, she created the costumes for *Antigone* (1922), *Train bleu* (1924), and *Orphée* (1926). Picasso designed the stage curtain and programme for the first two productions.

Cocteau also asked her to dress the daughters of Oedipus. In February 1923, *Vogue* observed, in its French and American editions, that: 'Chanel becomes Greek but remains French...'.[38] Generously, she later paid for the care and funeral of Cocteau's protégé, the young Raymond Radiguet, author of an award-winning novel entitled *Le Diable au corps* (1923), who died of typhoid at the age of 20. For Chanel, white became the colour of mourning.

Rivals

Misia was not an easy friend; she was easily overcome by passion, and could be invasive. Learning that Misia wanted to protect her from poet Pierre Reverdy, Coco Chanel noted that the only person she needed protection from was Misia. Where Misia had loved, she said, the grass no longer grew.[39]

Misia was certainly jealous of Coco's relationship with the poet, because she was the one who discovered him first. Reverdy was probably in love with Misia. He was six years younger than Chanel, who became the first to read his poems, and dedicated his manuscripts to her. Even when living the life of a recluse in the monastery at Solesmes, towards the end of his life, he continued to write to her. And he never made a negative comment on Coco's own poems and other works, during the period when she thought she would become a writer. On the contrary, he encouraged her to write maxims, such as: 'If you are born without wings, do nothing to impede their growing' and 'For a woman, betrayal has only one meaning, betrayal of the senses'.

---

[37]Laty, Dominique (2009, p. 10). Free translation from the original French.
[38]Picardie, Justine. *Op. cit.*, p. 124.
[39]Picardie, Justine. *Op. cit.*, p. 124.

Misia was convinced she had been the first and only person to recognize Chanel's potential as a fashion designer. She said so in very definite terms: '. . . I felt it deeply, from our first meeting, and I never stopped until I had opened other people's eyes. I have the privilege of having helped her emerge from her matrix and – in my heart – of having been the first to be dazzled'.[40]

In her professional world, Coco Chanel had good reason to dislike Misia's invasive propensities. When the famous perfume Chanel No. 5 was launched, Misia claimed she was the one to have inspired it. When Coco Chanel read the chapter of Misia's memoires that described Misia's self-proclaimed role in inspiring and creating the perfume, she demanded that it be removed from the book.

Chanel's Flair

As she got to know Misia's friends, Coco Chanel discovered a world of which she quickly became a part: the world of arts and culture. She read more, and learned to sing, dance and play the piano. At 31, Rue Cambon, her collections reflected not only her personal growth, but also a way of seeing and thinking about the world that was increasingly influenced by the artistic community and artistic creation.

Chanel showed great ingenuity in incorporating new trends successfully into her collections. She identified and recruited people with outstanding skills, and with them, went on to develop new products. Her growing sphere of influence, which encompassed a world to which designers did not usually have access, was also reflected in the design of her products, which became associated increasingly with cultural and artistic events and activities. The unusual nature of her network allowed her to become the most innovative designer in her field.

Incorporating New Trends

Between 1919 and 1924, Coco included embroidered patterns, crystals and lace in her designs. It was true that, under the influence of the Russian Ballet Company in Paris, traditional and symbolic patterns had been popular since 1909 thanks in large part to Paul Poiret, the precursor of many of the trends revived by Chanel. Poiret had lived in Russia and was already using embroidery to decorate his creations. Coco Chanel would go even further.

At her villa at Garches, where Coco was now living with Grand Duke Dimitri Pavlovitch Romanov and his sister, many of the staff were Russian.

[40]Misia Sert, cited by Picardie, Justine. *Op. cit.*, p 139.

After the 1917 revolution, large numbers of Russians emigrated to France, and by 1921–1922 demand was high for garments with Russian or Asian touches. In Chanel's 1922 fall-winter collection, the coats were even decorated with fur.

Embroidery was a skill in short supply in France, so Coco Chanel set up her own embroidery workshop, under the supervision of Dimitri's sister, Maria Pavlovna. Maria, who felt there was no chance of ever returning to Russia, threw herself into the project. She overheard Coco arguing fiercely with Madame Bataille, her in-house embroidery expert, who wanted to be paid 600 francs to embroider a blouse with silk thread. Maria offered to do the work for 450 francs. She bought an embroidery machine and learned how to use it. Her embroidery was instrumental in the success of Chanel's 1922 spring collection. Eventually, she oversaw a team of roughly 50 employees, many of Russian origin, and became famous for the quality of her work.

Identifying and Recruiting Talent

By the 1920s, Coco was already rich and was perceived as having a lot of power and influence. Everyone knew she would not compromise her reputation with projects that were doomed to failure.

Coco Chanel went out a lot. The Roaring Twenties were an intense experience for her. She had her finger on the pulse of Paris, the city that was inventing the future. She felt she was in the right place, at the right time, with the right product. Thanks to her experience, her networks and the things she had learned, she had developed a kind of 'sixth sense', an intuition of what was on the horizon.

Coco was an opportunist, and an expert in managing synchronism – the art of good timing. She was able to define and give structure to latent elements in her field, and seemed instinctively to know what was in the air, invisible to other people. It was this that allowed her to stay ahead of the pack. She relied on her intuition to create the things she felt should 'be'. Through this instinctive ability to predict trends, she was able to design products that were constantly ahead of the market. It was as though she let herself be carried by the 'spirit of the time'.

Her instinct was what kept her at the top of her field for so long. Other designers achieved fame, including Paul Poiret, and new names emerged in the luxury and fashion industries: Jean Patou, Jeanne Lanvin, Molyneux and Rochas, to name but a few. However, Chanel remained the choice of elegant ladies:

> When my customers come to me, they like to cross the threshold of some magic place; they feel a satisfaction that is perhaps a

> trace vulgar but that delights them; they are privileged characters who are incorporated into our legend. For them this is a far greater pleasure than ordering another suit. Legend is the consecration of fame.
>
> Coco Chanel (1935).[41]

Coco Chanel always maintained aesthetic control over her creations and over the quality of the work done by her employees and models.

On the other hand, over time she agreed to delegate certain aspects of the creative and business management processes to people who, in her opinion, had sufficient taste and skill, and above all, adequate social networks. Most were upper-class immigrants, people from high society who subsequently became customers.

According to Isabelle Fiemeyer, this allowed her to promote her fashion house without spending money, and like Proust, to be well-informed without leaving home.[42,43]

One of her chosen people was Count Étienne de Beaumont, a philanthropist known for his fabulous social events. It was Misia who engineered their meeting by forcing them both to attend a ball where name cards were obligatory. Coco Chanel hired him in 1924, to develop a collection of jewellery made of both real and false stones, which elegant women would wear during the day, instead of their 'real' jewels. As she noted: 'What really matters isn't the number of carats, it's the illusion'.[44] Coco Chanel had already democratized women clothing, she did the same with the jewellery.

Another of her employees was ruined Sicilian Duke Fulco di Verdura, who created a line of magnificent enamel bracelets. As for Picasso's goldsmith François Hugo, he created a line of clips and broaches.

In May 1931, Coco appointed Ilia Zdanevitch to manage her Asnières factory, which made hats as well as the famous knitted and jersey garments that were still extremely popular. Ilia Zdanevitch was originally hired as a designer, in March 1928. He had been forced to leave Russia because of his radical criticism of the system, and subsequently pursued a career as a writer and researcher. To earn a living, he learned about fabrics and colours, and Chanel entrusted him with the task of creating and perfecting knitting machines that would improve the texture and colours of her knits and jerseys.

However, by far the most productive and financially successful of Coco Chanel's collaborations would be those that led to the creation of her flagship perfume, *Chanel N° 5.*

---

[41] Picardie, Justine. *Op. cit.*, p. 7.
[42] Famous French novelist.
[43] Fiemeyer, Isabelle. *Op. cit.*, p. 92.
[44] Fiemeyer, Isabelle. *Op. cit.*, p. 92.

Dimitri Pavlovitch Romanov and the Perfume That Became the Most Famous in the World

One should spray it wherever one wants to be kissed.
– Coco Chanel[45]

When her 'idyllic' relationship with Igor Stravinsky ended, Coco Chanel met Grand Duke Dimitri Pavlovitch Romanov, who introduced her to Russian-born Ernest Beaux, the manager of a perfume factory in Grasse and also the official perfume-maker to the Tsar. Perfume was used extensively by the Romanovs and in the Russian court. Ernest's brother Édouard was a director of Rallet, the largest manufacturer of soap and perfume in Russia. Coco was interested by Ernest's research, as he attempted to reproduce '... the unique sensation he experienced north of the Arctic Circle, as he breathed in the unique and supremely fresh scent of rivers and lakes under the midnight sun.'[46]

Coco had a highly developed sense of smell and claimed she could recognise the odour of her childhood forests in Compiègne, on a branch or flower given to her as a gift. She wanted to create a perfume that would be appropriate for the style she had developed and the new women she dressed: 'An artificial perfume, yes, artificial like a dress – in other words, something that is made. I'm an artisan of couture. I don't want roses or lilies of the valley, I want a composed perfume'.[47]

In 1921, Ernest Beaux submitted two series of samples, numbered from 1 to 5 and from 20 to 24. She chose two: Number 22 and Number 5. *Chanel N°5*, with 80 components dominated by a floral scent of jasmine from Grasse, was launched on 5 May 1921, in the now-famous square bottle with black lettering on a white background.[48] *Chanel N° 22* was launched a few months later. However, it would be the No. 5 – Coco's favourite – that would make her fortune.

To promote the perfume, she invited friends to eat at restaurants, and sprayed them discreetly. She enjoyed watching their expressions change from surprize to pleasure. The perfume was also sprayed in the fitting rooms at her stores and at the *House of Chanel*. For Christmas 1921, she gave a bottle to her 100 best customers, who were the first to hear of the product's existence. In no time at all, everyone who was someone in Paris wanted it.

---

[45]Picardie, Justine. *Op. cit.*, p. 131, citation: Pierre Galante, Les années Chanel.

[46]Leymarie, Jean. *Op. cit.*, p. 87. Free translation from the original French.

[47]Galante, Pierre and Philippe Orsini (1972, p. 80). Cited by Wikipedia http://fr.wikipedia.org/wiki/N%C2%B05_de_Chanel#cite_note-0. Free translation from the original French.

[48]The format of the glass bottle would change five times: its original shape from 1921, with changes in 1930, 1950, 1970 and 1986.

Pierre Wertheimer: A Stormy Relationship

In 1923, Théophile Bader, the owner of Galeries Lafayette, felt the perfume was unique enough to offer to his customers. It then became a question of producing enough of it to satisfy the demand. Bader was also convinced that the perfume should be offered to a broader market than Chanel's usual, richer customer base. Ernest Beaux's laboratory was not large enough. He persuaded Coco Chanel to meet with Pierre Wertheimer at the Deauville racetrack, one Sunday.

The Wertheimer brothers already owned the House of Bourjois, a cosmetic and perfume company, and were very familiar with the industry's requirements for success. They had considerable capital, their factory was large enough to produce a significant amount of perfume, and they already had an extensive distribution network for their own products. Between 1905 and 1920, their network had grown to include roughly 100 distributors throughout the world. An agreement was quickly signed – too quickly, as it turned out.

The Chanel Perfume Company was created in 1924. Under the agreement with Coco Chanel, Pierre and Paul Wertheimer owned the rights, formulas and production methods for the perfumes. Coco Chanel became the company's president and held 200 shares (10% of the total). Each share was worth 500 francs. She was also guaranteed 10% of the shares in all producing companies outside France.[49] Pierre Wertheimer undertook to finance the entire operation in return for a 70% share. As for Theodore Bader, he and his partners, Adolphe Dreyfus and Max Grumbach, shared the remaining 20%. Ernest Beaux continued as the company's Artistic Director.

Coco Chanel soon began to regret the agreement. In fact, she would regret it bitterly throughout her life. She had agreed to use the same lawyer as the Wertheimer brothers for the agreement, and the partners already had business ties of which she was unaware. In her personal life, she was going through a difficult time, emotionally upset by her hopeless love affair with poet Pierre Reverdy and her break-up with Grand Duke Dimitri. The contracts, negotiations, agreements and money issues bored her to death. As she later admitted: 'Pierre was a bandit who screwed me royally'.

When she realized her mistake, Coco Chanel became so bitter that the Wertheimer brothers had to hire a lawyer to protect themselves from her, and even renegotiate some elements of the agreement. Pierre Wertheimer was probably in love with Coco Chanel. At the time, he was 36 years old and she was 44. According to René de Chambrun, who became Coco Chanel's personal legal counsel in 1934, the partnership was always a turbulent one:

> Thirty years of cold war, divorces and reconciliations (...) I nicknamed Coco 'Louis XIV', and Pierre Wertheimer, 'Cardinal Mazarin'. They danced around one another until the summer of 1939. At Longchamp, (...) Pierre's box was next to ours. When Coco came to see us on Sundays, he always sat near her.

[49]Vaughan, Hal. *Op. cit.*, p. 30.

> My wife Josée and I invited them to dinner one Friday evening at Maxim's. And then to lunch, at our home in Place du Palais-Bourbon. At lunch, Pierre spoke to me in confidence. He wanted me to do everything I could to make sure Coco understood that he always wanted to serve her without ever hurting her . . .[50]

The business relationship would continue to be difficult. It would cast a dramatic shadow over the role Coco Chanel may have played in the Second World War. Even so, when the conflict ended, Pierre Wertheimer came to the rescue of his difficult partner, helping to save both her company and her reputation.[51]

Other perfumes were created in subsequent years: *Gardenia* in 1925, *Bois des îles* in 1926, *Cuir de Russie* in 1927 and lastly, *Chanel Nº19* in 1970 (named for Coco Chanel's birthday). The style of the bottles did not change much. The *Chanel Nº 5* bottle had been designed by the Grand Duke Dimitri, and was inspired by the vodka flasks used by the Russian Imperial Guard. The perfumes that followed in the wake of *Chanel Nº 5* were presented in the same type of sober packaging, and were always the result of rigorous research. In 1984, Jacques Polge, trained by Ernest Beaux, created *Coco*, 13 years after the death of the woman who inspired him.

Bendor, Duke of Westminster: The Political World and Incalculable Wealth

> . . .He is simplicity made man, the most timid I'd ever seen. He has the shyness of kings, of people who are isolated through their circumstances and through their wealth.
>
> – Coco Chanel[52]

By the early 1930s, Chanel had begun decorating her short, straight, low-waisted dresses with strips of material. For her long evening dresses, she had reverted to organdy and sequins or pearls. Fur reappeared in her collections, confirming the social status of the wearer. Arthur Capel had introduced her to England, and the country became a source of inspiration for her.

During Christmas 1923, Coco Chanel went to Monaco with Vera Bate, a 33-year-old woman she had hired to oversee the House of Chanel's relations with London. Vera had excellent connections to the royal family and Britain's aristocracy. It was she who introduced Coco Chanel to Bendor, the Duke of Westminster, considered to be the richest man in England. Chanel said of him: '... unlimited wealth is not vulgar. At that level, affluence is beyond envy and takes

---

[50]Derrière l'empire Chanel... La fabuleuse histoire des Wertheimer: http://elsassexpat.blogs.com/histoire_chanel.pdf. Free translation from the original French.

[51]Yann Kerlau: Pierre Wertheimer, l'homme qui a sauvé la House of Chanel: 11/01/2011

[52]Coco Chanel to P. Morand, cited by Picardie, Justine. *Op. cit.*, p. 185.

on almost catastrophic proportions. I'm saying this because his wealth has turned Westminster into the last product of a disappearing civilization, a paleontological curiosity whose place is in people's memories'.[53]

Bendor owned a large part of Mayfair and Belgravia, in London. When his grandfather died in 1899, he inherited the Grosvenor fortune (his own father had died when he was just four years old). Bendor was a sportsman and an insatiable ladies' man. Between 1925 and 1930, he and Coco travelled around the Mediterranean, parts of France and Norway, and cruised throughout Europe on the Duke's yacht. They fished for salmon in Scotland, and stayed at the magnificently restored Eaton Hall castle. The Duke's estates were huge, and the couple loved to ride on horseback through the British countryside. In the summer of 1927, Chanel opened a store in London. Her target customers were the British aristocracy, the royal court, the horseracing community and high society's debutants.

For the 10 years they were together, the Duke showered Coco Chanel with jewels and bouquets of gardenias, her favourite flowers. He brought her fresh strawberries in the middle of winter and set aside a house for her in Mayfair, one of London's most sought-after neighbourhoods. His gifts were extravagant, and included a famous emerald and diamond necklace that she took apart after the war and remade into bracelets and broaches for her friends. Whenever he was unfaithful, he would give her another hugely expensive piece of jewellery – which she, in her fury, was likely to toss into the sea without a second thought.

In 1928, the Duke paid 1.8 million francs (more than US$3.6 million in 2012 figures) for a five-acre site at Cap-Martin, near Roquebrune and Monte Carlo, where the couple built a sumptuous residence known as *La Pausa.* He apparently handed ownership of the property over to Coco on 9 February 1929, when the estate was valued at six million francs (more than US$12 million in 2012 figures). At least, this was Hal Vaughan's version of what happened, but Justine Picardie disagrees, noting that it was clearly Gabrielle Chanel's name on the notarized deed, and the entire amount of 1.8 million francs came out of Chanel's bank account.[54] According to Picardie, Chanel's financial independence was already well-established when she bought La Pausa. She owned her store near Cannes as well as a significant portion of the Rue Cambon premises.[55]

Coco Chanel expanded her network of relations in England, branching out into the political community. At hunting parties, Bendor introduced her to the Duke and Duchess of Windsor and Winston Churchill. Coco was fascinated by the Duke, a fabulously wealthy man who was so indifferent to his property that he did not know what it was worth and felt absolutely no need to display his wealth. However, the Duke wanted an heir; his only son had died in 1909. Coco refused to marry him; she was almost 40 years old and unable to have children despite numerous visits to doctors and midwives, and a harsh exercise regime. There were rumours that she had been damaged by an abortion in her youth.

[53]Coco Chanel, cited by Picardie, Justine. *Op. cit.*, p. 197.
[54]Vaughan, Hal. *Op. cit.*, p. 48.
[55]Picardie, Justine. *Op. cit.*, p. 205.

However, Coco was also aware that her roots would do her no favours in the Duke's circle. In 1946, long after their relationship had ended, she described him as a 'skilled hunter', despite his somewhat clumsy appearance. As she pointed out, he had to be skilled to keep her for 10 years – a period she said was full of tenderness. The couple remained friends even after they separated. 'I loved him', said Coco. 'Or at least I thought I did, which is the same thing'. Westminster, she said, was 'kindness personified'.[56]

But the Duke needed an heir and his friend Winston Churchill reminded him of his obligations. He ended up marrying a member of the British aristocracy.[57]

The 'Little Black Dress' and the Great American Dream

In 1926, when other designers were bringing bright colours back into fashion, Coco Chanel surprized the world and the market once again with her famous 'little black dress' made of crepe, with long, fitted sleeves and a knee-length hemline. In the United States, it was referred to as 'Chanel's Ford', in a reference to Henry Ford's famous black car.

Like Henry Ford, Coco Chanel was a leader and agent of change in her field. By the early 1930s, she was employing 2,400 people in her workshops, and her textile factory was successful.[58] According to Vaughan, her workforce grew to more than 4,000 between 1931 and 1935.[59] In 1935, she had sold 28,000 dresses. She did business in Europe, the Middle East and America. For the Americans, she was the perfect example of elegance, style and success.

It was for this reason that the American film community began to pay court to her. In 1930, in Monaco, Grand Duke Dimitri introduced her to Sam Goldwyn, the American film magnate, who offered her a million-dollar annual contract to dress his stars. The contract came at just the right time, because fortunes were not what they had once been as a result of the 1929 stock market crash. Even Chanel had to cut her prices, often by half.

Coco arrived in New York on 4 March 1931, accompanied by Misia, who was somewhat depressed after her separation from Sert.[60] In Hollywood she was welcomed by Greta Garbo, who became her friend. Like Marlène Dietrich, Garbo was an occasional customer. Chanel also met several movie directors, including Erich von Stroheim and Cecil B. De Mille. Upon returning to Paris, she made Gloria Swanson's costumes for the musical *Tonight or Never* (1931).

---

[56]Coco Chanel to Paul Morand, cited by Picardie, Justine. *Op. cit.*, p. 197.

[57]Haedrich, Marcel. *Op. cit.*, pp. 109–110.

[58]Fiemeyer, Isabelle. *Op. cit.*, p. 103.

[59]The number of people employed by Coco Chanel varied considerably over the decades. Historians do not agree on the number at the height of her success, which would appear to be somewhere between 3,000 (Lauritano, 2018) and 4,000, between 1931 and 1935 (Vaughan, 2011). See note 1 at the end of the Epilogue.

[60]Sert left Misia for Roussadana Mdivani, known as Roussy, an exiled Georgian princess whom Misia also liked. Roussy was 19 years old and Sert was 50. Chanel featured her creations on Roussy's 'young and perfect' body.

However, she was disappointed by the falseness and superficiality of Hollywood: 'It's the Mont Saint-Michel of tit and tail', she said one day. Although she did not like the idea, she nevertheless felt that one day, fairly soon, Paris would no longer be the leader of fashion.[61] New York, she said, would invent it, Hollywood would publicize it and Paris would suffer it.[62] She was bemused by American materialism, even though it boosted her perfume sales. 'America is dying of comfort'.[63]

During her trip, she learned a lot about how New York's large department stores worked, and made some valuable contacts with women who directed the city's fashion magazines. She also met Paul Iribarnegaray (Iribe), a satirical Paramount artist born in the Basque country who was about her age. His illustrations and caricatures appeared in some of the more prestigious weekly publications, including *Le Témoin*, which she financed. He went on to design furniture, fabric, carpets and jewellery, and was responsible for producing the first-ever fashion catalogue (for Paul Poiret).[64]

Paul Iribe would play an important role in her life, and was the only lover she ever came close to marrying.

Tweed and Diamonds

Coco Chanel missed the creative process, and when she returned to Europe in May 1932, she presented 130 models inspired by life in England: berets, Scottish tweeds, and sports coats. The Duke of Westminster loaned her a nine-roomed house in London, to help her become established in the United Kingdom, and spent more than eight thousand pounds on decorations, so she could present her collection for the benefit of the Royal British Legion.

The event was praised by Churchill, who came to see it in person. Between 500 and 600 people attended the show each day. Coco Chanel allowed her models to be copied, but would not sell them. 'It's not a success if it isn't copied', she said. There were many newspaper columns about her work, and coverage in the American newspapers increased significantly after her visit, helping to establish her reputation there.

From November 7–9, 1932, back in Paris, she worked with Paul Iribe to present *Diamond Jewels*, a daring and highly original collection of authentic jewellery that could be converted into bracelets or broaches using virtually invisible mounts and fasteners. The spectacular show took place at Mademoiselle Chanel, at 29 Faubourg Saint-Honoré, in one of the most prestigious neighbourhoods of Paris, near the British Embassy and the Presidential palace.

Despite the serious economic situation, thousands of visitors spent 20 francs each to admire a collection of luxury diamond jewellery that only Coco Chanel

[61]Picardie, Justine. *Op. cit.*, p. 233.
[62]Coco Chanel to Paul Morand, cited by Picardie, Justine. *Op. cit.*, p. 233.
[63]Coco Chanel to psycho-analyst Claude Delay, cited by Picardie, Justine. *Op. cit.*, p. 234.
[64]See: http://www.histoire-costume.fr/paul-poiret/.

had the means to create. She did so at the request of the International Diamond Manufacturers' Association, which provided the stones, for the benefit of two Parisian charities.

Jewellery began to come back into favour, and Chanel's customers once again felt able to wear valuable necklaces over their woollen sweaters or with their tweed jackets. Justine Picardie noted that Chanel demonstrated her true power and showed that the fashion industry, at least under her leadership, could be more firmly-grounded than the financial institutions that had been victims of the stock market collapse.[65]

In 1931, Janet Flanner wrote of Chanel that: '. . . she tries to outdo not only her competitors, but herself too . . .'[66] Chanel's turnover at the time was estimated at roughly 120 million francs (or US$4.5 million).[67] It was always difficult to estimate her personal fortune and her companies' results because her money was spread among several banks in several different countries, and the capital was private. The best estimates at the time put her fortune at around $200 million in 2010 figures.[68]

When Coco Chanel celebrated her 50th birthday in 1933, she was fabulously rich, seductive and elegant in her own, original way. She was someone who did not follow the established rules: she challenged the norm and created new rules.

In spite of the economic and social problems of the time, and in spite of a series of riots, one of which took place on 6 February 1934, the day after her collection was presented, her elegant evening dresses came back into fashion. Chanel worked with subtle draping, used colour carefully, and handled tulle and muslin better than anyone else. Her hats now sported veils. Chanel adapted her garments to the lifestyle and financial means of her customers, bringing back tweed and jersey suits, short, lightweight afternoon dresses, and sportswear. As she often said: 'The woman I dress must be a caterpillar during the day and a butterfly at night'.[69] 'There's nothing more comfortable than a caterpillar and nothing more suited to love than a butterfly. Women need dresses that slither and dresses that fly'.[70]

To defend the fashion industry in those times of crisis, Coco Chanel probably used or was inspired by Paul Iribe's communication skills when she addressed the readers of the St. Paul Pioneer Press in February 1933, pointing out that fashion created employment in the textile industry (wool, cotton and silk), the accessory sector (artificial flowers and feathers) and the paint and weaving sector, and supported jobs in brokerage, customs, sales and storekeeping.

---

[65]Picardie, Justine. *Op. cit.*, p. 240.

[66]Vaughan, Hal. *Op. cit.*, p. 72.

[67]The equivalent of US$60 million in 2012 figures.

[68]Vaughan, Hal. *Op. cit.*, p. 72.

[69]Fiemeyer, Isabelle, op.cit. p. 103. Free translation from the original French.

[70]Coco Chanel, cited by Leymarie, Jean. *Op. cit.*, p. 196. Free translation from the original French.

Coco Chanel at Home

> Interior design, said Chanel, is the natural projection of a soul, and Balzac was right to regard it as being as important as clothing.[71]

In addition to clothing, jewellery and perfume, Coco Chanel was interested in homes, decoration and everything that now comes under the heading of 'interior design'. She was sensitive to the beauty of the homes and residences of friends and relatives. The apartment she shared with Capel was decorated with objects from his many trips abroad, and also with books – lots of books – that she placed everywhere on tables. Whenever she had a few minutes to herself, she would read. Among the collectors' items she treasured most were 20 Coromandel screens, lacquered and decorated with white flowers, which Capel had brought back from his trips to India.[72] She sometimes used them to divide the rooms in her apartments.

In her home, it was important to her that the furniture and accessories could be moved around easily. Her preferred colours were sober: beige, black and white. But she also liked lampshades, carpets, heavy velvet drapes and settees on which she could stretch out, even when receiving visitors. Her interiors at her home in Garches, at the Faubourg Saint-Honoré, at *La Pausa* in Roquebrune, and at the Ritz, were comfortable and welcoming. Coco Chanel loved to be at home and receive friends. She enjoyed being a hostess, and was good at it.

Mirrors played a very specific role in her private apartments and at her fashion house. At her fashion shows, it was a well-known fact that she always sat on the last steps of the famous staircase, from where she could observe the individual models, the show as a whole and the public's reactions, thanks to a series of carefully placed mirrors.

Prelude to War

Paul Iribe died suddenly in 1935, and Coco's life became difficult. In the couture industry, competition was strong and aggressive. Coco spoke slightingly of Elsa Schiaparelli, whom she referred to as 'that Italian women who makes dresses', and criticized her use of vivid colours. Above all, however, far-reaching social changes were announcing the end of the era with which she was now identified.

In 1936, to her dismay, the workers at her factories and workshops went on strike. Coco regarded their action as the ultimate personal affront. While she, as the employer, felt she paid them well, gave them privileges and even offered a month of paid vacation time instead of the statutory 15 days, with the possibility of staying at the workers' vacation resort she had set up in Mimizan, the workers

---

[71]Coco Chanel, cited by Leymarie, Jean. *Op. cit.*, p. 158. Free translation from the original French.

[72]See: *Celebrity Homes: Coco Chanel*: http://www.youtube.com/watch?v=cZ2VNimpCV4&feature=related.

themselves were more interested in their work schedules, wages and vacation conditions. They even prevented her from entering her own fashion house during the strike. Eventually she gave in to several of their demands, partly because she wanted to save the collection that was being prepared (her famous ultra-nationalist red, white and blue collection).

As always, she had several projects on the boil. In 1937, she attended the International Exhibition of Art and Technology in Modern Life and created the costumes for Cocteau's Oedipus Rex. Her maxims were published in Vogue magazine in September 1938. She also met Dali and hosted him at La Pausa, where she set up a special studio for him at the bottom of the garden.

The Second World War broke out on 3 September 1939. Coco Chanel closed her fashion house, claiming that the era of the dress was over. Only her accessory and perfume boutiques remained open. Some saw this as a kind of vengeance. Perhaps she was trying to punish her workers for going on strike? Or was it simply a good business decision?

Coco Chanel: Building an Empire – Chanel in Three Acts Act Three: Revival and Survival (1953–1971)

> I'll never rest as long as I'm alive. There's nowhere I'd be more bad-tempered or tired than in a rest home. I know I'd be bored stiff in heaven; I'm more bored on a plane than on the ground.
>
> – Coco Chanel[73]

In 1946, Coco Chanel was 63 years old. From 1946 to 1953, she lived in voluntary exile in Lausanne (Switzerland), where she went to escape the unpleasant post-war 'atmosphere and settling of scores'.[74] It was the place she said she would like to be buried one day. She went back to France from time to time, staying at her home in Roquebrune, or in Paris. While in Switzerland she lived in hotels, always with her wartime lover, Hans Günther von Dincklage, known as Spatz.

In Switzerland, she was surrounded by rich exiles, royalty and illustrious artists including Maurice Chevalier, Sacha Guitry, Somerset Maugham, Yvonne Printemps, Gary Cooper and Gregory Peck.

Creative Boredom

The same thing happened to her in Switzerland as had happened during her time with Balsan: surrounded by the 'beautiful people', Coco Chanel became bored. Playing the piano, accordion or cards . . . she was ill-suited to a life of leisure. She

[73]Coco Chanel to Paul Morand, in *L'Allure de Chanel*, p. 204, cited by Fiemeyer, Isabelle. *Op. cit.*, p. 132. Free translation from the original French.

[74]Fiemeyer, Isabelle. *Op. cit.*, p. 130.

missed her scissors, and in the darkest times began to sleepwalk. She was haunted by the spirits of her dead friends: her family, and more recently, Diaghilev, who died in 1929, Paul Irebe (1935), Dimitri (1942), Sert (1947) and Misia in 1950, followed by Westminster and Balsan. Dincklage, rejected by Switzerland after the war, went back to Hanover and ultimately went to live on Spain's Balearic Islands.

Coco Chanel always kept an eye on her business. In 1946, she went to New York to review the contracts binding her to some of the city's stores. By then, virtually all her income was derived from her perfumes. In Europe, she renewed contact with the arts community, with directors Franco Zeffirelli, Roger Vadim and Christian Bérard.

In New York, she had a very specific reason for going over her contracts: she had appointed a lawyer, René de Chambrun, to act for her, and was preparing a transaction with the Wertheimer brothers. The United States was, in her view, a market with infinite potential. While in Switzerland, and unbeknownst to the Wertheimer brothers, she had quietly created three new perfumes (No. 3, No. 2 and No. 31), under the name *Mademoiselle Chanel.* They were ready to launch in 1946, in round bottles, with red labels and white lettering. As for the Wertheimers, they had set up a new company, *Chanel Inc.*, in 1942, and had begun to promote a new perfume sold under the American colours (red, white and blue), named *Courage.*

In 1947, René de Chambrun negotiated an agreement with the Wertheimer brothers, and Coco Chanel became immensely rich as a result. The brothers showed no resentment about the three new perfumes created in Switzerland. In fact, one of them, No. 31 (renamed No. 19), went on to become a huge success. As a result of the agreement, Coco Chanel received 2% of world perfume sales (at least $1 million per year) in exchange for her 10% shareholding in the Chanel perfume company. The Wertheimer brothers were responsible for paying all her living expenses, including her apartment at the Ritz Hotel in Paris. A lump sum was also paid to cover the arrears owing until the agreement came into force in May 1947.

Coco Chanel convinced herself that she would never work again, and that she had retired. France had changed. The great fashion houses were now led by men, including Christian Dior, whose *New Look* was all the rage. Off-the-peg fashions demanded production conditions that Coco Chanel did not think she could support, and she did not understand why fashion had fallen into the hands of men. Almost all of them were homosexuals. How could they possibly understand what women needed?

The Return of Chanel

Nobody suspected that Coco Chanel was preparing a comeback. In 1953, following Westminster's death, she sold her Roquebrune villa *La Pausa.* Étienne Balsan had also been killed in a car accident, bringing back painful memories. And then her brother Alphonse also died. This intense period of mourning, somewhat paradoxically, seemed to give Coco Chanel a new lease on life.

And in fact, she still had more to say. She travelled to New York to see her friend Maggy Van Zuylen, who lived permanently at the Waldorf Astoria hotel. She renewed her contacts with the city's fashion journalists, and felt intuitively that she still had a place in the world of fashion, alongside Dior, Balenciaga and Givenchy. She reopened her fashion house on Rue Cambon, in Paris, hired workers for her workshops and decided to present a new collection in Paris on 5 February 1954.

The entire experience was a letdown. But rather than being crushed by the critiques, some of whom described her as a 'has-been', Coco Chanel got back up, dusted herself off and set to work. France, she said, hated her, as did England. The message was clear. In an interview with journalist Lillian Ross of the *New Yorker* magazine, Coco Chanel claimed she had 'laughed' at the critiques' reaction to her collection as being outdated. 'Wait and see', she said![75]

France may have rejected her, but America welcomed her, and a photograph of her chosen model, Marie-Hélène Arnaud, dressed in a dark blue jersey jacket over a white blouse, appeared in *Vogue* in 1954. It was an image reminiscent of her former self, rejuvenated, defying time. She rebounded with quilted bags, two-tone pumps and corded jackets. Her dresses were short and light. She was right: America loved her. The Americans bought the Chanel look.

Unlike the French critiques, who treated her with contempt, Bettina Ballard of Vogue said Chanel's models were reminiscent of all that was best in the 1930s – elegant lace evening dresses and suits that were easy to wear and refreshing after the cluttered look of previous years.[76] Customers quickly followed.

Bettina Ballard justified the market's enthusiasm for all things Chanel, noting that it was precisely because the 'Chanel Look' had not changed that women liked it so much. Women, she said, wanted clothing that made them feel confident, and this was where Chanel excelled. For years, fashion had made women look ridiculous. Chanel was like a breath of fresh air. She gave women attitude and style, not fashion.[77]

In Dallas, in the fall of 1957, Coco Chanel received an award, the Oscar of the fashion world, from the hands of Stanley Marcus, owner of the Neiman Marcus stores. He described her as the most influential fashion creator of the century, and the most courageous for coming back to the top at the age of 74, 'like a former champion'.

The columnists from the most popular fashion journals and magazines came faithfully to her twice-yearly shows. This time, it was the New Wave actresses who wore her creations, on screen and in the city: Jeanne Moreau, Delphine Seyric and Romy Schneider. Marilyn Monroe said the only thing she wore at night was Chanel No. 5. The Chanel jacket became a classic, and became forever associated with President Kennedy's assassination: Jacqueline Kennedy, dressed in a bloodstained pink Chanel suit, was unforgettable.

[75]Picardie, Justine. *Op. cit.*, p. 337.
[76]Bettina Ballard, cited by Picardie, Justine. *Op. cit.*, p. 329.
[77]Bettina Ballard, cited by Picardie, Justine. *Op. cit.*, p. 330.

Looking to Eternity

In the 1960s, Coco Chanel was horrified by the miniskirt, since it revealed the knees, which she had always felt were ugly. She criticized women for forgetting what elegance was. Trousers, she felt, should be worn only for sport, on the beach or when alone at home. Her famous maxims, which she had written during Pierre Reverdy's time, revealed the secrets of true elegance and good taste: 'Always take off, never put back – no button without a button hole – the inside as beautiful as the outside'.[78]

In 1962, photographer Douglas Kirkland captured Coco Chanel's dynamism and seductive charm. As Karl Lagerfeld noted:

> He removed from her image all its evils and the bitchy side popular imagination has attached to her persona. (...) Hating them and letting people know publicly how much she loathed the fashions to come, she put herself instantly in the position of the has-been oracle of style and fashion.
>
> The years to come were clouded by her gloom and bitterness. They were also the years of respect, homage (a word the French love) and all those evident signs which tell you your time is over. (...)
>
> (...) This young man was a perfect target to test for the last time her once famous powers of seduction. There are hardly any photos of her – even when young – with such a winning smile, with such a lightness in her expression.[79]

Coco Chanel hardly ever went out now, except for her once-daily trip to Rue Cambon. In the street, she was bothered by the people who recognized and greeted her. After all, she did not know them. She always wore a suit and boater hat in straw or felt, depending on the season. She also wore too much makeup: too much rouge, too much eyeliner, too much of everything. And always her broaches and pearls.

Mademoiselle, as she was known, had become grouchy and hard on both herself and other people. She pushed everyone around her. The living models on whom she worked became exhausted. She was still creative and determined, and always seemed to be battling her own creations. She had begun to use more lamé and more colour: her base colour was still beige, but it was now enhanced with red, green, blue and gold.

Coco Chanel took regular trips to Switzerland, 'a clean country where one feels safe'. She bought a modest home near Lausanne, which she intended to renovate but never did. After Paul Iribe's death in 1935, she had never been able to sleep without taking Sedol, a form of morphine on which she had come to rely.

---

[78]Leymarie, Jean. *Op. cit.*, p. 224.
[79]Kirkland, Douglas and Karl Lagerfeld. *Op. cit.* Not paginaged.

She took it to keep going, so as not to feel as though she were dying, to keep herself safe from the shadows that haunted her and the hands that shook the heavy curtains of her Ritz bedroom. She occasionally slashed her own pyjamas with scissors, while she was sleeping. She thought of going to America. Her arm became paralysed after a minor stroke. She almost found it funny.

On 10 January 1971, her friend Claude Delay-Tubiana found her standing in front of her mirror, scrawny and old, but so full of enthusiasm and projects for the day: lunch at the Ritz, as usual, followed by a trip to the races. The following day, she sent her friend away, because she had so much to do. When she returned home on the Sunday, she complained of a suffocating chest pain, and went to lie down. And that is how she died: 'neat, made up and well-dressed'.[80] 'This is how you die', were her last words. She was alert until the very end. She was 87 years old.

Her great-niece, Gabrielle Labrunie, and two of her faithful workers, sat with her. They said they tried to protect her, to make sure her last moments were calm, but according to Justine Picardie, during the night of Chanel's death, a stream of mysterious visitors left with bags containing most of her jewellery.[81]

The day after her death, *Le Monde* and the *New York Times* both published columns and acknowledged the work of Chanel the woman, entrepreneur and creator. After her death, Coco Chanel was acknowledged and acclaimed by a host of designers who spoke of her influence. Her funeral took place at La Madeleine, but in accordance with her wishes she was buried in the cemetery at Lausanne: 'The life we live is not much, she believed, but the life we dream, that is important, because it will continue after our death'.[82]

Throughout her life, Coco Chanel used creativity as a way of overcoming the profound humiliation of her childhood and adolescence. She helped to redefine women as people who were able to free themselves from suffocating social norms. She left the world with a concept of elegance that has been handed down by women over the generations. Without realizing it, she created an entire industrial sector that would become a major player in several economies, generating thousands of jobs in the process.

Survival . . .

The survival of the *House of Chanel* had been secured in the winter of 1954, when Coco Chanel went to New York with her great-niece Gabrielle Palasse-Labrunie, to meet with Pierre Wertheimer and suggest that he should take over as its leader.

Under the agreement, she kept her rights over the perfumes, and her lifestyle was maintained and paid for, but she handed over financial leadership of the

---

[80]Perrignon, Judith, Coco Chanel, possédée par sa légende, dans Le Monde, le 23 (15 h 50) et le 27 (16 h 39) août 2012: https://www.lemonde.fr/culture/article/2012/08/23/coco-chanel-possedee-par-sa-legende_1750784_3246.html.

[81]Picardie, Justine. *Op. cit.*, p. 11.

[82]Leymarie, Jean, *Op. cit.*, p. 243. Free translation from the original French.

House of Chanel to the Wertheimer family, keeping only the artistic leadership, which she held until her death.

The Wertheimers took over the entire fashion house, all the workshops and stores, plus the rights to the image and name. In the 1960s, the Pantin factory made everything, from the lipstick first produced in 1924, to the corks used for bottles of Chanel N° 5.

In doing this, Coco Chanel made sure her life's work would continue on in the hands of a solid, dynamic family firm created in the 19th century by Jewish tie-maker Ernest Wertheimer. The third-generation Wertheimers, grandsons of Pierre Wertheimer, have continued the legacy to the present day. The two brothers control the entire enterprise, Alain from New York and Gérard from Geneva. They are among the richest people in the world.

Karl Lagerfeld was the artistic leader of the *House of Chanel* from 1983 until his death on 19 February 2019. The name, logos and graphics that Coco Chanel chose for her products and her company have survived, and her private apartments on Rue Cambon have been preserved. Even Karl Lagerfeld's office door has always shown the name *Mademoiselle*. Visitors half expect to see her standing at the top of the famous staircase.

Last Will and Testament

Coco Chanel loved life: her life. Sometimes she expressed regret at having never had either a husband or a child. She once told her great-niece and her friend Claude Delay that, regardless of age, 'every woman needs a man who looks at her with love (...) without such a look, she is dead'.[83]

And if she had something to say to the women of today:

> I want to tell you something important. Fashion is always the fashion of the time in which we live. It doesn't happen in isolation. The problems faced by fashion in 1925 were different. Women had barely begun to work in offices. I launched the fashion of short hair because it was suited to the modern woman. I told working women to take off their corsets because they would not be able to work otherwise. I invented tweed for sportswear, as well as pullovers and baggy shirts. I encouraged women to take pride in their appearance and to love perfume. A woman who doesn't wear perfume has no future![84]

Coco Chanel's affairs were in order when she died. She had embraced philanthropy in the last few years of her life. In 1965, for example, she had created the COGA Foundation (CO for Coco and GA for Gabrielle) to take care of her employees and the artists who had remained faithful to her, and to pay a pension

[83]Picardie, Justine. *Op. cit.*, p. 379.

[84]Coco Chanel to Lillian Ross in the *New Yorker*, cited in Picardie, Justine. *Op. cit.*, p. 337.

to her cook, chauffeur, butler and maids. COGA is based in Vaduz, Liechtenstein, where it is sheltered from income tax.

She also became involved in a number of social causes: 'By the time she died in 1971, Chanel had become one of the richest women I the world. She left an estimated fortune of more than $10 million to a trust that would distribute it to charities, one of which was a fund set up to help workers who accidentally lost their hands'.[85] She had set up this fund when her own right arm was paralysed.[86]

In 1966, her Parisian lawyer Robert Badinter was replaced by Swiss counsel. From then onwards Mr Badinter only took care of small details and licences, and also defended her from personal attacks. He was patient and would listen quietly while Mademoiselle raged against mini-skirts, women who wore pants, and new fashion trends.

Coco Chanel prepared her will shortly after the death of Pierre Wertheimer in April 1965. Its executors were Mr Gutstein, a lawyer from Zurich, and the Swiss Banking Union. Her fortune was estimated at $75 million francs.[87]

Pierre Wertheimer bequeathed the *House of Chanel* to his only son Jacques, who was 56 years old at the time. However, Jacques, an art collector, hypochondriac and horse enthusiast, had little interest in the family business and was replaced in 1974 by his son Alain, who was just 26 years old. Alain invited his brother Gérard to join him, and they went on to develop what would become a flagship company in the luxury empire – although not without some difficulties, since competition was fierce.

In 1983, after restructuring, acquisitions and attempts to revitalize the company, Chanel was teetering on the edge of bankruptcy. As a last resort, the two brothers hired Karl Lagerfeld as their artistic director: 'It was like *Sleeping Beauty* when I arrived – completely outdated. Wertheimer told me: Chanel! It's no fun as it is. If you're able to do something with it, so much the better. If not, I'm going to sell it'.[88] Karl Lagerfeld '... was taken by the idea of bringing the Queen back to life'. Virginie Viard, a close collaborator of Karl Lagerfeld for roughly 30 years, took over the position after his death.[89]

In 2018, Alain and Gérard Wertheimer, along with other family members, owned 100% of the *House of Chanel*. While they remain discreet, their company is one of the largest in France, with an estimated value of roughly $10 billion – almost as much as Louis Vuitton, and far more than Gucci.[90]

---

[85]Artuso, Anthony. W. and A. Zalesnik (1987) op. cit., p.322.

[86]Artuso, Anthony. W. and A. Zalesnik (1987).

[87]About US$15 million at the time.

[88]Perrignon, Judith, Coco Chanel, possédée par sa légende, in *Le Monde*, August 23 (3:50) and 27 (4:39) 2012: https://www.lemonde.fr/culture/article/2012/08/23/coco-chanel-possedee-par-sa-legende_1750784_3246.html.

[89]Birken, Maxime, Qui est Virginie Viard, successeur de Karl Lagerfeld chez Chanel, Huffpost, 19/02/2019 14:23 CET | Updated February 19, 2019: https://www.huffingtonpost.fr/2019/02/19/qui-est-virginie-viard-successeur-de-karl-lagarfeld-chez-chanel_a_23672816/.

[90]Public information officially published for the first time in 2018.

Coco Chanel: Building an Empire – Chanel in Three Acts Epilogue: The Chanel Mystery (1939–1945)

> Jews or not, she didn't care (. . .) She was a selfish woman who had no empathy for human beings, and who despised both the Germans and de Gaulle's resistance.
>
> – Isée St. John Knowles[91]

In 1940, Coco Chanel was living in a pied-à-terre at the Paris Ritz. By all accounts, she was helping friends to hide intellectuals and artists who were wanted by the Germans. In the summer of 1940, she joined the Palasse family, whom she regarded as her only relatives, in Corbères, France, where she sheltered some of her own workers, sending gifts to any of their family members who were soldiers. She also became the war sponsor of French actor and director Jean Marais.

She seemed to be leading a quiet life, but American and German archives discovered after the War suggested that she was in fact involved in top-secret missions with Churchill, and in peace negotiations instigated by German officers afraid for their lives as the end of the War became imminent. This somewhat ambiguous period of her life was not explored by Coco Chanel's biographers until much later, and there are still many grey areas and unanswered questions, as though France as a whole were trying to keep this particular skeleton firmly ensconced in its cupboard.

Baron Hans Günther von Dincklage, known as Spatz, was an aristocrat, a third-generation member of a family of German officers, who had fought alongside his father on the Russian Front during the First World War. His family's values were deeply nationalist, racist and militarist, and he was extremely bitter about the defeat and humiliation inflicted on the German people by the Versailles Treaty at the end of the First World War.

Spatz was a member of the Revolutionary Party of German Communist Workers, an extremist group responsible for assassinating Jewish intellectual and Marxist militant Rosa Luxemburg in 1919. Shortly afterwards, Spatz was recruited and trained by the German Secret Police, becoming Agent 8680F. He was part of a *Freikorps* composed of civil and military combatants whose main combat tactics were harassment and stealth.

Spatz was well-mannered, cultivated and seductive. He spoke both French and English, and had typically Aryan looks: blond hair, athletic build, and blue eyes. He was resourceful, curious, an excellent observer, and blended easily into groups. In other words, he was the perfect spy. Beneath his carefree exterior, the thing that interested him the most was the Mediterranean port of Toulon, where the French navy was stationed.

---

[91] Isée St. John Knowles, President of the Baudelaire Society to which Coco Chanel made a donation. Cited by Catherine Schwaab in Paris Match: http://www.parismatch.com/Conso-Match/Mode/Actu/Chanel-intime-335563/Free translation from the original French. See also: Muggeridge, Malcolm, *Chanel's only interview about her war, in September 1944:* http://www.baudelaire-chanel.com/malcolm_muggeridge_entretien.php.

When did Coco Chanel and Spatz meet? The answer is: probably in 1941. She was 57–58 years old, and he was 13 years younger. As Coco Chanel herself pointed out, 'When you're nearly 60, you don't look at a gentleman's passport'. According to Gabrielle Palasse-Labrunie, he was the shoulder her great-aunt needed to lean on, and the man capable of bringing home her nephew André Palasse, who had fought on the Maginot Line and been taken prisoner in 1940.

Despite her reticence and doubts about Spatz's military activities, Coco Chanel apparently asked him to help free Palasse. Unable to intervene directly, Spatz introduced her to a friend, Theodor Momm, who was responsible for Germany's textile activities in France. He was able to obtain Palasse's freedom by putting him in charge of a factory owned by Coco Chanel and reopened for precisely that purpose.[92] However, this was only the beginning of an extremely complex story.

The German archives clearly show that a certain 'Frau Chanel', a perfume factory owner, was in fact recruited by the German secret services. In 1941, her name appeared in a German Intelligence Service file as Agent F-7124, under the code name Westminster. She knew Churchill sufficiently well and could persuade him to prepare for peace. She was described as an enemy of Soviet Russia, a simple citizen who felt it was her duty to help France.

A woman known as Frau Lombardi was supposed to serve as the intermediary between Frau Chanel, the German contingent, and Churchill.[93] However, rather than simply delivering the message to Chanel, who would then take it to Churchill, Frau Lombardi decided to denounce Chanel to the British authorities.

Others have also suggested that Coco Chanel played a much more active role in the War. For example, it was she who is purported to have asked Theodor Momm to negotiate peace with Churchill in 1943. The operation would have had a particularly apt code name: 'Chapeau de couture' or 'Fashion Hat'. Apparently, a meeting regarding this possibility took place in Berlin in 1943, with Walter Friedrich Schellenberg, head of the SS Intelligence Service, and an acolyte of Himmler. A 119-page document summarizing Schellenberg's interrogation by the British Secret Service (MI6), in 1945, is kept in the National Archives in Washington.

According to this document, Chanel knew Churchill sufficiently well to start political negotiations with him. She described herself as an enemy of the

---

[92]This was the Chanel fabric factory, located in Maretz, in the Nord-Pas-de-Calais region. The Chanel Fabric Company had been created in 1930 and would remain in business until 1950. Rodier, from which she purchased jersey, was also located there, but was swallowed up by Chanel. The building has since become a museum, and still contains two looms and a sample of Chanel's early jersey fabrics. Source: Isabelle Bernard: Sur les traces de Coco Chanel, Thursday, May 7, 2009: http://www.lunion.presse.fr/article/a-la-une/sur-les-traces-de-coco-chanel.

[93]Frau Lombardi, who used the name of her Italian husband, Alberto Lombardi, an officer and Colonel in the cavalry, was in fact Chanel's former colleague Vera Bate (when using her first husband's name), or Sarah Arkwright (her own name). After marrying Alberto Lombardi, she became an Italian citizen and later a member of the Fascist party that supported Mussolini. She was arrested in 1943 and accused of spying for the British.

Bolsheviks who wanted to help France and Germany fulfil their shared destiny. Schellenberg, Chanel, Spatz, Theodor Momm and Schiebe, an SS officer, were all present. Coco Chanel never denied being questioned in Berlin, but she never clarified either her role or her contacts.

In Paris, on 16 April 1946, Coco Chanel was called before Judge Roger Serre and questioned about her relationship with Baron Louis de Vaufreland, a traitor who had worked for the Gestapo. In a detailed 50-page report, the Judge stated that Coco Chanel had in fact been recruited by the Abwehr (the German Intelligence Service), had been a spy, and had also belonged to a circle of pro-Nazi politicians in England and Spain.

Judge Serre was not able to uncover the extent of her collaboration with SS Walter Schellenberg, nor was he able to establish her complicity with Baron Hans Günther von Dincklage (Spatz). The post-war period was a time when many scores were settled in France, and when many cruel and tragic events took place. As the French took their revenge on the collaborators, they showed absolutely no mercy towards women who had maintained sexual relationships with German soldiers.[94]

The biographers who studied this period of Coco Chanel's life based their charges of anti-Semitism and pro-Nazi behaviour on a variety of facts and scenarios, and on documents from the French and German archives when they became available. However, many documents were destroyed during the War, and others were factually incorrect.

Some people have claimed that Coco Chanel's deep-seated anti-Semitism was connected to her Catholic upbringing, the Dreyfus Affair of which she had undoubtedly heard, and the anti-Semitic opinions of her lovers and collaborators, including the Duke of Westminster and Paul Iribe. Iribe, for example, had clearly demonstrated his ultra-nationalistic leanings in 1933, when he published a drawing showing a 'Marianne' (a representation of the Goddess of Liberty) who looked very like Coco Chanel, naked, wearing a Phrygian or 'liberty' cap, lying in the arms of Hitler, under the caption 'France is still breathing'.[95] The drawing was published in *Le Témoin*, a magazine supported financially by Coco Chanel.

Today, in spite of all the stories of what she said and what she did, many questions still remain unanswered: Was Coco Chanel anti-Semitic? Was she a Nazi sympathizer? Did she collaborate with the Gestapo?

In his book *Sleeping with the Enemy*, Hal Vaughan notes that Frau Chanel was sufficiently involved to have an agent's number, and was allowed to circulate

---

[94]Picardie, Justine. *Op. cit*, p. 305.

[95]The Dreyfus Affair: A judicial error involving betrayal and spying, against a background of anti-Semitism. Captain Alfred Dreyfus, a Jew from the Alsace region of France, was accused of spying for Germany. His trial, covered extensively by an anti-Semite press, divided France into two camps: the 'Dreyfusards' who believed in his innocence, and the 'Anti-Dreyfusards' who thought he was guilty. The trial took place from 1894 to 1906. Captain Dreyfus was found not guilty and was rehabilitated by an order of France's Court of Appeal.

freely in Switzerland and Germany, using a pass that only the Gestapo could issue.[96] He also noted that her lover had managed to find accommodations for her at the Ritz, a veritable German fortress at the time. She lived not in a single room, but on the second floor, in apartment 227-228, in a section reserved exclusively for friends of the Reich. Her neighbours included Marie-Louise Ritz, the wife of hotel owner César Ritz, in apartment 266-268, and the pro-Nazi Dubonnet family, in room 263. The Ritz was a regular haunt of Göring and Goebbels, Joachim von Ribbentrop and Albert Speer.

Those who lived at the Ritz wanted for nothing. Meals were generous and sophisticated, and wine was plentiful. While the people of France raided garbage cans or died of hunger, Coco Chanel was able to provide lavish entertainment for her guests, including Serge Lifar, whom the Germans had appointed to lead the Paris Opéra ballet company, as well as Jean Cocteau and Jean Marais, who lived near the Ritz and, like many others, depended on their benefactor to live.

Was she forced to collaborate with the Germans? Was it the price she paid for André Palasse's freedom? Or, as Vaughan suggests, was she simply being opportunistic?[97] Would she have used her contacts or her 'Aryan identity' to take back control of the Chanel Perfume Company and get rid of the Jewish Wertheimer family, whom she felt owned too big a portion of 'her' company?

The Wertheimer brothers had escaped from Europe via Spain, and after a brief stay in Brazil, took refuge in New York with their wives and children. In 1940, the Bourjois factory in Croydon, England, which produced more than 600,000 bars of soap per month, in addition to talcum powder and perfume, was destroyed by the Luftwaffe. Fortunately the Chanel perfumes, produced in Pantin, France, were not affected. In Paris, Coco Chanel was said to have given bottles of perfume to the American soldiers as gifts during the Liberation.

The Wertheimer brothers had already experienced their share of problems with Coco Chanel, and had hired a full-time lawyer to manage their agreements with her. Before they left for America, they handed over control of the company to nominees, including Félix Amiot, a French industrialist and aircraft builder, with whom they would have considerable trouble after the War. The Wertheimer brothers were able to deceive the Nazis and maintain control over their family businesses. If Coco Chanel ever had any intention of trying to take back control of the Chanel Perfume Company, they had once again managed to outsmart her.

After the War, she always cut short any attempt at conversation on this subject, and when biographies were subsequently published, the *House of Chanel* firmly reiterated that Coco Chanel was neither a Nazi sympathizer nor

[96]Vaughan (2011, p. 131).

[97]Vaughan, Hal, author of *Sleeping with the Enemy,* Coco Chanel, Anti-Semite and Nazi Agent: (August 16, 2011) http://www.dailymotion.com/video/xkkpoz_coco-chanel-antisemite-et-agent-nazi_news.

anti-Semitic. As for the Wertheimer family, they came to her aid when she tried to re-establish herself in France's post-War fashion community.[98]

Following the abortive exchange of letters for her supposed meeting with Churchill to begin discussions aimed at ending the War, Coco Chanel fell out with Vera Bate. Later, during the Liberation, she was arrested and detained ... for an hour. Churchill is said to have intervened in her favour. Shortly afterwards, she left France to go and live in Switzerland, possibly as a requirement for her release.

She always maintained contact with Walter Schellenberg, who was tried in Nuremburg and sentenced to six years in prison. His sentence was relatively light because he had helped save thousands of prisoners from the concentration camps, and had come over to the prosecution. Coco Chanel continued to write to him on a regular basis, and supported him financially when he was released from prison in 1950. He died the following year, and once again Coco Chanel paid for her friend's funeral.

Even after her death, her ghosts came back to haunt her. Madame Pompidou, a fervent admirer and customer of Coco Chanel, had prepared an exhibition, due to open in October 1972, on the life and work of Coco Chanel. According to Hal Vaughan, Hebe Dorsey, editor of the *International Herald Tribune* and a popular fashion columnist, threw the first rock: Was France in fact preparing to celebrate a woman who had slept with a dangerous Gestapo agent? This was, and will probably continue to be, part of the 'Chanel Mystery'.[99]

Selected Bibliography and Notes About Coco Chanel

Artuso, Anthony W. and A. Zalesnik (1987) 'Coco Chanel (1883–1971)' (Harvard College). Case study written by Anthony W. Artuso under the supervision of Professor Abraham Zalesnik. Translation into French by Geneviève Sicotte, under the supervision of Professor Laurent Lapierre. Published in: Lapierre, L. (1992) *Imaginaire et leadership*, Volume 1, pp. 321–345, p. 322.

Birken, Maxime, *Qui est Virginie Viard, successeur de Karl Lagerfeld chez Chanel*, Huffpost, 19/02/2019 14:23 CET | Updated February 19, 2019: https://www.huffingtonpost.fr/2019/02/19/qui-est-virginie-viard-successeur-de-karl-lagarfeld-chez-chanel_a_23672816/

Chaney, Lisa. *Chanel (2011) – An Intimate Life*, London, Fig Tree, Penguin Books, xvi-496 pages.

Charles-Roux, Edmonde (1974) *L'irrégulière ou monitinéraire Chanel*, Paris, Grasset. Also: L'irrégulière – L'itinéraire de Coco Chanel, Collection Le Livre de Poche, no: 4825, 2009, 661 pages.

Fiemeyer, Isabelle (2004) *Coco Chanel – Un parfum de mystère,* Paris, Éditions Payot & Rivages, Paperback Edition, 173 pages.

[98]Kerleau, Yann, author of *Dynasties du luxe*: Pierre Wertheimer, l'homme qui a sauvé la maison Chanel (January 11, 2011): http://www.myboox.fr/video/yann-kerlau-pierre-wertheimer-l-homme-qui-sauve-la-maison-chanel-5387.html.

[99]Vaughan, Hal. (2011, p. XV).

Gidel, Henry (2000) *Coco Chanel*, Paris, Éditions Flammarion, 375 pages.
Haedrich, Marcel (2008) *Coco Chanel*, Paris, Éditions Gutenberg, 236 pages.
Kirkland, Douglas and Karl Lagerfeld (2009) *Mademoiselle – Coco Chanel Summer 62*. Photos by Douglas Kirkland, text by Karl Lagerfeld, 1st Edition, Glitterati Incorporated, New York, Steidl Publishers, Götingen, not paginated.
Laty, Dominique (2009) *Misia Sert et Coco Chanel*, Paris, Odile Jacob, 252 pages.
Leymarie, Jean (2010) *Chanel*, Paris, Éditions de La Martinière, 246 pages.
Madsen, Axel (1990) *Chanel – A Woman of Her Own*, New York, St Martin Griffin, 1990, x-388 pages.
Morand, Paul (1996) *L'Allure de Chanel*, Paris, Hermann, 248 pages.
Perrignon, Judith (2012) *Coco Chanel, possédée par sa légende*, in Le Monde, August 23 and 27: https://www.lemonde.fr/culture/article/2012/08/23/coco-chanel-possedee-par-sa-legende_1750784_3246.html
Picardie, Justine (2011) *Chanel: sa vie*, translated from English by Lionel Leforestier, with input from Sabine Charvet, Aude Fondard and Magali Pès, 2nd Edition, Göttingen, Steidl, 395 pages.
Simon, Linda (2011) *Coco Chanel*, London, Reaktion Books Ltd, 2011, 203 pages.
SOCIÉTÉ.COM: https://www.societe.com/societe/chanel-542052766.html Presentation by the company Chanel. Chiffres-clés des entreprises.
Usine Nouvelle (L'), https://www.usinenouvelle.com/article/chanel-implante-sa-r-d-a-pantin-pres-de-paris.N26337 'Chanel implante sa R&D à Pantin, près de Paris', October 10, 2008.
Vaughan, hal (2011) *Sleeping with the Enemy - Coco Chanel's Secret War*, New York, Alfred A. Knopf, 279 pages.

Coco Chanel – Audiovisual Documents

Linternaute, Paris pendant les années folles. http://www.linternaute.com/actualite/histoire/paris-pendant-les-annees-folles/
Maison Chanel – Portal, http://www.chanel.com/fr_FR/
Marie-Claire TV Découvrez les secrets de création d'une robe Haute Couture Chanel. http://www.vogue.fr/mode/news-mode/articles/chanel-haute-couture-le-making-of/3759
On Paris in the 1920s: Allen, Woody. *Midnight in Paris.* United States and Spain, 2011.
Paris in the 1920s. 100 minutes. http://fr.wikipedia.org/wiki/Minuit_%C3%A0_Paris

About Coco Chanel

(1) Coco Chanel: The Legend and the Life by Justine Picardie. http://www.youtube.com/watch?v=i9WwBP0JPqg
(2) Bitoun, Eric (2020) Chanel l'insoumise. Documentary, SKOPIA Films, Paris. (53 minutes)

(3) Fontaine, Anne. *Coco avant Chanel* Paris, 2008.
(4) Video recording HEC - DVD (110 minutes) Electronic access: Visionnement
(5) Duguay, Christian, Coco Chanel Video Series: Chanel from 1 to 10 Collection with Shirley Maclaine. http://www.dailymotion.com/video/x7ycng_coco-chanel-1-10_webcam
(6) Ten capsules on different stages of Coco Chanel's life Inside Coco Chanel's Private Apartment. http://www.youtube.com/watch?v=xpinr4Uts-8
(7) Lauritano, Jean (2018) The Wars of Coco Chanel (Les guerres de Coco Chanel), 55-minute documentary. Includes several excerpts from interviews with Coco Chanel (1883–1971), the year before she died (1970). Arte France, Slow Production. French, German, English.

Sandrel, Micheline

Mademoiselle Chanel. http://www.ina.fr/art-et-culture/mode-et-design/video/CAF86015245/mademoiselle-chanel.fr.html

Chanel, 86 years old, in an interview. Document containing: archive images, fashion shows, society critiques, elegance, popular trends including trousers for women, ugliness of knees, American customers, youth cult and money.

Vaughan, Hal: Coco Chanel antisémite et agent nazi: *Sleeping With the Enemy* ('Coucher avec l'ennemi'). http://www.dailymotion.com/video/xkkpoz_coco-chanel-antisemite-et-agent-nazi-lvmh-se-separera-t-il-de-chanel-comme-de-john-galliano_news

Note 1

Interview in French on the life and work of Coco Chanel, as told by Véronique Borboën

Title of the programme: *Aujourd'hui, l'histoire*
https://ici.radio-canada.ca/premiere/emissions/aujourd-hui-l-histoire/segments/entrevue/52185/coco-chanel-mode-haute-couture-parfum-tailleur-veronique-bor-boen. December 20, 2017 (Audio dated Thursday, December 21, 2017).

Excerpt from the interview (translated from the original French)

The Chanel Revolution: Perfume, Suits and Little Black Dresses

Creating Modern Fashion

Coco Chanel had watched as women had to wear corsets and elaborate hairstyles, and decided to create a line of clothing that she herself would enjoy. Her garments allowed women to move freely, without feeling over-dressed.

Chanel was a hard-worker and ruled both her company and her employees with a fist of iron. She quickly earned a reputation for her talent and intuition. By 1919, she had 300 employees.

During the fabric shortage caused by the First World War, Chanel made stretch dresses in the jersey fabrics used by soldiers. She also introduced women to the sailor shirt.

Véronique Borboën is a specialist in costume history and teaches at the *École supérieure de Théâtre* at the *Université du Québec à Montréal* (UQAM). Her areas of expertise include: Theatre costumes – Costume history – Scenic arts - Theatre – International cities

Concerning the nickname 'Coco', she has a firm opinion, which she expresses at the end of the interview: The nickname derives from the song *Qui Qu'A Vu Coco,* which Chanel used to sing in concert cafés: *Qui Qu'A Vu Coco?* https://www.youtube.com/watch?v=-twn0-JBcpM

See also: *Coco avant Chanel*, film produced by Anne Fontaine, which can be seen at: https://www.google.com/search?q=coco+avant+chanel+film+complet+francais&rlz=1C1SQJL_enCA899CA899&oq=coco+avant+Chanel&aqs=chrome.4.69i59j46j0l6.10384j0j8&sourceid=chrome&ie=UTF-8

Maxims and Sayings by Gabrielle Chanel[100]

Fashion is always a reflection of its era, but we forget it if it is stupid.
You look sillier if you pretend to be naïve than if you admit your ignorance.
Taking care of your appearance is a victory of mind over common sense.
Goodness is love; generosity is a form of passion.
Nature gives you the face you have at twenty. Life shapes the face you have at thirty. But at fifty you get the face you deserve.
True generosity lies in accepting ingratitude.
Appearance, what a science! Beauty, what a weapon! Modesty, what elegance!
Fashion can sometimes be a queen, and sometimes a slave.
Your face is a mirror that reflects the movement of your inner life; take care of it.
You can become used to ugliness, but never to negligence.
Published in Vogue France, 1938 (translations).

Case Discussion

Below are some questions that you can use to start a discussion about this case study. You may also add others that are tailored to your particular learning context or field of study if you wish. The questions below are meant to encourage you to think about innovation-related activities. If you are using this case study in a classroom context, it may be useful to start the discussion in teams of two, before opening them up to the group as a whole. Students may also wish to change partners for each case discussion. It is important to note that there are many potential answers to each question.

---

[100]Maximes et sentences de Gabrielle Chanel. Published in Vogue Magazine – Paris, France, 1938. Selection of 10/31 by the authors of this case study.

Coco Chanel

(1) What are the indications in Coco Chanel's background to suggest that she could become an entrepreneur? Identify at least three.
(2) What did she learn from her family? From her education by the nuns?
(3) How do you assess the influence and the support she received from her lovers who were entrepreneurs? How did these role models influence the development of her interest in innovation?
(4) It was some time before Coco Chanel found her way into the fashion and clothing industry. What do you think led her to choose that sector?
(5) She spent a lot of time with artists. What influence do you think these relationships may have had on her creativity? On her capacity to innovate? Explain your answer.
(6) Coco Chanel had relationships with several political leaders. What do you think was the impact of her relationship with Winston Churchill, who became Prime Minister of Great Britain?
(7) Coco Chanel was a solitary person in some ways. Was this an advantage or a disadvantage for someone inventing products that had not previously existed? Why? Explain your answer.
(8) Chanel revolutionized women's clothing and changed the way actresses were dressed in the nascent film industry in Hollywood. What did she do to renew her capacity to work as an agent of innovation?
(9) What advice would you have given regarding the way she functioned and the way in which she introduced her innovative products to the market?
(10) What are the main lessons you have learned from Coco Chanel's story? Name four. How will these lessons support your own development and prospects as a potential innovationist? As a potential agent of innovation?

References

Artuso, A. W., &Zalesnik, A. (1987) *Coco Chanel (1883–1971)*. Harvard College.
François, L. (1961). *Comment un nom devient une griffe*. Gallimard.
Galante, P., & Orsini, P. (1972) *Les années Chanel, Paris, Mercure de France* (pages 340, p. 80).
Gallante, P. (1973). *Mademoiselle Chanel* (p. 213). Henry Regnery Co.
Haedrich, M. (1971). *Coco Chanel: Her life, her secrets* (p. 199). Little Brown and Co.
Laty, D. (2009). *Misia Sert et Coco Chanel* (pages, 252, p. 15). Odile Jacob Editor.
Leymarie, J. (2010). *Chanel, Paris, Éditions de La Martinière* (pages, 246, p. 7).
Picardie, J. (2011 [2010]). *Coco Chanel: The Legend and life* (p. 352). Harper Collins.
Vaughan, H. (2011). *Sleeping with the Enemy - Coco Chanel's Secret War* (pages, 279 p. 8). Alfred A. Knopf.

Chapter 2

Alain Bouchard, Couche-Tard/Circle K: Conquering the World of Convenience Stores

Joëlle Hafsi and Louis Jacques Filion

Abstract

Alain Bouchard was born in 1949. He bought his first convenience store in 1978, when he was almost 30 years old. By then, he already had nearly 10 years of experience in the sector. He had already been involved in the start-up of more than 200 convenience stores. He understood that if he was to transform his newly acquired store into a chain and build something big, he needed to set up a team of people with complementary skills to help him make acquisitions.

In 2023, there are roughly 15,000 convenience stores operating under the Circle K/Ingo/Couche-Tard banners, employing 130,000 people in more than 30 countries. Annual sales are more than US$60 billion. Alain Bouchard officially retired from his position as President and CEO in 2014 and became *Founder and Executive Chairman of the Board.* He continues to be a major shareholder. He is still actively involved in strategic orientations and in identifying potential acquisitions. He has become a 'Chief Culture Officer' involved in executive leadership mentoring. He has never stopped communicating the importance of innovative, creative and intrapreneurial behaviour at all levels of the enterprise.

This case study presents Alain Bouchard, the man and the entrepreneur. It shows how he learned and mastered the craft of starting, acquiring, managing and developing convenience stores. It looks at how he encouraged the people around him to act as facilitators and intrapreneurs. It describes his values, how he works and learned to live with risk.

Keywords: Entrepreneur; acquisitions (buying enterprises); convenience store; proximity store; teamwork; international business

Agents of Innovation, 49–87

doi:10.1108/978-1-83797-012-420231002

Case
Alain Bouchard, Couche-Tard/Circle K: Conquering the World of Convenience Stores[1]

> Being an entrepreneur means wanting to invent and keep reinventing your life.
>
> – Alain Bouchard[2]

Alain Bouchard was born in 1949. He bought his first convenience store in 1978, when he was almost 30 years old. By then, he already had nearly 10 years of experience in the sector. He had already been involved in the start-up of more than 200 convenience stores. He understood that if he was to transform his newly acquired store into a chain and build something big, he needed to set up a team of people with complementary skills to help him make acquisitions.

His first important acquisition – a chain of 11 Couche-Tard convenience stores in the Québec City region – took place in 1985. In the 15 years that followed, he and his team acquired a dozen more chains, bringing the total number of Couche-Tard stores to roughly 1,000 and transforming the enterprise into the leader of the convenience store sector in Canada.[3]

In 2003, Couche-Tard took over 2,200 Circle K stores operating in 16 American states, doubling its size in the process. This major acquisition would be followed by more than 100 additional ones, mainly in the United States but also elsewhere in the world, especially in Europe and Asia, making Alain Bouchard's chain one of the top-ranking convenience store enterprises in the world.

In 2023, there are roughly 15,000 convenience stores operating under the Circle K/Ingo/Couche-Tard banners, employing 130,000 people in more than 30 countries. Annual sales are more than US$60 billion. Alain Bouchard officially retired from his position as President and CEO in 2014 and became Founder and Executive Chairman of the Board. He continues to be a major shareholder. He is still actively involved in strategic orientations and in identifying potential acquisitions. He has become a 'Chief Culture Officer' involved in executive leadership mentoring. He has never stopped communicating the importance of innovative, creative and intrapreneurial behaviour at all levels of the enterprise.

This case study presents Alain Bouchard, the man and the entrepreneur. It shows how he put together a team to help bring his ambitions to fruition. It begins with his early life and motivations, and shows how he learned and mastered the craft of starting, acquiring, managing and developing convenience stores. It goes on to examine his learning process and looks at how he encouraged the people around him to act as facilitators and intrapreneurs. It also describes his values and how he works. Overall, it tells the story of a courageous, tenacious and daring entrepreneur who has learned to live with risk. The selection of reflections

---

[1]Case written by Joëlle HAFSI and Louis Jacques Filion.

[2]Unless otherwise mentioned, citations selected for case studies were taken from interviews conducted by the authors with each subject of the case study concerned.

[3]https://corpo.couche-tard.com/en/

presented in Appendix A at the end of this case provide information on his creativity, market analysis approach, business intuition, management philosophy and views about being an entrepreneur and developing a business. Appendix B shows a selection of awards and recognitions received by Alain Bouchard.

A Strong Entrepreneurial Family Culture

> The most valuable thing my father taught me is responsibility. I've always felt responsible. Everything I've done, and everything I do today, is my responsibility. That's why I'm successful in foundations, fundraising and the like. I take care because it requires a lot of effort. My father really worked hard. I learned a lot from his tenacity and effort. He was a great inspiration for me.

Deep down, Alain Bouchard had always dreamed of working for himself. It was a family tradition that he fully intended to continue. Even as a teenager, he showed an unusual amount of interest in the tobacconist's store owned by the parents of one of his friends. He describes himself as 'fascinated by the ins and outs of the business', and saw the potential for a chain of similar stores. Even then, as a child, he had big dreams.

But before those dreams turned into reality with his first convenience store franchise, before his 30th birthday, Alain Bouchard would learn many lessons, all of which would serve to forge his determination and broaden his horizons.[4]

Entrepreneurship – A Family Tradition

Alfred Bouchard, Man of the Forest and of the North

When asked if he has an entrepreneurial model, Alain Bouchard has no hesitation in naming his grandfather Alfred, whom he describes as a 'very hard man'.

Alfred Bouchard was born in the Lac-Saint-Jean region of Québec, and like many of the region's lumberjacks and entrepreneurs, he earned a living from timber.[5] Not only did he harvest it, but he also travelled to the neighbouring town of Chicoutimi to sell it. To get to the forests of Northern Québec, he also built roads through a landscape composed of wild and hostile mountains. No conditions were too much for him.

---

[4]In Saint-Jérôme, a small town, 65 km north of Montreal.

[5]250 km north of Québec City, considered.to be a region of lumberjacks like the state of Maine in the United States.

Jean-Paul Bouchard and the Ups and Downs of an Entrepreneur's Life

Alain Bouchard's other inspiration was his father, Jean-Paul Bouchard, a tireless entrepreneur who invested a fortune in machinery to excavate and build roads for forestry companies in the Lac-Saint-Jean region, which was truly a 'lumberjack pioneer country' at the time. He sometimes worked with a general contractor, and it was this occasional partner who eventually turned the Bouchard family's life upside down by filing for bankruptcy in 1957. Jean-Paul Bouchard, who had not been paid for the work he had done to build a new forest road, lost his machinery and was also forced to file for bankruptcy the following year. It was a huge shock for the entire family, especially for the two oldest children, Gilles and Alain.

Goodbye Chicoutimi, Goodbye Beautiful House, Goodbye Cadillac and Luxury Life

> Leaving Chicoutimi was a shock for the older members of the family and the transition was hard. From my point of view as a nine-year-old child, it was very clear that life was a lot better when my father was an entrepreneur, and a lot worse when he began to work his fingers to the bone for someone else, just to keep a roof over our heads. In Chicoutimi, we had a position in the town's society. My father drove a Cadillac and my mother was proud to take us out and about. When we moved to Baie-Comeau – well, let's just say it was a huge step down from life in the fast lane. I had no doubt that I was going to become an entrepreneur.[6]

Jean-Paul Bouchard, his wife and their six children left behind 'their beautiful house, the Cadillac, family, friends and the good life in Chicoutimi' and moved a few hundred kilometres north-east, to the North Shore region, along the St. Lawrence River. The area was booming at the time; Hydro-Québec was building series of huge dams on the St. Lawrence tributaries, and for Jean-Paul, a skilled mechanic, it was a case of 'going where the work was', travelling even further north to remote places such as Wabush and Labrador City to repair cars, trucks and mining equipment.

Finally, in 1963, he managed to obtain regular employment with Hydro-Québec, on one of its dam construction sites, and the family moved into a mobile home. During all the years he worked as an employee for other people, his father never stopped dreaming of the day he would once again become an entrepreneur. His son remembers the family's Sunday afternoons:

> Although my father worked in garages, he never lost his desire to go back into business. Every Sunday, the family went to look at every imaginable type of business: garages, restaurants, mobile

[6]200 km north of Québec City.

home parks, campsites – you name it, we saw it. My father tried to figure out a way to buy them. Obviously, it was something of a pipedream for him, because the Bankruptcy Act was very harsh in those days. He had to repay all his debts to his creditors first, and a good part of his income went on that.

Years later, gradually, he restored his own honour and that of the family. He worked on a hydraulic pump to inject cement into dams and became an international consultant. He trained people overseas, mainly in Africa, on mechanical maintenance. He left a surprizing amount of money to his children when he died.

Life on the Manic Sites and the Emergence of a Budding Entrepreneur

The family moved to Hauterive where rented apartments were cheaper and the Bouchard children could attend school in the neighbouring small town of Baie-Comeau.[7,8] Alain had his first experience as an entrepreneur during the summer of his 14th birthday (1963), travelling around the construction sites on the Outardes and Manicouagan Rivers, selling sandwiches and drinks that he prepared at home with his mother. 'I had the idea because I wanted to earn some money', he says. This was his first-ever experience of selling, which he 'thoroughly enjoyed'.

The following summer, however, after the family moved to live in the Manicouagan workers' village, there were no sandwiches to sell. Instead, Alain formed a band that played in dance halls on construction sites and paid for its instruments out of the commissions it received.

Although he had always loved music, he found he was better at organizing than at drumming and took responsibility for negotiating the band's contracts with the clubs' directors. This was not as easy as it seemed, because the band members were all minors and he had to be very convincing to obtain the contracts. However, as he points out, 'the 18–20 year-olds preferred our band to the other groups, which played old music and square dances. Our band became fairly popular at the local level'.

Rivière-du-Loup: The End of His Academic Career

Because the family had moved so frequently, Alain found it hard to concentrate at school. In his Grade 10 science lessons, the nun who taught mathematics nevertheless managed to capture his attention, although he was so disruptive that she often had to call him to order. 'Alain Bouchard, you're a mathematical genius, but you waste your own time and everyone else's. Concentrate on what you're

[7] 560 km northeast of Québec City along the St-Lawrence River.
[8] These two small neighbouring cities, Hauterive and Baie-Comeau, merged in 1982: 26,000 people.

good at!' She became a catalyst in his life, allowing him to complete his courses and graduate from high school.

He wanted to go to university, but first he had to complete a preparatory programme. Although better able to concentrate by then, he still liked to make his classmates laugh and always tried to be the 'class clown'. This behaviour, and his clashes with an 'overly strict' teacher, eventually caused him to be expelled from both the programme and the school.

This might have marked the end of a dream for a young man who had thought of becoming an engineer or a pilot. Jean-Paul Bouchard, although he worked hard, could not afford to pay his son's way through university – it was expensive, and there were few scholarships available at the time. However, Alain did not give up. For example, he spent a weekend with the monks in Québec City, hoping that this would be a way for him to get to university, but he quickly realized he did not have a religious calling. And so he applied to the Army – a process that showed his ability to dispense with formalities:

> I wrote to the Army because I'd always dreamt of becoming a pilot, and I wanted to study at the military school in Saint-Jean (province of Québec) to become an officer. I waited for over a month, but still didn't receive an answer, so I packed my suitcase and went to the Army recruitment office in Québec City. 'I wrote to you and you didn't answer – so here I am!' 'Listen, young man, that's not how it works.' 'So put me in the ranks and when you've finished with the paperwork, send me to the military school in Saint-Jean!' 'We can't do that!'

All the gateways to university seemed to be closing, and Alain eventually went back to the Outardes 4 Dam Complex, where he worked at the site's forestry outlet for a while. 'I was wondering what to do. But one thing never left my mind: I knew that one day, I would be an entrepreneur. I would grow my own business because, after what happened to our family, we needed vindication, and I was determined I would get it'. The Sunday afternoon family rides, when his father looked for a business to take over, had made a major impression on him.

Discovering the World of Convenience Stores

From Bush Country and Small Towns to Montreal

When Alain Bouchard turned 18 years old, he decided to move to Montreal.[9] He was 'so impressed to see 40-storey buildings' that he 'spent days just walking around, looking upwards' and dreaming. For the next 2 years he worked at a

[9]When Alain Bouchard first came to Montreal in May 1967, he discovered a city that was booming, with an underground rail system, a huge Arts Centre and several other public attractions developed to receive visitors who came from all over the globe to the World International Exhibition that had just opened (EXPO 67).

succession of jobs in the city's textile sector, the Chabanel Street sweatshops, doing everything from sewing to shipping. He saw changing jobs as a way to improve his lot in life and earn a bit more money, while learning and saving 'so I could eventually start my own business'.

The Emergence of a New Concept: The Convenience Store

It all began with Frank Bazos, a young Greek immigrant who came to Toronto from the United States in 1926. In 1932, he bought a dairy firm that he renamed Devon Ice Cream, and quickly began selling his products throughout the province of Ontario. Twenty years later, Frank Bazos and Bruce Becker joined forces to create Becker's Milk.[10] The new firm became popular, and its activities grew well beyond those of a traditional dairy, creating a new concept known as the 'corner shop' or 'convenience store'. The new stores became so successful in Ontario that Robert Bazos, Frank's son, decided to start his own chain of stores in Montreal in 1960, which he named 'Perrette Dairy'.

Thanks to His Older Brother, Alain Bouchard Discovers a New World

In 1969, Alain Bouchard was 20 years old. He had been working in the sweatshops for 2 years. Although he did not know precisely what he wanted to do with his life, he hoped for better things and still dreamed of becoming an entrepreneur and operating his own business. One weekend, he went to visit his older brother, Gilles, who managed a Perrette Dairy franchise in Bois-des-Filion, a small town located on the outskirts of Montreal. His reaction was the same as it had been to his friend's tobacconist's store in Hauterive: he fell in love with the business. Gilles asked Alain to take care of the store on weekends, Alain jumped at the opportunity. For the next few months, he spent his weekends working up to 14 hours a day:

> I went with my brother to Presto, which was a kind of warehouse. When I saw a display of little brooms made of marshmallow and chocolate, I told him we had to try them. We put them on the counter, and customers snapped them up. It was a very profitable experiment. I enjoyed seeing how the customers reacted and realized that if we wanted to sell products quickly, we had to attract more people to the store.

---

[10]Frank Bazos was originally from Ohio, and worked for his father-in-law's company, which developed a revolutionary new way of selling milk in reusable containers. Frank Bazos, who prided himself on his avant-garde approach to innovation, quickly saw the concept's potential and joined forces with Bruce Becker to introduce it to Toronto. In the 1970s, Becker's Milk owned 500 stores, and the figure grew to nearly 900 by 1990. The banner was sold to Silcorp in 1996.

Alain worked long hours every day of the week but weekends were different, all the more so because his brother left him plenty of latitude. Alone in the store, he worked in an environment where he enjoyed the freedom to do what he wanted and to do it in his own way.

A Major Change in His Life: Freedom to Be Creative

> My brother's store was really a terrific opportunity for me. I enjoyed the job and the contact with the general public. I moved products around. I liked seeing the customers' reactions to the moves, and I realized we sold more when the products were presented more advantageously. I also realized that customers would buy products on impulse when they were displayed on the counter.

He took advantage of this unique situation to give free rein to his creativity. His observations of the store's customers – how they reacted to certain products and how they moved through the store – confirmed his desire to start his own business in the same sector. He listened carefully to the customers' comments, absorbing information like a sponge.

Every day was a new learning experience. He remembered everything he saw and heard, and continually thought up new ways to use the information to increase sales. The store became his university, the place where he was able to learn the basics of a new and imaginative craft: operating a new type of store in a creative way. The things he learnt would subsequently be applied in his own stores – not least, to give store operators the latitude they needed to adjust to their own specific context.

Mr Hébert Recognizes a Potential Star Who Could Improve Perrette's Operations

The Perrette chain's owner, Robert Bazos, had big dreams. As his company expanded, stores had to be opened and managed. He hired Mr Hébert to do this, and it was not long before the task became too much for only one person: the chain opened stores throughout Québec and Mr Hébert no longer knew which way to turn. Over the months, he had noticed Alain Bouchard's initiatives and offered him a job in development. Alain describes it as follows:

> I started off as a store opening assistant, and gradually became responsible for all new store openings in Québec. I then became the district supervisor and manager. However, I soon realized I wasn't doing development work at all – I was simply an operator. By the time I came on the scene at a store, construction was finished. My job was to take care of the equipment and merchandise.

Between 1970 and 1974, not only did Alain Bouchard open approximately 100 stores, all of which were under his supervision, but he also renovated and reopened others that were on the point of closing. He often stood in for managers who left the company or had been fired. He learned a lot, both from Mr Hébert and from his own activities. He literally worked until he dropped. During all that time, he never stopped thinking about running his own business and saved hard to accumulate capital. He was a naturally frugal person who could live with very little.

He married in 1972, and Robert Bazos gave him a car: a Kingswood Estate Station Waggon, with wood side panels, very useful for carrying goods. However, the vehicle came with even more responsibility. In 1974, he disagreed with his boss about a policy he felt was unfair and had to be changed to reduce staff turnover, since he would inevitably find himself with the burden of finding and training replacements:

> I saw the numbers. They didn't show Perrette in a rosy light. For one thing, the dealerships had to pay the head office for any products lost due to shoplifting – and it wasn't the wholesale price they wanted for the stolen items, but the retail price… It cut into revenues that most dealers already thought were too low. I lost dealers constantly, and I lost good ones.

One day Alain Bouchard had the opportunity to speak directly with Robert Bazos and told him that the turnover rate for dealers was much too high and that replacing them was costing the company a lot. He suggested 'finding a formula for them to make more money, and that will make them stay with us longer'. Bouchard can still hear Bazos' response, as clearly as he did that day: 'Mind your own business…' 'The next day, I handed in my resignation. Bazos said: 'Give me your car keys' (Gendron, 2016, p. 54). Alain had to go home in taxi. He was convinced the way Bazos operated was not the right way to manage and to develop a business. Several years later, he bought Perrette from Bazos.

He wanted to own a store but he knew he was not yet ready, for two reasons. First, all the stores he felt were suitable for conversion into convenience stores – a format he believed held great promise – cost a lot more than the $20,000 that he and his wife had saved. And second, although he had started and trained operators for more than 100 convenience stores at Perrette, he felt he still needed more experience. He decided instead to find another job and work for someone else in the same sector for a few more years.

Intrapreneur and Developer With Provi-Soir, Provigo's New Convenience Store Division

He went to see a headhunter who offered him several possibilities, including Pepsi and also Provigo, first in the Wholesale division, and then in the newly launched Convenience Store division, which had just opened its first store in Québec City.[11]

---

[11]The headhunter also happened to be a part time lecturer at HEC Montréal, the Montreal Business School affiliated with the University of Montréal. He convinced Alain Bouchard to take his course on 'Decision Making Theories' the following year.

Alain Bouchard chose the Convenience Store division: 'After everything I'd learned at Perrette about opening new stores, I'd made up my mind. My ultimate goal was to start up a network of convenience stores of my own. However, Provigo, a major player in the food sector in Québec at the time, had just done precisely that. So, at 25 years of age, I felt I should continue to improve my understanding of the sector and I decided to work for them. At the very least, I'd gain some useful experience, and then I'd decide what to do next'.

However, at that time, few people believed there was a real potential to develop lucrative business operations in the convenience store emerging sector: 'The Pepsi guy was angry that I didn't accept their job offer. "You made a bad decision. In the food trade, the money's in production, not in retail. If you really want to go into business for yourself, learn how to manufacture things and you'll make more money." I don't know what I'd have become if I'd taken his advice!'

Hired in 1974 as a maintenance and construction coordinator, Alain Bouchard soon moved on to development. To build the first stores, which he handed over turnkey to the operators, he used the experience he had gained with Perrette, and he also developed his own market analysis model using variables such as market research, competition, store environment demographics, traffic direction and intensity, as well as development and production costs, equipment and rental or construction value.

His first analysis model, divided into several columns, was very finance-oriented and he continued to refine it. When a store was to be attached to a service station, his boss was responsible for negotiating with the oil companies, but the site was always chosen in a group session. Group discussions were often difficult. Alain Bouchard was the youngest member of the group, but the one with the most experience of the sector. He was never afraid to say what he thought.

He was responsible for negotiating contracts with builders, and for purchasing equipment and maintenance. For the first time in his life, he had a secretary! She taught him several basic skills, including where to sign on contract documents. Making the most of the freedom available within the company's administrative limitations, he built store after store. 'We were very successful', he says, 'because nobody else was doing it, except for Frigo, a Petro-Canada company'. In reality, he was learning 'to work in a large, organized corporation structured into multiple divisions that was growing and developing very quickly', alongside reputed food sector strategists.

Alain Bouchard had a great deal of freedom in his work. Although it was no less demanding than his job at Perrette, his hours were more reasonable and he no longer worked on weekends. Taking advantage of his free time, he enrolled for evening classes at HEC Montréal, where he took a Certificate course in supply management. He also travelled to the United States to learn about convenience store trends in that country.

Big Dreams

Alain Bouchard always had dreams. As a teenager they were limited, but once he was established in Montreal, as he acquired experience in his sector, they began to grow and take shape. This was especially the case during his years with Provi-Soir, as he worked with many professional people. From his dreams, he developed a vision of a high-growth company, and he used it to devise an ambitious development project for Provi-Soir, which he submitted to his divisional vice-president:

> In 1978, I placed a file on my vice-president's desk and told him: 'This is what we need to do to develop and grow more quickly.' My idea was to buy existing stores instead of only building new ones. I was told: 'It's not our way; we build nice new 2,400 square-foot stores. It's what we do.'

Between 1974 and 1978, Alain Bouchard worked on approximately 100 new Provi-Soir convenience stores. Although he wanted to move more quickly, he felt cut off in the big, bureaucratic corporation and decided to leave the company. His departure package included two franchises and the requirement to train his successor over a period of several months. In reality, he was replaced by three people: an engineer for construction, someone to oversee maintenance issues, and a third to oversee development.

From Intrapreneur to extrapreneur[12]

> It was clear in my mind: 'I have to be an entrepreneur because life is better that way!' It was obvious to me. In spite of the shock of what happened to my family in Chicoutimi when I was a kid, all six children in our family wanted to work for themselves. All my brothers and sisters were self-employed at one point or another during their life.
>
> After opening 100 convenience stores with Perrette and 100 more for Provigo, the only thing on my mind was to start on my own so that I could have a management office and grow my own company.

For Alain Bouchard, the 1970s had been a time of learning for the future. He had learned the managerial craft, first in his brother's store and then with Perrette, before moving on to development with Provi-Soir. After setting up more than 200 convenience stores, he had acquired the foundations he felt he needed to start his own company. He was almost 30 years old and on the verge of achieving his dream of building a chain of convenience stores throughout Québec, and eventually Canada, and perhaps even the world.

---

[12]An extrapreneur is an intrapreneur who keeps doing as an entrepreneur working on his own what he did as an intrapreneur working for others.

1980s, a Key Decade: Developing His Own Entrepreneurial Activities

The Saint-Jérôme convenience store – Alain Bouchard's first, under the Provi-Soir banner – was located at the Highway 15 exit near where he lived, in the Laurentian Mountain foothills one hour north of Montreal. The investment was a considerable one for him: $10,000 for the franchise and $30,000 for the inventory.

In 1978, the convenience store concept was still new, and because the store was located in a former garage that had been converted into a service station, potential customers had still not realized that it was in fact a store as well. At the same time, Alain Bouchard was not always present on site, since his time was split between his obligations with Provi-Soir and his activities at his own store. However, he was able to make some changes so that people would see it was now a store. It soon became one of the most profitable stores in the entire chain.

He received his second franchise the following year, in Blainville, a small town located between St-Jérôme and Montréal. It was clear to Alain Bouchard that he would not be content with just two stores. Based on the principle that 'more is better', he purchased a third, le Marché Jérômien. This was an independent store, supplied by IGA, a major competitor of Provigo.[13] Their prices were lower than Provigo's. He was at the point of considering a fourth store when Provigo decided to enforce a non-competition clause in his contract, forcing him to sell his two Provi-soir franchises. He kept the Marché Jérômien, which became his first independent store.

However, his company really took off 2 years later, in 1980, when he purchased another store, followed by a tobacconist, and finally a supermarket in the Vimont neighbourhood of Laval, another suburb north of Montreal.[14] These early stores were grouped together under the *Orano* banner. Alain Bouchard continued to apply his principle of 'more is usually better', even in the recession of the early 1980s, buying several other convenience stores in the Montreal region. His financial institution, the National Bank of Canada, was less than pleased, warning him of the dangers and demanding increasingly large guarantees. This is what Alain Bouchard has to say on the subject:

> The major recession of 1981–1982 brought interest rates of between 17% and 18%. It was very hard, but we made a lot of money because the inflation rate was between 10% and 12%. I signed three acquisitions without talking to the bank. They weren't pleased. 'Alain, you're growing too fast. Have you seen the interest rates?' 'There's inflation as well,' I told them. 'Just look at my financial statements, I'm making money.' 'Yes, but if we set goodwill to zero, you'd be technically bankrupt!' I paid a lot of goodwill for my stores. In the end, I had to put up my buildings and personal property as a guarantee.

---

[13]Independent Grocers Alliance.

[14]Alain Bouchard converted the two stores (which were neighbours) into one large convenience store, the Renaud store, which was managed by his younger brother Serge.

Team Building: Choosing and Integrating Partners

With his sights firmly set on development, Alain Bouchard knew he could count on his younger brother Serge, who had served his management apprenticeship with the two Provi-Soir franchises. However, he also knew that their combined skills and strengths were barely enough to lead the stores and focus on the type of growth strategy he had in mind. He decided to contact Jacques D'Amours, a young, resourceful man who had worked part-time with him at a Perrette store as a jack-of-all-trades when he was a 14 year-old student. Not only did D'Amours offer to invest in the new company, but he also agreed to take over responsibility for the supermarket.

Alain Bouchard was comfortable with his brother Serge and Jacques D'Amours, 'an extraordinarily hard worker', but he was also aware that he tended to become impatient with his bank. Aware of his lack of expertise in this area, he approached Richard Fortin, a longstanding friend whom he had met when he worked at Perrette, and now a 'confirmed banker' who decided to invest in the firm in 1982, becoming its fourth partner.[15] They had never worked together before but they quickly developed a good relationship based on trust. However, his brother Serge left the enterprise shortly afterwards.[16]

The year 1985 became a turning point for Alain Bouchard when he purchased a small chain of 11 convenience stores in the Québec City region under the 'Couche-Tard' banner, paying only $20,000.[17] The following year, the name of his chain of 34 stores, including 31 franchises, became 'Alimentation Couche-Tard', and on 26 June 1986, the firm went public. Alain Bouchard converted Orano into a personal portfolio.

From Imaginative Strategist to Visionary Builder: Fast Growth Through Acquisitions

> When we came back home from Québec City, we started looking at the experiences of other big firms. Should we decentralize, or not? We liked the Bombardier model, with a small corporate

---

[15]Richard Fortin, who had previously worked for the Bank of Montreal and the Mercantile Bank, was vice-president in Canada for a major French bank (Société Générale) at the time.

[16]It turned out that two Bouchards in the same organization was one too many. Serge left at the end of 1984. Alain's relationship with his older brother, Gilles, had been excellent. Gilles' health was fragile and he passed away in 1979.

[17]Couche-tard is a French term meaning 'Go to bed late'. It had been the name of a popular weekly evening TV show led by two bright and witty humorists who presented late shows in night clubs. Couche-Tard's website contains information on more than 70 acquisitions that followed this first one and transformed Couche-Tard into a world leader of the convenience store sector. This case study presents the early acquisitions so that readers can understand how the acquisition methodology and pattern was developed and implemented. See: https://corpo.couche-tard.com/en/.

> group and many divisions. Réal, who was an engineer and had an MBA, had read more than me on the subject. We eventually chose decentralization, and it was this that made us so successful. 'We have good managers, so we'll give them the power and visit them regularly. We'll coach them – let's see if it works!' It's our operations that bring in the profits.

Alain Bouchard and his small team gradually gained expertise in identifying promising stores and mastering the 'art of the deal'. Acquisitions became his trademark. From that time onwards he focused on buying not only individual corner stores but also chains of convenience stores. In 1987, Couche-Tard swallowed up all 75 stores under the Métro-Richelieu 'Seven-Days' banner. In 1992, 37 'Mac's' and 72 'La Maisonnée' stores in Québec, owned by Silcorp (based in the Scarborough – Toronto area), were also taken over.[18] That same year, Couche-Tard became the biggest convenience store banner in the province of Québec, with 271 stores.

In 1993, Couche-Tard bought an additional 54 'Mac's' and 'La Maisonnée' stores from Silcorp. The following year, in 1994, shortly before Perrette filed for bankruptcy, Couche-tard took over the 84 stores that were left, and in 1996 it acquired all 245 Provi-Soir stores, meaning that, ironically, Alain Bouchard now owned dozens of convenience stores that he himself had started when working for Perrette and Provi-Soir.

In addition, as part of the Provigo transaction, he obtained 49 'Wink's' stores, 21 in Ontario and 28 in Alberta, marking the firm's first foray outside Québec. Other major coups followed. In 1999, Couche-Tard acquired Silcorp and became the major player in the Canadian convenience store sector. The transaction included 974 stores located in Ontario and Western Canada operating under the Mac's, Mike's Mart and Becker's banners.

During the 2000s, Couche-Tard became a major player in the United States, under several banner names.[19] The American adventure began in 2001, with the purchase of 225 Bigfoot stores in the states of Illinois, Indiana and Kentucky. Later that year, Couche-Tard bought 287 Dairy Mart stores operating in seven Midwest states. In 2002, in addition to his convenience store activities, Alain Bouchard moved into a new niche in Québec, with a series of non-traditional stores located in airports, shopping malls and underground stations.

In 2003, the company extended into 16 American states with the acquisition of 2,200 stores from Conoco-Phillips, including 1,650 Circle K stores, at a cost of more than $1 billion.[20] This was Couche-Tard's biggest acquisition so far. With 4,600 stores, the company doubled in size and sales increased from $3.6 to almost $9 billion. At the end of 2003, a report from Deloitte Touche revealed that Couche-Tard 'had more growth in five years (1998–2003) than any other large

[18]Original name: 'Sept-Jours' banner.
[19]See: https://corpo.couche-tard.com/en/.
[20]Circle K was created in El Paso, Texas, in 1951.

company on the planet. Its annual average increase in sales – an incredible 55% - was double that of Starbucks, and just edged out the darling of online commerce, Amazon'.[21]

The dance of acquisitions continued. Eleven years later, there would be an even bigger transaction in the United States:

> On December 18, 2014, just a week before Christmas, Couche-Tard announced that it had completed the biggest acquisition in its history in North America. The price tag: USD $ 1.7 billion. The Pantry was a company that owned more than 1,500 convenience stores, concentrated in the Southeast United States, near the Gulf of Mexico, and mainly under Kangaroo Express banner. The deal would add $7 billion to Couche-Tard's sales and lengthen its list of employees by 15,000.[22]

Entering Asia, the European and Other International Markets: Discovering, Understanding, Acquiring and Sharing

In 2007, Alain Bouchard began to visit Europe to examine the different markets, and at one point he bid on an English network. The bid was unsuccessful, but he kept looking because he was convinced that Couche-Tard needed a European base for its acquisitions.

In 2010, Statoil, a highly integrated company controlled mainly by the Norwegian government, announced its intention to sell off its retail unit via an IPO (initial public offering).[23] Alain Bouchard registered his interest, met with the organization's banker and sent a letter of interest. Statoil noted all this but continued with its IPO. It was 2 years before matters came to a head:

> In 2012, an opportunity arose to buy a network of roughly 300 units from a major oil company in one of the eight countries covered by Statoil. We visited and hired a local firm of accountants and lawyers, because the second round of negotiations was already underway. While I was there, I received a call from the financial manager of Statoil's parent company. He was aware of everything that was going on, including the fact that we were there, and he said: Don't sign anything, come over, we need to talk!

The negotiations led to one of Alain Bouchard's largest acquisitions: in the end, he bought not just the original 300 stores, but all 2,300 Statoil stores, thereby

---

[21]Gendron, Guy (2016, p. 218).
[22]Gendron, Guy (2016, p. 278).
[23]Statoil is a world leader in the oil and gas sectors.

gaining a presence in eight Northern European countries: Denmark, Estonia, Latvia, Lithuania, Norway, Poland, Russia and Sweden.

How did he feel in the early months after the acquisition? Not very good: he slept badly, something that had not happened often in his life. The cost of the acquisition – more than US$3.6 billion, including $1 billion of debt – was considerably more than the company had paid in the past. However, what bothered him was not the cost involved but how to adjust the operating activities between North America and Europe. The adjustment was difficult for everyone:

> In the early months, we studied and tried to understand one another. The newly acquired stores worked in markets and cultures that were very different from the prevailing markets and cultures in North America. There was a kind of dual methodical impact and procedures that lasted many nights. One of the parties was a company with an IPO, controlled by the Norwegian government, and the other was a large, integrated entity. We weren't familiar with their methods, and vice-versa. To effect the separation, they'd hired McKenzie and had built a good business model, but one based on knowledge and heritage specific to governments and large firms. It was hard to understand it all.

And yet, his experienced operator's eye quickly spotted the changes that had to be made to the stores to make them more profitable. The results soon spoke for themselves:

> I have to say their operation was a good one, and the network certainly wasn't in decline. They were better than us in several respects. Things were done well. We felt we needed to correct the storefronts because this was an aspect they hadn't considered. They looked like converted garages, but when you got in there, you said to yourself: Wow, what an extraordinary range of ready-to-eat products!

What Did He Learn From the Process?

> Working alongside people who were very focused on procedures helped us realize that we weren't focused enough. I started to sleep better when I realized that procedures can sometimes be good, for example if they allow you to adopt methods that have been analyzed carefully and are well thought-out, then implemented quickly in the network.
>
> As for them, they learned something too: They just didn't 'have it' when it came to their storefronts! They sent 40 people to our most

> effective division, in Arizona. They stayed for ten days. They studied our methods, and then went home to their respective countries to build and test a plan. They achieved roll-out in record time – something that would have been hard to do here because we're so decentralized. Sales went up immediately and kept increasing over the years, despite the fact that the European economy wasn't in good shape.

Seeing how quickly the changes were introduced in the European stores, and the 'phenomenal' results that ensued, Alain Bouchard realized he needed to be a bit less 'lean'. Although he had always resented head offices and procedures, especially those that made operations more cumbersome, he decided to introduce some organization-wide and peripheral procedures 'because I realized we couldn't just manage on the go'.

In fact, Alain Bouchard enjoyed action and results, and gave stores the latitude to adjust quickly to changing contexts. He certainly did not like bureaucracy, describing himself as being 'allergic to people who only do internal consulting without really understanding operations'. It went against his management philosophy. He entrusted these people with responsibility but made sure they understood that 'the store is your customer – nothing ever happens in your office'.

He saw the gaps that existed between 'head offices' and operations when he made acquisitions, especially when he took over Silcorp in Canada and Circle K in the United States. The information technology project 'Connect' was completed in May 2014, and Alain Bouchard was pleased with 'this great acquisition' and the people who were receptive and understood' his business model.[24] He says he is now ready to look at other European markets.

The firm's international activities outside North-America included agreements of all kinds that allowed it to enter foreign markets, including Cambodia, China, Costa Rica, Egypt, Guam, Honduras, Hong Kong, Indonesia, Ireland, Jamaica, Japan, Macau, Mexico, Mongolia, New Zealand, Saudi Arabia, the United Arab Emirates and Vietnam.

Building an Entrepreneurial System

> The frenzy of fast development! We needed to build quickly so we could grow, and I needed partners to help me out, manage the stores and bring in capital. I was willing to share in order to achieve fast growth.
>
> Fortunately, I tried to surround myself with good people early in my career. I set up committees, identified thinkers, hired graduates and hoped they could help me in practical terms.

A Tenacious Leader Focused on Growth Supported by a Resilient and Complementary Team

Very early in his career, Alain Bouchard was able to make decisions quickly, even when they were difficult. At Provi-Soir, for example, he even overruled his Vice-President, who was sick at the time, because, as he points out, 'If you're wrong, we'll know it soon enough!' Citing the example of the decision tree, which he describes as 'the only thing I really learned from my time at the business school', he encouraged everyone to make decisions when necessary:

> I don't remember the exact figures, although I used them for years. 'If you have four good decisions out of ten, you become an intermediary manager. If you have five good decisions out of ten, we'll start keeping an eye on you. If you have six out of ten, you'll be promoted. With seven out of ten, you're appointed to the executive level. Eight out of ten is truly exceptional, and ten out of ten is impossible. So make your decisions and look at where you are in the organization that employs you. You'll soon see if you're no good, or if you're not in the right place, or in the right sector, or if you've reached the limits of your abilities!' I used the decision tree as much as I could. At Provigo, it brought me to the attention of the vice-president.

At the same time, Alain Bouchard does not shy away from risk. More than once, he has 'put the firm on the block' to make an acquisition:

> You have to take risks. As one of my favourite members of the board, Jean Guertin, said to me one day: 'Alain, you're putting your company at risk!' 'Jean,' I said, 'I've been doing that all my life!' 'Yes, but it's no longer a small company!' 'Well, for me it's a micro-company. I'll be putting it on the block again in the future!'[25]
>
> The left-hand side [of the brain] removes the ability to take risks. But you have to take risks ... I did it when we bought Circle K, which went on to be a phenomenal success. Brian Hannasch, then our American vice-president, told me: 'Alain, I've seen you put up a billion and a half ...' It was enormous, considering our means.

From the very beginning, if he was to grow at the pace he had in mind, Alain Bouchard understood he needed a team. He chose partners whose expertise was complementary and who were never afraid to express their views although there was always a high level of respect between them. He clearly established his

---

[25]The late Jean Guertin was a Harvard DBA, a brilliant professor of finance who became Dean of HEC Montréal.

position with between 57% and 58% of the voting shares, although he considered major decisions should be the result of team work:

> By 1980, the firm had three partners who were operators rather than financiers. I wouldn't go in a specific direction if I hadn't been able to convince them. If something like that happened, however, the final decision would be mine.

The recession of the late 1980s affected the Canadian convenience store sector, as did the new seven-day (and often 24-hour) opening hours for supermarkets and the activities of Actigaz, with its gasoline booths along the lines of Sergaz. The following years were difficult. The company was not as successful as had been hoped, and a series of other events also tested the four partners' endurance while confirming Alain Bouchard's leadership.

Here is an example of one of the important turning points that had to be overcome to keep development going:

> Times like these really strengthened our shareholding and our partnership. In 1992, Réal Plourde told everyone: 'There are too many of us executives right now. We have two choices: either we have to let one of us go, or we have to cut back all our salaries to the level they would be if there were only three of us'. We unanimously chose to cut our salaries by 25% ... With hindsight, it was a great decision. It really was a turning point for the company's founders. It put management into a position of strength and took us to where we are today.

They did the same thing following the financial crisis of 2008, cutting their salaries by 10%. Indeed, because he could not offer high salaries, Alain Bouchard had decided early on to pay some of his own income and that of his partners in the form of company shares. In the long run, it proved to be an excellent decision.

A Corporate Culture of 'Small Is Beautiful'

Réal Plourde, who joined Couche-Tard shortly after Serge Bouchard left at the end of 1984, was responsible for store construction and development. According to Alain Bouchard, his philosophy could be summarized as follows:[26]

---

[26]In 1983, Réal Plourde, an engineer by training, had just completed an MBA. He was involved in small businesses and in consulting. This is how, in September 1984, he was referred to Alain Bouchard who was - as part of his numerous activities – owning and operating a telephone and console reconditioning plant. Réal Plourde joined Couche-Tard at the end of 1984. See the following case study: '*Réal Plourde, Couche-Tard, Circle K and Entrepreneurial Facilitation*'.

> Réal Plourde was a great supporter of the 'small is beautiful' approach for the chain. When you go to your local Circle K, you're not bothered about the ones in other cities because you don't know them and probably never will. And because you, as the customer, are only interested in your local store, we as its owners have to adjust it to the local customer base. That's the 'one store at a time' approach. Let every unit adjust to its market. Réal was a great teacher for me.

From a financial standpoint, banker Richard Fortin was also a valuable resource. In 1985, the enterprise already had 20 stores, but Alain Bouchard intended to increase that figure to between 500 and 600 in the following years. The financial requirements were likely to put off most account managers. He describes a meeting he and Richard Fortin attended with their bank:

> 'Why don't you have a separate entity for each store? It'd be much easier for us to finance a government guaranteed SBF loan for $200,000!' So we decided to have an incorporated company for each store. I submitted an application and we received our SBF loan. We've done it for about 20 stores. In reality, each corporation had two or three stores, no more.[27]

By incorporating the stores, not only was Alain Bouchard able to obtain development funding more easily, but he also achieved compliance with regulations concerning liquor permits, which had long been an obstacle to the development of some convenience stores and most supermarkets.

Decentralization also allowed them to place management and operations as core elements of the company. He felt strongly that: 'It's the manager who knows, not the people at head office. It all starts in the stores'. Store managers were responsible for drawing up their own budgets, after being given the company's financial statements. 'Finance is very important. You can organize things around it. Operations are what bring in the money', says Alain Bouchard, emphasizing the fact that the success of the entire system is based on the company's operations from the bottom up – in other words, on the store managers:

> The first time I visited the Circle K stores in the United States, people were astonished to see me and even more surprised that I would talk to them about how to improve their operations. They'd rarely seen a company executive from Head Office in their lives, even if they'd been working there for 15 years!

Alain Bouchard often found that the convenience store chains he visited prior to acquiring them were not always as well managed as they could, with high

---

[27]Small Business Finance loans could get preferential rates.

employee turnover, coffee machines that were 'out of order', half-empty shelves, the whole place in need of cleaning, and so on. But when he visited the head office, it would be modern and well-maintained. He was always struck by the contrast.

Whenever he found a chain with potential, he did not hesitate to invest. The same applied to anything that might help to improve operations. In 2000, for example, to 'improve our network's competitive edge and reduce its distribution, storage, handling and delivery costs', he set up a leading-edge distribution centre in the Montreal area, considerably improving the efficiency and economic performance of its Québec network supply chain.

Building a Decentralized Multinational Corporation – But Not at Any Cost

Alain Bouchard was constantly in touch with his environment and made development his priority. He describes development through acquisitions as being 'his cup of tea'. Although the acquisition process was relatively simple in the early years, it became more complex when he entered the US market and he had to review his methods. He explains this as follows:

> I'm not sure we can describe ourselves as an acquisition machine, or even a growth machine, but we're nicely structured for acquisitions. Our way of positioning the company to take advantage of the available opportunities was to decentralize it into several divisions. Each division has its own vice-president and managers for its stores. For instance, in Québec and the Maritimes, the VP is responsible for roughly 800 stores. Many people know me around here. When somebody calls me for something that has to do with Québec, I refer this person to the regional VP.

The acquisition process is well-honed and takes place internally for the most part, since each region has its own managers who are responsible for development. For example, the store support office that serves the 800 or so stores in Québec and Eastern Canada, providing accounting, computer and other services required for the network to function properly, shares the same building in Laval as the *corporate office* and its 55 staff members.[28] When an acquisition is about to be completed, management takes over and applies the acquisition model, a due diligence tool used to examine roughly 500 elements. Ultimately, however, the entire workforce of more than 130,000 employees is always on the lookout for potential acquisition opportunities.

Alain Bouchard's ultimate goal was not necessarily to become the world convenience store leader, but he believed it could happen. He felt the European market

[28]Alain Bouchard does not use the term '*Head Office*'. He is allergic to it. To him, there is a '*Corporate Office*' to support operations, since it is operations that generate sales and profits.

was 'more complex than the North American market, but still offers some excellent opportunities'. He never stopped exploring potential business opportunities.

A New Generation in the Wings

Richard Fortin retired in October 2008 but remained Chairman of the Board until 2011. Brian Hannasch had already been identified to succeed Réal Plourde as Head of Operations in 2010 and Alain Bouchard as President and CEO in 2015. Brian and Réal had worked closely together for almost 10 years. Réal Plourde stayed on as Executive Vice-President and President of the Board, 2011–2014. Jacques D'Amours retired in 2014.

In September 2014, at the annual meeting of shareholders, Alain Bouchard confirmed an announcement made in March of that year, to the effect that he would resign at the end of the year as President and CEO in order to take up the position as Founder and Executive Chairman of the Board in 2015. What changes will this new title bring? When he is no longer involved in everyday management, Alain Bouchard hopes to devote most of his time to the aspect of his work that he enjoys the most: scanning the environment for potential new acquisitions. Convinced that Couche-Tard/Circle K still has considerable potential for expansion, in the summer of 2015, a few months after he traded in his role of CEO for that of chairman of the board, he said: 'I want to double the size of the company before I leave it in 10 years'.[29]

Identifying and making acquisitions was always the activity that brought him the most satisfaction, fuelling his passion for growth and making the biggest contribution to his business empire. For a developer like Alain Bouchard, acquisitions were always a source of enjoyment. In addition to this, however, he still intended to remain present at the firm after his 'retirement':

> I'll still be at the office every day, and I'll be involved in the four-weekly market reviews and in the budget process. I'll also be taking part in strategic discussions and will act as mentor and coach for our new generation of managers.[30]

Alain Bouchard always liked to remain close of the operations. There are many stories about this in the enterprise. He always found something to adjust or to improve. Jacques D'Amours notes that 'Alain and I began our career as specialists in demolition'. As soon as a store had been acquired, they put on their old clothes and went with their tool boxes to tear down walls and replace whatever was broken. They made sure the place would be attractive. Sales usually doubled within a few months.

---

[29]Gendron, Guy (2016, p. 282).

[30]Press release – Couche-Tard announces changes to its senior management structure. Laval (Québec), 18 March 2014, p. 1 (translation of the original French).

It is interesting to observe that, after their retirement, the four partners remained on the board and were still actively involved in important decisions:

> According to Hannasch, that's fairly exceptional for companies that have reached that size. Not only are the founders still present after 35 years, but their egos have failed to expand along with their bank accounts and their bonds of friendship are intact. It contributes greatly to the positive environment in the company, says Hannasch. 'In 15 years I've been with these guys, I have never seen a situation where a problem occurred and caused a break in their relationship or one of them being upset for a long period of time.'[31]

The Next Generation: President and CEO Brian Hannasch

Brian Hannasch joined the management team after Couche-Tard bought 225 Bigfoot stores for US $66 million in 2001. He had worked for BP (British Petroleum) for 12 years, including a stint in London, England. He left BP when he had to return to the United States to take care of his father, who was sick, and obtained a position with Bigfoot. He had been there for less than a year when the chain was acquired by Couche-Tard. As an experienced MBA who had been involved in complex international operations, he was surprised that convenience store management was so demanding.

He had never heard of Couche-Tard and was still learning about convenience store management when the takeover occurred. He was not sure he wanted to stay; the new owners spoke limited English and had a very different management style, 'spending far too much time in the stores'. However, he knew they would need him for at least a few months, to make the transition.

In July, two weeks after the takeover, the Couche-Tard team invited him to visit them in Montreal and to join them for their yearly fishing 'pilgrimage' to Northern Québec:

> He had expected an American-style fishing trip: a few boat outings for formality's sake, interspersed with long sessions of beer drinking and card games lasting well into the night. But he was in for a surprise. For one, the four men took fishing very seriously. Beer was conspicuously absent. There were, however, plenty of excellent wines, Hannasch recalls. After a meal washed down with a number of bottles, Réal Plourde went to the other room. He returned not with a deck of cards, but with a stack of songbooks, 'I thought it was a joke' says Hannasch. 'We were going to sing.

[31]Gendron, Guy (2016, p. 281).

> And I DO NOT sing! They almost lost me with that one,' he says with a laugh.[32]

The ball started rolling quickly. Immediately after the acquisition was finalized, Alain Bouchard said he wanted to open 600 additional stores in the Midwest division within the next five years. Brian Hannasch was puzzled: it had taken 20 years for Bigfoot to open 200 stores, and he did not see how it would be possible to speed up the process.

However, he quickly discovered the well-oiled Couche-Tard acquisition machine, with its own culture and techniques, along with a highly refined and structured approach to negotiation and fast growth that he had never imagined could exist in the convenience store sector. His quiet life at head office was well and truly over. He quickly developed a real passion for what he was doing. Although his income continued to increase, it was not his main motivation anymore. He did not even have the time to think about it.

The target of 600 new stores was reached and exceeded within a few months. Alain Bouchard wanted the new store managers to adapt the Couche-Tard approach, so a training centre was set up in Columbus, Indiana. In the following months, Brian's hands were more than full, and remained so. He quickly became a 'member of the family'. He went on to become a key player and major builder of one of the planet's largest multinational convenience store empire, and was ultimately appointed to the top position as its President and CEO.

Standardizing the Organization's Name: A Necessity?

By 2015, Couche-Tard had become an umbrella organization for dozens of banners, as a result of acquisitions in Canada, the United States, Europe, Latin America, the Middle East, Africa and Asia. Canada was divided into four geographic business units composed mainly of the Couche-Tard banner in Québec and Mac's in Ontario and Western Canada. The Circle K banner served the United States, with eight geographic business units covering virtually the whole of North America.

Internationally, stores were licensed under the Circle K banner in 12 countries and territories. The stores acquired from Statoil, which operates a vast retail network with service stations in eight countries, did business under the Statoil and Ingo banners.

Although the fact of operating under different banners had never been a problem for Alain Bouchard in the past, the Statoil acquisition changed that. Here is what Alain had to say after the Statoil acquisition:

> The 'Statoil' name will no longer be available to us ten years after the IPO. It's part of the contract. We'll definitely have to make a

[32]Gendron, Guy (2016, p. 195).

decision before then. We've started talking about it already because the deadline is looming.

Was he considering standardizing the name of the organization, or simply standardizing his European acquisition under the Circle K banner, which dominates the English-language business units and is used extensively in Asia too? In 2014, Alain said he did not yet know. But in 2018, the board supported the proposal to use the name 'Circle K' everywhere in the world except in Québec, where the name of the original founding enterprise, Couche-Tard, remained.

Reconciling Family and Work

> I find it easy to forget the office because I live in the present. It's not a very sophisticated approach. My family is my balance and my passion. I've always managed to maintain a very, very good balance between work and family. When I leave the office, I can't wait to get home.
>
> – Alain Bouchard

Over the years, Alain Bouchard has learned to manage work and family time. His first years at Perrette Dairy were not easy because he had to work from early morning until late at night, six days/week, sometimes seven. He does not want his employees to go through anything like this. Guy Gendron, during the interviews he conducted for his book on the story of Couche-Tard and Circle K, noted that all employees were gone by 6 p.m.:

> A late-day visitor to the Couche-Tard/Circle K service center in Laval – the very heart of a multibillion-dollar multinational company of extended-hours stores – would be astonished to find the premises looking like a ghost town at 6 p.m.: The vast parking lot empty; every one having gone home for the day.
>
> The example came from the very top. Bouchard had personally reproached employees 'caught in the act' of working too many hours. One night when he passed by his office to pick up a file, Bouchard found an attorney recently hired by the enterprise legal department, busy preparing a contract. He lectured him at length. 'You have a family, a wife and kids. What are you doing here at this hour? Go home!' he ordered... 'You have to have a balanced life to be able to reach your potential. I'm paying you to have clear ideas. Go home... and don't let me see you in the office this late at night again.'[33]

[33]Gendron, Guy (2016, pp. 164–165).

Alain Bouchard's children – one boy and three girls – are very important to him. He gives them his time and attention and monitors their development. He has some leisure activities: the occasional round of golf and some fishing trips. He finds salmon fishing, from a boat or from the shore of a river or lake, to be the best way of unwinding.

The Sandra and Alain Bouchard Foundation

In 2012, the Bouchard couple created the Sandra and Alain Bouchard Foundation mainly to support people living with an intellectual deficiency, something that is particularly important to Alain Bouchard as his only son is intellectually disabled.[34] The Foundation also supports people and organizations devoted to arts and culture.

The Foundation is funded by personal donations from the Bouchard family. It is managed by a board of directors whose six members are all volunteers: Sandra and Alain, two of their daughters, Alain's assistant Martine Coutu, who studied part time several years to get a degree in philanthropy, and one professional. The Foundation performs well. It was able to make many significant donations of several millions dollars since its creation.

Circle K/Couche-Tard: Looking to the Future

Alain Bouchard's position as Founder and Executive Chairman of the Board is not an indication that he intends to retire. He has simply changed his role in the organization. He loves what he does, and has tried to free up time to explore potential new acquisitions while continuing to play a real role in the organization's activities:

> There are two things. Everything connected with organic development will continue to report to me, and all new store plans have to go through me. This hasn't changed – it's always been that way. Every week, I consider, authorize or question two or three projects. Every time I start looking at the history of a new site or acquisition, it's like reading a novel! It requires a lot of time. And given that I want to speed things up, it's going to need even more time …
>
> I'll travel to countries where I think we should have a base for acquisitions, to meet with people, forge contacts with bankers and companies, and eventually identify targets. Acquisitions don't usually happen by themselves. It's extremely rare for someone to call and say they want to sell!

---

[34]See http://fsab.ca.

What will the future be? For most people, time is an increasingly important factor and the take-away food sector may well keep expanding as a result. There may be a place for Circle K in this sector, to provide something different from what already exists on the market, perhaps with a formula that lies somewhere between fast food and slow food. Will we see more stores developing food specialties?

Gasoline and cigarettes account for more than 50% of all Circle K/ Couche-Tard sales, and both these products are set to decline in the coming decades. In Europe, and especially in Norway, many stores now have stations where electric cars can be recharged. How will the Circle K/Couche-Tard group make the energy transition? In Canada and in growing numbers of American states, cannabis has become legal in the last decade. Will convenience stores be allowed to sell cannabis, in the same way as they currently sell beer, wine and cigarettes? Whatever happens, the search for new acquisitions will keep going, as will the construction of new stores. In addition, Alain Bouchard continues to think about how to make store operations more innovative and entrepreneurial.

Case Discussion

Alain Bouchard

(1) What influence do you think his father's bankruptcy had on Alain Bouchard? How did it help to trigger his interest in innovation? How did it help to support his own thinking about becoming an entrepreneur? What were the consequences for the way he would operate his business?
(2) What kind of an employee was he? What did he learn as an employee? How do you think the things he learned in his various jobs affected his capacity to generate innovations?
(3) What do you think of his method of developing a business through acquisitions? Please list the advantages and disadvantages.
(4) What do you think of the profiles of the people with whom he chose to surround himself?
(5) Is Alain Bouchard an entrepreneur, a developer or a one-of-a-kind agent of innovation? Explain your answer.
(6) Alain Bouchard spent most of his time meeting with and training store managers. Was this a good use of his time as an agent of innovation and as the leader of a giant multi-national corporation?
(7) Alain Bouchard often exposed his enterprise to risk when he made new acquisitions. What do you think about the way he dealt with and managed that risk?
(8) (A) Would you define Alain Bouchard as a visionary? Why?

A. Would you like to work with Alain Bouchard? Why?
B. Would working with Alain Bouchard help to improve a person's interest in innovation? Would it encourage that person to become an agent of innovation? Explain.

(9) How do you assess Alain Bouchard's values as they relate to social responsibility and sustainable development?
(10) What did you learn from this case history that might help: A) to improve your ability to design and implement innovations? B) to motivate you to start a new venture?

Reference

Gendron, G. (2016). *Daring to succeed. How Alain Bouchard built the Couche-Tard & Circle K convenience store empire* (p. 54). Juniper Publishing.

Appendix A

Life Lessons

Complementary Quotes From Alain Bouchard

Extracts From Interviews and Encounters

Tenacity

When I was nine or 10 years old, our family's life took a very different turn. Until then, we'd been happy and things had gone well, thanks to my father's activities as an entrepreneur. But he lost everything, and it all became much harder. I learned something from it: from that point onwards, I knew I wanted my own business, but I also knew I didn't want to lose it. I think there's a lot of this, especially the need not to fail, in the type of energy I have.

Inspiration From Entrepreneurs and Continuous Learning

I read everything that was ever written about Paul Desmarais and how he built Power Corporation. He was a very powerful example for me. I met him twice. He was a very discreet person who didn't make many public appearances. He was better in a 'one-on-one' context. I admired how he positioned his companies both locally and internationally by developing a lot of business relationships. This is something I've not developed at all: perhaps I'll have time to do so eventually.

It was important for me to understand how these successful entrepreneurs envisioned their development internally, and how they interacted with customers and other people.

A Constant Concern for Growth and Acquisitions

Over the years, the mechanisms used by the company to assess potential acquisitions have been refined. Due diligence is still the method of choice, combined with visits to a sample set of stores in cases where the proposed acquisition is a chain. However, a new tool, geolocation via Google Earth, is now used to identify the ecosystems of the various units and classify them into categories, because 'buying isn't the only thing – we need to know what we'll be doing with the asset once we've bought it':

> We use Google Earth for both acquisitions and developments, to understand the site's location. I ask my people to put all the photos of all the stores on our electronic development site, which is hosted outside the organization. It's an extraordinary tool that saves a lot of time and gives us more assurance regarding what we can do afterwards.
>
> In addition to the sample of 20 % to 50 % of stores that are visited, I can look at the outside appearance of other stores, simply by clicking. We look at the surrounding area to see if the site is big enough for expansion or redevelopment, to see whether it's situated in an industrial, residential or commercial area, and so on. The photos allow us to understand the environment and give us two or three other views of the site. We make fewer mistakes. Apart from this, the process is fairly traditional, in the sense that we still believe due diligence is best performed in-house. I've seen firms hire a hoard of lawyers and accountants to perform due diligence. We do use specialists, but only for very specific subjects.
>
> When we consider a potential acquisition, we classify the stores as A, B, C and D, where A refers to stores we want to keep for the long term, B to stores we are considering keeping, C to the stores we want to keep until they've attained a satisfactory EBITDA and then redevelop or sell them, and D to stores we want to sell immediately.[35] It's often a mixed bag – for example, an acquisition might include 20% of A stores, 20% to 30% of B stores and 50% of C and D stores.

Alain Bouchard insists that location is always a key criterion in the success of a convenience store 'as you have to keep in mind that when people come to a convenience store, they are also buying time. It is usually near where they live and they expect it will be quick'. You need each store to be designed and organized to operate accordingly.

Estimating Fair Value and Setting Ego Aside in Negotiations

The last step in an acquisition is the negotiation process, which requires both skill and restraint. As Alain Bouchard points out:

[35]EBITDA or *Earnings* before *Interest, Taxes, Depreciation and Amortization* is an indicator of a company's profitability, or a store's profitability in Couche-Tard's case.

> Simply deciding to buy isn't enough – you have to do it scientifically! You need to be able to negotiate and set your ego aside. It's important not to fall in love with your target. As one of our directors says, when we pay a lot of money for something, it's always because it's strategic! It's easy to use the word 'strategic' to mean different things: 'because it's easy', 'because it's complementary to what we already have' or 'because we want to enter a new market'. There's always a good reason to pay too much! I have to admit that there are some occasions where we should have stretched a bit more, because we've missed opportunities by being too conservative. Overall, though, I'm fairly satisfied.

A Look at Unionization

In Europe, Alain Bouchard learned to work with the unions and acknowledges that 'it's much easier to manage when the rule is the same for everyone. I don't want to be the only unionized company in our industry – it wouldn't work'.

The Constant Development of a Lively Entrepreneurial Culture

Alain Bouchard believes his firm's stability is due to the fact that he was able to surround himself with the right people, in his immediate circle, on his board of directors and in the enterprise at large.

> I toured the network every fall. By Christmas, I always had a bad cold and was bedridden for several days. I was completely exhausted. Travelling and working from early morning to late at night is physically very demanding. I don't do it anymore. I want to save my energy to support the firm's growth strategy and future. However, I've agreed with Brian (my successor) to visit around 30% of the divisions each year.

Facilitators: A Crucial Role in Couche-Tard's Growth

Alain Bouchard may have been the leading innovator of the social system built by him, but his partners enjoyed a lot of freedom, becoming facilitators and process innovators to help realize their leader's vision. To Richard Fortin, the financial facilitator, and Jacques D'Amours, the trouble-shooter for operations and activities, life was becoming increasingly demanding. At one point, there were so many acquisitions that Jacques needed help.

Réal Plourde became Alain Bouchard's acquisitions integrator in the mid-1980s. As growing numbers of stores were added, Plourde, as Vice-President for Operations (V-P and COO), had to be very creative, not only for the integration itself, but also for staff training, to convey Couche-Tard's culture to all the newcomers. Alain Bouchard describes Plourde as an 'outstanding operator', and presents his role as follows:

> The operator's involvement in the acquisition process begins way before the transaction. He's involved at the planning stage, since he's the one who will be managing it all afterwards. He has to 'digest' it. Now, because of our size, this often takes place in the divisions. For example, if we buy 500 stores in the United States, two or three divisions will be affected: we'll put 100 in one division and 150 in another, or we'll create a new division. It's much easier today, because we have operations in every North American market. It might be different if we were entering other markets on other continents where the rules differ in each jurisdiction. You need local people to help you learn each of these regional systems.

From Top to Bottom, Always Keep the Succession Process Alive

Brian Hannasch joined the organization in 2001, following the Bigfoot acquisition in the American Midwest. He worked with Réal Plourde and quickly learned the Couche-Tard culture. Alain Bouchard describes him as follows:

> He's incredibly intelligent and extraordinarily adaptable. He's very Cartesian – a real numbers man. He has an MBA from Chicago University. He learned other aspects of the business with Réal and with the Human Resources people. It became clear not long after he began working with us that he was the ideal person to take over from Réal and eventually from me.

Brian Hannasch is also very field-oriented. Like Alain, he prefers to meet with managers in their own environment. As a consequence, Brian also travels a lot. Working closely with Réal Plourde, he was always involved in the integration of acquired stores not only in North America, but also in several countries.

The highly structured succession plan drawn up for Brian Hannasch is also used at other levels of the organization. According to Alain Bouchard, it helps 'identify the directors who have the skills to become Vice-Presidents over a 1-to-2 year period, or a 3-to-5 year period.'

Permanent Renewal and Reinvestment

> Understanding operations is fundamental for an entrepreneur. You can live your entrepreneurial dream through your academic

qualifications, but you have to learn the trade for the kind of firm you want to start. If not, there's a significant risk of failure.

You need to be naïve to a certain extent. You'll never do anything if you need to know everything and need to have a perfect model. Our education system is built to stop us from making decisions. Of course, there are risks to anything you may think of doing.

As I've become older, I've developed a desire to invent my life. That's what entrepreneurs do – they invent themselves! There are no courses for that, and it's not like a profession for which you can train. If you're an entrepreneur, you keep inventing and reinventing who you are and who you want to become!

... Acting as an Intrapreneur and Testing Boundaries

At Provigo, most of my contacts were with the Managing Director. He had a plan to group all the equipment purchases from all Provigo's divisions in order to get volume discounts. He and I had some epic battles that had to be settled in the President's office. I remember being absolutely against some of the sites proposed by my superior. We had some very harsh discussions. I always said what I thought.

When making decisions, I always went above my own level and above my boss's level. For example, my boss was sick and we were a few months behind as a result. So I would decide to commit $100,000 or $200,000. It was the kind of decision that should have gone to the vice-president. I wanted to do something that was meaningful for the company. I was hauled before the vice-president twice, and I asked him: 'What would you have done?' 'The same as you,' he replied. 'There you are, then. If my decisions are wrong, tell me.' In the end, my decisions saved the company time and money.

... Finding Business Opportunities

I was in Chicago last week to see some acquisition proposals, and I'll be in Ohio next week. It's always my priority. I'm the developer and I make acquisitions with my people in the regions.

I called the Suncor president when they announced their merger with Petro-Canada. 'We're interested in buying all your stores in Canada. If you decide to sell part of your network, we'll be there!' I make this kind of approach, and I stay in contact with the larger organizations.

… Achieving His Dream Through Hard Work and Savings

I've always worked and tried to improve my lot by earning a bit more money. I saved up so I could eventually go into business for myself.

I didn't spend anything and I kept sending money to my mother, who deposited it in the bank … I put aside all the money I could – enough to be able to start a business on my own. Some weeks, I lived on my expenses accounts and my mom deposited my pay checks in the bank.

One evening, not long after we were married, my wife told me the employees at the bank where she worked could get interest-free loans. There was no limit on mortgages. I told her: 'It's free money, we need to do something with it!' We loved the area in the country side to the north of Montreal, so we bought a cottage there in the mountains, which we renovated and sold the following year for a $5,000 profit. And then I bought another one. Along with my job, the property renovations were my second source of capital. Renovations kept me busy over the weekends.

… At Provi-Soir: Birth of a Market Analysis Model

It was all based on experience at first, and then a young university graduate and I developed all the paperwork for a market analysis model … I gave him my experience and that of the other Provi-Soir operations managers.

We were responsible for market analysis, development, production costs, equipment, rental improvements and construction.

As far as the analysis is concerned, it's a model that includes market research, photos of the store and its environment, the competition, and the store's demographics.

I still use the model today, although it's been refined with technology such as Google Earth.

Acknowledging the Importance of People: Responsibility, Power and Culture...

... So I go to see the store manager. 'Hi, how are you doing? How many employees do you have? Introduce them to me!' I shake hands with the employees – it's never been an effort to do that. Now everyone in the company does it. Some of them are natural at it, others not so much, but at least they do it.

First question: number of employees and staff turnover. Oddly, employees think it's not a bad thing to have a turnover rate of 50% for full-time employees and 150% for part-timers. A rate of 50% means you're completely renewing all your staff in the store every one and a half years. It's not good at all! We have a large turnover, especially about part time employees, and that's why I'm interested in it. It's the nature of the beast. For general staff, and for managers and assistants, we're in just about the best position in the industry, because we monitor the situation.

Second question: customer service, percentage. In the early days, I would go on blitzes. When I wasn't satisfied with the customer service, I'd go into the stores. If I saw an example of bad service, I 'flew off the handle', as my daughter used to say when she was a teenager. Two months later, when customer service had improved, I was happy. But blitzes don't work all the time, so I would have to fly off the handle again six months later. Customer service is a daily challenge – it has to be.

... On Power: The Importance of Accountability and Decentralization

Another turning point came when we bought Silcorp in 1999. They had 900 stores from Ontario to Victoria, British Columbia, under the Mac's and Becker's banners, which they'd bought in 1996 and were in the process of converting ... Réal, the COO, and myself, we were at a loss as to how to manage and operate those 900 stores, in addition to the 600 we already had in Québec, and the number of employees increasing from 4,500 to 11,500. As far as operations were concerned, Réal and I were all we had. Our initial idea was for one of us to move to Toronto, and then Réal suggested meeting with management to get a better idea of what should be done.

We sacked the entire Silcorp executive team since we already had one at Couche-Tard. We also sacked all the bureaucratic employees; there were a lot of people working on statistics for the board.

We kept all the operations managers, though, and met with them individually, for an hour or two each, to learn about their experience and what they wanted to do in life. We were left with the Operations Vice-Presidents in each market. They were good, and we said we'd keep them on and review the structure ... People in Alberta and the West were not pleased. They said decisions were made in the head office in the Toronto area without consideration for their suggestions.

When things are going well ... it's very stimulating in the stores for the manager and assistant manager ... You need back-up, a good balance of working hours, so that someone's available to replace a colleague who's sick. The power always starts in the store. Even if we give power to the regional vice-presidents – and we do – if they don't transfer it to the stores, it doesn't work properly ... Everything starts in the stores.

... Creating a System and Getting Organized for Growth

In the regions, there's a Director of Development and two or three development managers or development coordinators. So we don't need consultants because we have dozens of people internally who work full-time on development.

[Being surrounded by people who think]: It can work, but it's important not to rely too much on people who build their power by bringing in other people who aren't needed. I experienced this kind of thing with my first employers, and it's helped me to put things into perspective. We really need to stay light so we can focus on the basics: What brings in the business? Let's start with the stores: How much power should they have?

This isn't a head office, it's a service and support centre for the stores with a lot of people in operations ... We call it a 'corporate office'. It's fairly small, with 55 people including the executives. Our 'corporate office' supports operations ... Compared to the rest of the industry, it's very lightweight, considering we employ more than 130,000 employees. I haven't yet decided to have a real head office like many big enterprises have, because I don't want top executives to be too far from the operations.

. . . Innovation

I tend to go and see innovative convenience stores for myself. Some of the independent stores and chain members are better than others, but many of them copy us … With our leading position in the market, we tend to be the ones who are copied … I read articles about innovations made by specific stores. Last week, when I was visiting some stores in Chicago that we're thinking of buying, I did a detour to go and see a couple of innovative ones. We're not the only ones to have good ideas. It's always interesting to see what other people are doing.

Becoming an Entrepreneur: Intention, Sector Expertise, Being Naïve, Risk, Analysis. . .

I'm an emotional guy, but I'm very rational as well. Really, I rationalize everything. I was the same when I was 18 years old. I've always analysed things. When I go fishing, I count how many fishermen came to a given spot, and I've always thought there's no money to be made with an outfitting operation. When I go to a restaurant, I count the number of covers. Same thing when I go to a campsite. Everything!

You need analysis. As an entrepreneur, you must be able to understand what you're looking at. You can't improvise and become an entrepreneur if you haven't rationalized what you want to do. If you don't bother, it's like not bothering with your own life.

Here's something else I tell my people: You have to love what you do. If you like the sector, you're more likely to succeed than if you choose a sector just because you think it'll be profitable. As an entrepreneur, you need to enjoy what you do!

Becoming Involved and Sharing Values With Young People...

> Young people have to be exposed to business ... For two years, I devoted a lot of time to giving speeches throughout Québec – in all regions – to try and motivate local decision-makers, teachers and others, so they'd include the principle of exposing young people to entrepreneurs and businesses.

Appendix B

Selection of Awards and Recognitions

Alain Bouchard has received a number of awards, recognitions and distinctions, some of which are listed below:

Québec

- 1998 Entrepreneur of the Year Award (Retail)
- 1999: Enterprise of the Year – (*Les Affaires* Newspaper)
- 2004: Outstanding CEO of the Year – (*La Presse* Newspaper)
- 2014: 'Architect of Québec's Economy' Award – (Institut sur la gouvernance)
- 2014: Officer of the National Order of Québec
- 2015: Outstanding Philanthropist Award (Association of Fundraising Professionals – Québec Section)
- 2017: Honorary Doctorate, Consumer Sciences – Université Laval – Québec
- 2018: Tribute Award, *Cercle des grands entrepreneurs du Québec*
- 2019: Honorary Doctorate, Management – McGill University – Montreal

Canada

- 2005: Retailer of the Year – (Convenience Store Petroleum Magazine)
- 2006: Appeared on the list of Canada's Most Admired Corporate Cultures
- 2008: Industry Leader Award – (National Convenience Stores Distributors Association – NACDA)
- 2013: Canadian CEO of the Year
- 2014: T. Patrick Boyle Founder's Award (Fraser Institute)
- 2017: Companion of the Canadian Business Hall of Fame
- 2018: Officer of the Order of Canada

USA

- 2007: Chain of the Year – (Convenience Store News)

International

- 2014: NACS Insight International Convenience Leader of the year

National Association of Convenience Stores, NACS (nacsonline.com) is the international association for convenience and fuel retailing.

- 2017: International Horatio Alger Award

https://www.newswire.ca/news-releases/alain-bouchard-wins-the-2017-international-horatio-alger-award-604985826.html.

Acknowledgements

Alain Bouchard has earned a reputation as a great entrepreneur, especially in Québec and Canada. The authors have had many opportunities to see and hear him, via the media or in person. Some of the information used in this case study was taken from his public appearances and from dozens of magazine and newspaper articles.

Additional information for this case also came from a speech given by Alain Bouchard to CIRANO (an inter-university centre devoted to research into organizational practices) on 7 April 2009. After his speech, Mr Bouchard took time to answer questions from the audience. The presentation was followed by a meeting and a dinner with Mr Bouchard and some attendees. One of the authors of this case attended the speech and both the meeting and the dinner with Mr Bouchard.

Most of the information and citations for this case study came from three interviews conducted by the authors with Alain Bouchard at the Couche-Tard/Circle K organization's main office in Laval, on the outskirts of Montreal, on 22 May and 23 June 2009, and on 4 September 2014. Each of these interviews lasted several hours. They were recorded and transcribed. The citations were translated from the original French. An additional interview was conducted on 11 December 2019.

The case study was completed in 2020. It includes most of the material from previous case studies written by the authors between 2011 and 2015. Copies of the first two case studies produced in 2011 are available at the HEC Montréal Case Center (http://www.hec.ca/en/case_centre):

9 40 2011 007 – Alain Bouchard et Couche-Tard: à la conquête de la planète à petits pas – Cas A.

Translation: Alain Bouchard and Couche-Tard: Conquering the World, Step by Step – Case A.

9 40 2011 008 – Alain Bouchard et Couche-Tard: la poursuite d'une conquête jamais achevée – Cas B.

Translation: Alain Bouchard and Couche-Tard: The Conquest Continues – Case B.

Additional information and quotes were taken from the following book: Guy Gendron (2016) *Daring to Succeed. How Alain Bouchard built the Couche-Tard and Circle K Convenience Store Empire.* Montreal: Juniper Publishing.

Many thanks to Alain Bouchard for his patience in answering all our questions over the years. The authors also thank Alain Bouchard's assistant, Martine Coutu, for her efficient support, her advice and her patience in revising all the materials we produced on the subject of Alain Bouchard over more than a decade, including this case study.

Section 2
Life Stories of Facilitators

Many different categories and types of facilitators work with entrepreneurs, on different aspects of management, technology or other aspects of organizational and market development. For the purposes of this book, the focus was placed on highly creative facilitators who devise innovative managerial processes to support an entrepreneurial project.

Almost all successful entrepreneurs are supported by one or more facilitators who play a key role in their projects. This was the case for Coco Chanel, especially in the early part of her career, when she received support from Balsan and Boy, both of whom were her mentors and coaches for many years. Later the Wertheimer brothers helped her to market her perfume. The same applies to Alain Bouchard, who surrounded himself with three facilitators who made major contributions to support him and bring his vision to fruition.

Today, entrepreneurship is as much a team activity as an individual one. New ventures are increasingly created by teams that include facilitators. These people are mostly process innovators who are usually more like collaborators (in the true sense of the word) than aides. Many become partners who share or have a stake in the firm's ownership.

Facilitation is a complex, multidimensional task. A facilitator must first understand the entrepreneur's vision and be familiar with the organization and its resources, and with the sector, the competitors, the markets and the technology.

Entrepreneurs and facilitators maintain different types of relationships. For example, the entrepreneur will express visions and ideas, and the facilitator will work to make them happen. Or the facilitator will propose ideas and/or innovations that the entrepreneur uses as inspiration to adjust the vision. These are the most common types, and there are, of course, different degrees and levels of collaboration.

The entrepreneur–facilitator relationship may follow different patterns. Three patterns in particular stand out: secrecy, discretion and tactics. A pattern of secrecy would apply to a relationship where the entrepreneur and facilitator talk about ideas or projects that they do not want to disclose to anyone else, inside or outside the firm, including potential acquirers.

The pattern of secrecy would also include 'silent design' of new products and contacts with potential new clients, subcontractors or suppliers. A pattern of discretion is similar to a pattern of secrecy, with the addition of people being informed inside or outside the firm. As for a pattern of tactics, this would include exploratory action by the facilitator following conversations with the entrepreneur to obtain information or assess potential reactions within the firm or sector, or on social media.

Facilitators must be inventive and resourceful, since they will be asked to solve difficult problems and devise original solutions to ensure that the entrepreneur's innovations are successful. Facilitators often become experts in achieving activities that require fewer resources than is usually the case in the sector. They are imaginative, structured and can work with both judgement and finesse.

They must often do things that most other people in the firm would consider impossible. They are inventive thinkers, able to propose approaches and methods that will make a difference in realizing the entrepreneur's vision and, by extension, in the firm's performance. They are usually fairly quick to assess and evaluate situations and to act. Some work closely with their entrepreneur; this is the case for Réal Plourde. Others work outside the entrepreneur's sphere of activity; this is the case for Pierre Nelis.

Réal Plourde

Réal Plourde helped to oil the Couche-Tard/Circle K machine for Alain Bouchard, speeding up the pace of acquisitions and smoothing out the integration of newly acquired chains. As an engineer and MBA graduate with extensive international experience, he brought considerable added value to Alain Bouchard's team. Among other things, he helped to train many of the organization's senior executives, including the current CEO, Brian Hannasch, who joined the company in 2001, working closely with Réal Plourde for nearly a decade before replacing him as Head of Operations in 2011 and ultimately taking over from Alain Bouchard as CEO in 2014.

Although officially retired for some years now, Réal Plourde continues to sit on the boards of several organizations. He also Chairs the board of an engineering firm employing more than 2,000 engineers. His Foundation has received several awards for its social and community contributions.

Pierre Nelis

Pierre Nelis joined a small group of artists working for a creative entrepreneur who had invented software to produce movies. He brought a great deal of marketing expertise to a team of technology creators, and it was this that ultimately allowed the firm to sell its software to movie industry leaders throughout the world. The firm – Softimage – was bought by Microsoft, which hired Pierre Nelis to oversee the integration process and later to develop new communications products. Nelis has an outstanding ability to identify the elements needed by a firm to become more effective, and this led him to set up a one-of-a-kind external facilitation programme that went on to become a model for many business growth support organizations throughout the world, but especially in North America and Europe.

Chapter 3

Réal Plourde, Couche-Tard/Circle K and Entrepreneurial Facilitation

Joëlle Hafsi and Louis Jacques Filion

Abstract

Réal Plourde helped to oil the Couche-Tard/Circle K machine for Alain Bouchard, speeding up the pace of acquisitions and smoothing out the integration of newly acquired chains. As an engineer and MBA graduate with extensive international experience, he brought considerable added value to Alain Bouchard's team. Among other things, he helped to train many of the organization's senior executives, including the current CEO, Brian Hannasch, who joined the company in 2001, working closely with Réal Plourde for nearly a decade before replacing him as Head of Operations in 2011 and ultimately taking over from Alain Bouchard as CEO in 2014.

Although officially retired for some years now, Réal Plourde continues to sit on the boards of several organizations. He also chairs the board of an engineering firm employing more than 2,000 engineers. His Foundation has received several awards for its social and community contributions.

Keywords: Facilitator; entrepreneurial facilitator; facilitation; partner; business leader; negotiation

Case
Réal Plourde, Couche-Tard/Circle K and Entrepreneurial Facilitation[1]

From the very beginning, Réal played an important role in our company's growth. He was the one who oversaw our operational structure and was responsible for the success of our decentralized business model . . . I've worked with him for 25 years, and I can tell

[1]Case written by Joëlle Hafsi and Louis Jacques Filion.

Agents of Innovation, 91–109

Published under exclusive licence by Emerald Publishing Limited
doi:10.1108/978-1-83797-012-420231003

> you that he's a man of his word, with tremendous values and a big heart.
>
> – Alain Bouchard[2]

Réal Plourde was never one to turn his back on the unknown, either as a student or during his career as an engineer. While at university, he applied for a summer job that would take him to the northernmost reaches of Manitoba. After graduation, he gave up a permanent job with Quebec's Ministry of Transport to live out his dream of doing cooperative work in Africa, where he spent 4 years building roads mainly in Zaire and Togo, bringing back many wonderful memories and an outstanding set of professional and human experiences.

With a background such as this, Réal Plourde was used to wide-open spaces and large-scale budgets, and had no intention of settling into the routine of a subordinate job. Instead, he wanted to become his own boss or a partner in the development of an enterprise. What better way of achieving this, he thought, than by obtaining an MBA, which would give him the extra tools he needed to play this new entrepreneurial role.

After completing his MBA, he became a turnaround consultant. His first contract was in a metal products enterprise in the Montreal area, where he became a partner (1983–1985). In addition to this, he also became involved in his region of origin in Eastern Québec, where he turned around a door and window manufacturing company that had been closed down by the bank.

In the fall of 1984, he was referred to Alain Bouchard by a regional officer from the Ministry of Industry. Bouchard was looking for a consultant to resolve problems with a telephone and console reconditioning plant he had taken over. Réal Plourde had to use his engineering and managerial expertise to settle the problems. It took a few months.

At the end of 1984, Bouchard invited Réal Plourde to join his team at Couche-Tard. A few years later, he was again asked by Bouchard to troubleshoot Pro-Optic, a business that manufactured prescription glasses (obtained through a complex process of acquisitions), and he became its President and CEO in 1989–1990. Pro-Optic, which operated roughly a dozen laboratories in as many cities, employed 120 people and needed to renew its management. It was eventually sold and Réal was able to resume his full-time activities at Couche-Tard (1990), where he was COO for 23 years, from 1988 until he retired in 2011.

This case study tells the story of Réal Plourde, a man who, according to Alain Bouchard, is driven by the maxim 'Small is Beautiful', and who was part of the

---

[2]This paragraph is part of a memorandum sent by Alain Bouchard, then President and CEO of Alimentation Couche-Tard/Circle K, to all the company's vice-presidents on 10 April 2009, paying tribute to Réal Plourde, who had received the 2009 Dunamis Award (attributed yearly by the Chamber of Commerce and Industry of the City of Laval, a neighbouring town of Montreal. At the ceremony, held on 8 April 2009, Mr Plourde was presented with an Award of Merit 'for his professional and personal success during his remarkable career, and for his social commitment to the community of the City of Laval'.

team behind the growth of an enterprise that became one of the world leaders in the convenience store sector: 'An extraordinary story', he says.

Origin, Education and Early Work Experience

From Anse-au-Persil to Laval University (Quebec City)

> My three brothers all chose farming. My father used to tell me: 'It's a good life, Réal, I have freedom, I can do what I want, and I don't have a boss!' However, all I saw was the endless drudgery of milking cows, morning and night, seven days a week, with no time off. Even when I was a kid, I always knew I'd never be a farmer. Not ever. It didn't appeal to me. I decided to go to school instead.

Réal Plourde was born in 1950 in Anse-au-Persil, a small village near the town of Rivière-du-Loup, where his parents owned a dairy farm.[3] The seven children divided their time between school and the farm. The boys helped their father, Thomas Plourde, a self-taught self-employed farmer who had 'learnt to calculate interest rates and financing' and had made a success of his business. The girls helped their mother, Bertha Martin, who managed the budget and looked after the extended family as well. Diplomatic and eager to support her husband, she was never afraid to broaden either her own horizons or those of her children.

On the farm, Réal drove tractors, gathered hay and worked on the harvest, but rarely milked the cows, an activity he did not enjoy. During his time off, he read and played chess or cards with his brothers and sisters. In Anse-au-Persil, the children went to the local village school. When Réal was old enough to start high school, he followed his older brother to the boarding school run by priests in a suburb of Rivière-du-Loup. However, he did not like life as a boarder and left after the first year, enrolling instead in the science course in the nearby town of Rivière-du-Loup because he enjoyed mathematics and science. He was just 16 years old when he enrolled in the Geological Engineering programme at Laval University (Quebec City). 'Geology was an outdoor activity, rather like farming, and I could travel as well!'

Adventurer, Explorer and Man of Action

The most striking aspect of Réal Plourde's time at Laval University was not so much his hard work and learning, but the way he spent his summers to finance his studies. After his first year, he obtained a summer job with Quebec's Ministry of

---

[3]Anse-au-Persil near Rivière-du-Loup is a rural farming area on the south bank of the St. Lawrence River, just over 400 km (250 miles) east of Montreal and 200 km (130 miles) east of Quebec City.

Natural Resources and Wildlife, doing geological mapping, and spent a relatively quiet few months in the Quebec City region, working with the Ministry's geologists.[4]

However, his second summer was very different. He decided to answer a Manitoba Government advertisement for bilingual geology students. While 'able to read a bit of English', he did not speak the language 'at all'. Nevertheless, in his application he described himself as 'bilingual', assuming that the 'bilingual' applicants from Toronto and Western Canada would be no more fluent in French than he was in English.

And so Réal Plourde, an 18-year-old unilingual French-speaker, flew off to Winnipeg to take up a position that required him to speak both Canada's official languages. The change was brutal, as was his sudden immersion in the English-speaking world of Western Canada at South Indian Lake in Manitoba's Far North, where he went to join his team. The work experience – in geological mapping once again – soon took a back seat to the human experience. 'The first month was a bit rough', he says. 'My assumption proved to be correct: none of the other five people in the team spoke French! However, after a month I felt like one of the group, and I had a great summer. I learnt English, but the others didn't learn French!'

Regardless of where he was located – Quebec City or Northern Manitoba – the work he did (geological mapping) was the same. However, his taste for adventure gradually allowed him to learn the subtleties of the English language – often the hard way. As he continued to travel during his last two summers as a student, he became more of an explorer than a summer employee.

He worked on nickel deposits in Northern Ontario and Quebec for a Toronto-based company, as well as in the Labrador Trough, in Canada's North-East, where the Cartier Mining Company had claimed an iron deposit under Mount Wright. This diverse experience allowed him not only to learn, but also to prove that he could handle whatever was thrown at him. 'I probably got the job because I'd worked in Manitoba and had shown myself to be resourceful. I arrived in a town, I drew up my plan, I rented a plane or a boat to have a look at the outcrop, and I took samples that were then sent to the Toronto laboratory'.

Fulfilling a Dream: Exploring and Contributing to the African World

When he graduated as a geological engineer in 1972, Réal Plourde went to work for Quebec's Ministry of Transport. His job involved identifying materials for road-building. However, he was curious by nature, and in his spare time took Master's level courses in soil mechanics, a subject that would later become his specialty area.

His work at the Ministry was appreciated by both his co-workers and his superiors. And yet, a year later, immediately after obtaining permanent status, he

---

[4]His job was to identify and map visible rock formations. Maps such as these are used by mining prospectors or to identify construction materials for roads, bridges and buildings.

resigned. He had always been used to wide-open spaces, even as a child, and found it hard to imagine being confined to his office or his 'bungalow in the suburbs' for the next 20 years. He wanted to discover the world and decided to become a co-operant in Africa.

Originally, Réal Plourde thought his work in Africa would be a missionary initiative sponsored by the Canadian University Service Overseas (CUSO). In the end, however, he went as a paid engineer, and spent 18 months working in Zaire, beginning in January 1974. His employer was Desjardins, Sauriol & Associates, which had won a contract to design and build a 400-km road through the jungle between the towns of Kikwit, Tshikapa and Kananga.[5,6]

Réal Plourde was responsible for studying the foundation soils. In Kikwit, where he settled with his wife, he was able to use stereoscopy to study maps and aerial photographs. However, there was still a need for field surveys to check the materials used and the load-bearing capacity of the soil (pounds per square foot). As he explains: 'In Africa, there were no Blackberries and no Internet to communicate. At the time, all we had was a telex. I learned to get by, what to do to make things work, depending on the environment. My education certainly helped. But it was a combination of everything; I can't really put my finger on it. It was just easy for me'.

The couple lived in a trailer-tent in the bush for over a month. As they travelled from village to village, they were warmly welcomed everywhere they went. The hospitality in each village was similar: Réal sat on a large bamboo chair alongside the village chief, and his wife remained standing to listen to the villagers' stories. The family went back to Africa in 1978 – this time to Togo, for Gendron, Lefebvre & Associates, which hired Réal Plourde as a mission chief to oversee the construction of a 50-km stretch of road.[7,8] After that contract, he worked on different projects in Northern Québec as an engineer-geologist, studying how to turn rivers northwards to feed the huge dams built by Hydro-Québec in James Bay.

What does he remember of his years in Africa? Some good times, certainly, but a lot of unexpected events. Broken traffic lights, lost travel reservations in Zaire, and meetings with the Minister of Public Works in Togo. His sense of ethics was sorely tested. Although prepared to make small concessions in his everyday life, it was out of the question to do anything but the best possible job when supervising

[5]Zaire, a former Belgian colony, became independent in 1960. Following a troubled history, it became the Democratic Republic of Congo in October 1971, on the initiative of its President Mobutu. Its capital is Kinshasa.

[6]The project was funded by CIDA (Canadian International Development Agency). Desjardins, Sauriol & Associates changed its name in 2010 to Dessau Inc.

[7]The couple's son was born in 1977, and accompanied his parents in Africa.

[8]The World Bank, which financed the project, launched an international call for bids. Gendron, Lefebvre & Associates was commissioned to design the road and prepare the bidding file, including the plan and specification. A French consortium was contracted to build the road. Gendron, Lefebvre & Associates became part of Groupe Tecsult Inc. in 1992.

his site. The 18-month mission in Togo stretched to 30 months. When the family returned to Quebec, 'the road was built, the surface was according to specification, and everyone was happy'.

However, his international experience soon came to an end. After careful consideration, he refused an offer from the United Nations to move to New York to oversee French-speaking African issues. He decided to unpack his bags and settle in Quebec. It was time to go back to school and undertake some training that would prepare him to become an entrepreneur as he considered buying or starting his own business.

An MBA, a New Set of Learning and Credibility Improvement

> In engineering, there are two paths. You can be a pure technician on the design side, or you can be a manager. My projects led me more towards the managerial side of things, because they involved project management. Engineering programs don't really prepare you for that kind of thing, because they don't focus much on finance, marketing, clients or human resource management. We have to learn on the job. I felt I needed a few additional tools in my arsenal. An MBA is a good complement to an engineering background!

During this period, the family's evenings were given over to study. Réal, the father, was a full-time student in the MBA programme at HEC Montréal, with a double major in Finance and Operations Management (1981–1983). For an engineer who had always been involved in project management, 'the MBA upgraded my management skills. It was clear to me that I wouldn't go back to engineering'. His wife already had a nursing degree, and enrolled for a Master's programme in community health at the University of Montreal. And their son did his homework. It was a period of intense learning for the whole family.

Réal Plourde's Entrepreneurial Aspirations

Over the months, as he completed his courses, he became certain of one thing: he wanted to build something for himself by becoming an entrepreneur. This was by no means a new idea; in all his previous projects, he had always been his own boss. It was natural for him to turn to projects in which he could invest.

His first challenge was located in Rivière-du-Loup, where his family was from. A door and window manufacturing company belonging to one of his uncles had closed down the previous year due to bankruptcy. The bank was on the verge of liquidating all its assets and equipment as well as the building. Réal Plourde was asked by family members if he could do something to help.

He was able to guide it through to recovery. Using the knowledge he had learned during his MBA programme, he became a true entrepreneur: preparing a business plan and reworking the budget, raising $200,000 from within the family, reshuffling management, designing an efficient operations system, and carefully monitoring the new start-up. It succeeded (in 2020, the company employs more than 100 people and is doing very well). He did this mostly from a distance, since he lived and was involved in projects in the Montreal region.

While he inherited much of his intuitive thinking from his mother, he nevertheless appreciated the importance of his human resources management courses. However, emotionally speaking, in spite of everything he learned about human relationships in his MBA programme, he found it was ‘not easy to do business with the family’. On the other hand, ‘without the MBA, I’d never have been able to turn the firm around. It allowed me to learn about many aspects of organizational management and development and gave me some credibility. It also reassured the guy from the Federal Bank’.

His days and weeks were more than full. Other business turnaround projects followed. In his work for management consultants Maheu & Noiseux, his MBA production courses helped him to profile a kitchen cabinet manufacturer. Observing the flow of materials, production level and cost-benefit ratio, he quickly realized the firm was technically bankrupt and could not be saved.

Based on this broad experience acquired in Canada and Africa, and with his MBA in his pocket, Réal Plourde began to develop his own organizational design system with a view to becoming an entrepreneur.

Discovering the World of Convenience Stores

Facilitating an Entrepreneur’s Activities and Becoming a Partner in a Small Convenience Store Business

It was at this point in his life that Réal Plourde crossed paths with Alain Bouchard, about a year after he graduated from his MBA, in the fall of 1984. One of Bouchard’s many activities involved recycling telephone handsets for Bell in a warehouse in Saint-Jérôme, a small town 50 km north of Montreal:

> When I left the Rivière-du-Loup company, I met Alain Bouchard one Friday afternoon, through a guy from the Ministry of Industry and Commerce. I’d told the guy that if he knew of a small firm needing help, I’d be willing to do something, since I had a bit of time on my hands. He told me he’d think about it, and he talked to Alain about me. Alain originally called me about his telephone recycling business in Saint-Jérôme, not about his convenience stores.

Réal Plourde describes their first impressions of one another at their first meeting:

> From my point of view, I liked what he wanted to do with the telephone company, and he liked what I’d done … We got on. I

> didn't go through the whole evaluation process with psychometric testing to get the job. We understood one another quickly, and there really wasn't much risk, either for him or for me … Often, when I'm hiring someone, I look at their résumé and experience, naturally, but it's more about intuition and chemistry …

With his engineer's eye and production background, Réal Plourde wasted no time, and soon reorganized the warehouse. The telephones were checked and upgraded, minor parts were changed, and they were sent back to Bell quickly. Just three months later, the profits were excellent and it was time for Réal Plourde to move on to something else.

Alain Bouchard offered him a position with Couche-Tard, which at the time was a small business operating a few convenience stores:

> After two or three months, I told him: 'That's it, things are working, we're making a profit, I want to do something else'. He said: 'I have something else for you. With my convenience stores, I do business with a lot of oil companies, including Petro-Canada, Esso and Ultramar, and the contracts are all different. I'd like you to look them over, make a summary and see if we're missing something.' So that's what I did. Then, when I'd done that, he told me: 'I've bought a site to build a store. Can you take care of it?'

Réal Plourde looked over Couche-Tard's contracts with its oil companies, because Alain Bouchard wanted a clearer picture of the situation. However, before taking over the construction of a store – his new task – he decided to put his cards on the table:

> 'It's not a job I want, it's shares! If I'm not a shareholder, I'm not interested.' We agreed on a share in the Saint-Jérôme business, and in Couche-Tard. I wanted shares before the company went public, but it didn't work out that way … I bought public shares on day one, and they gave me some options later, so that I'd be rewarded … It was an excellent investment.

Alain Bouchard wanted a team to develop his business, and invited Réal Plourde to become the fourth partner, replacing his brother Serge Bouchard, who had just left the firm. A few weeks later, at the end of December 1984, Alain Bouchard opened his first new store and invited several dozen people to celebrate this special event, since all the partners had worked hard to make this happen:

> He thanked the employees for their continued efforts. Then he went on to deliver a prediction that left his audience stunned. Their company, he told them, would become the largest convenience store chain in Quebec. 'The other partners and I just stared at each

> other,' says D'Amours. 'We definitely had a long way to go to catch up with Provi-Soir, which had 200 stores, or Perrette, which had 125. We only had 12!'
>
> Gendron (2016, p. 87)

Alain Bouchard had ambitions, great ambitions. He usually did not share them, but it became clear after a few months that he had recruited a team to build something big; clearly, three partners were not needed to operate only a dozen tiny stores.

Whether in operations inside or outside the core of the firm, this was a time of diversification and growth.[9] The three partners were there to facilitate Alain Bouchard's dreams. For example, in the late 1980s he had to deal with two government decisions that hit the franchised stores hard. The first was a new Act governing business opening hours, which allowed the supermarkets to open in the evenings and on Sundays. The second was a 'sky-high' increase in cigarette tax, which had a devastating effect on the franchised stores' turnover, to such an extent that they began to lose money.

Alain Bouchard was involved in numerous activities and he needed 'Réal Plourde's brain'. In the early years, Réal was also asked to take care of different tasks outside Couche-Tard. For example, he spent 2 years (1989–1990) reshuffling and reorganizing Pro-Optic and then taking it public. He came back to Couche-Tard on a full-time basis in 1990.

After considering his situation and talking to the leader and senior partner, Réal Plourde offered to take over responsibility for half the company's operations, leaving the remaining half in the hands of Jacques D'Amours, the group's Vice-President of Operations and Administration. However, within 6 months he had taken over all the operations and had become COO, allowing Jacques D'Amours to concentrate on the reshuffling of stores after acquisitions and on specific aspects of administration.

A Corporate System, a Necessity as the Firm Grew: Courses and Training for Store Managers

Réal Plourde liked to 'see people grow', and decided to formalize the firm's training by introducing three courses designed to develop the employees' financial skills: Finance 101 (gross margin), Finance 102 (income statement) and Finance 103 (connection between the income statement and balance sheet). Thanks to the new courses, which went far beyond basic introductory training on the technical aspects of the job (cash register, marketing, etc.), the store managers were able to play a role in preparing their own business plans. Still not satisfied, however, Réal

---

[9]1984: Reconditioning of Bell telephones in a warehouse at Saint Jérôme.
1985: Summary of contracts with Petro-Canada, Esso and Ultramar.
1986: Technical service: store construction.
1989–1990: Pro-Optic Inc., a prescription glasses manufacturer, where he was Executive Vice-President and President.

Plourde went on to introduce a human resources management course that focused on hiring, incentives, evaluations and so on.

This increasingly specialized training was given by the company's best communicators, all former convenience store managers. From time to time, Alain Bouchard and Réal Plourde would visit the classroom, the former to talk about entrepreneurial aspects and the latter about operations. Gradually, the courses helped to improve the managers' efficiency. They also helped to generate a sense of belonging among the company's employees.

A Major Crisis

Despite the new training, however, the franchisees continued to experience problems that were exacerbated by the Government's failure to address the issue of contraband cigarettes, for fear of triggering a new crisis with the Amerindians. Aware that their situation was becoming increasingly problematical, Réal Plourde recommended buying back stores from franchisees in difficulty.[10] Although a franchisee was never forced to sell, the franchised stores were gradually bought back 'due to outside circumstances', and were converted into corporate stores.[11] In the meantime, the dance of acquisitions never stopped in Quebec and Réal Plourde was instrumental in improving the structure of the acquisition process (see the Alain Bouchard case study).

A major change in how the firm was operated and in the training of its store managers came in 1999, just after Couche-Tard bought Silcorp and its 980 stores in Ontario and Western Canada, under the Mac's, Mike's Mart and Beckers banners. Although Alain Bouchard and Réal Plourde briefly considered moving to Toronto, leaving Richard Fortin and Jacques D'Amours, the firm's other two partners, in Laval, at the operations centre, they quickly changed their minds, deciding it would be wiser to identify 'good players' and put them in charge, because 'people from Western Canada and Toronto are as different as Québecers and Ontarians'.[12] By doing this, each business unit would be able to create its own marketing.

The firm's breakthrough in the United States in 2001, which Réal Plourde considered to be a small acquisition even though it involved 180 stores in the American Midwest, took the training process to another level altogether. While

---

[10]In 1990, Mohawk communities in the Montreal region objected to the expansion of the Oka municipal golf course, claiming ownership of the land. Between March and September of that year, groups of Mohawks blocked roads that the provincial police and then the Canadian army tried unsuccessfully to clear. Commonly known as the Oka Crisis, the armed confrontation between the Mohawks and the provincial and federal authorities lasted 78 days, ending with the death of Corporal Lemay during a failed assault on 11 July 1990.

[11]In 2010, in Canada, Alimentation Couche-Tard had 1,530 corporate stores and 507 affiliated (franchised) stores. In the United States, it had a total of 2,866 corporate stores and 980 affiliates. In all, 53,000 people worked for the enterprise.

[12]Part of the urban area of Montreal, 440,000 inhabitants in 2020.

the system remained unchanged, the training unit became a real school, offering different modules for different markets.

Accountability Starting at Store Level: Belonging, Accountability and Flexibility

The success of Alimentation Couche-Tard/Circle K is due in large part to the decentralization of its operations, accountability, and the flexibility enjoyed by individual store managers. Alain Bouchard always wanted flexibility when he operated stores. He felt it was essential to be able to adjust to the culture and habits of customers at the store's location. By observing and listening to their customers, stores could adjust their marketing to suit the needs of their community.

Réal Plourde's intention, when he opted for decentralization of the managerial structure, was to transform all the store managers into intrapreneurs who would run their stores as though they owned them. This meshed well with Alain Bouchard's view of store management and it was built into the management structure at every level.

While Alain Bouchard and Finance V.P. Richard Fortin were busy making acquisitions, Réal Plourde introduced the newcomers to a culture of accountability. To facilitate and encourage intrapreneurial behaviour, and also to ensure that each unit's marketing was adjusted to its territory, he decided not only to introduce a decentralized management system, but also to develop training activities that would prepare store managers to operate in that way. A supervisory structure was designed and store supervisors were also trained to operate accordingly.

First, a position of coordinator was created: a person with some experience who would be responsible for approximately ten stores in a given area. Why ten? 'I felt it was the number that worked best'; the coordinator had to be located in physical proximity to the managers for whom he or she was responsible, and had to visit them on a regular basis. As Réal Plourde points out:

> When I went to see the person in the store and they said 'It's my store, they're my employees' or 'It's my area and my business', it made me happy! ... We felt that between 400 and 500 stores was the right number for a Regional Vice-President, because it would allow him or her to get to know both the stores and the market. Beyond 600 or 700 stores, you can't possibly remember them all or even visit them all. I wanted my Vice-Presidents to visit all their stores ... In a cash-based business, you have to be present to see what's going on. You need someone who has the gumption to control and visit a store and say, 'We've got a problem here ...let's think about fixing it as quickly as possible'.

For Réal Plourde, the capacity to adjust quickly was vital. When visiting chains with a view to acquiring them, the partners often found lots of small problems that they considered unacceptable, such as 'out of order' notes on coffee machines. An efficient supervisor who visited the stores frequently would help to fix this type of problem quickly.

Accountability became omnipresent throughout the company, from store manager to area coordinator to Regional Vice-President. A sense of belonging was also encouraged and maintained. For the four partners, this meant two fishing trips per year: a weekend family trip, often to a National Park, and a three-day trip for senior management. In this latter case, the trip served as a strategic meeting and team-building exercise. It took place in a different region of Canada each year – preferably in the North, in places such as Yellowknife and James Bay. According to company lore, the managers were even given songbooks and were invited to sing around the campfire at night in both French and English!

The managers also had access to the Ambassadors' Programme, which included two types of measures: one based on criteria such as steady results, the store's contribution, personal development and the general performance of both the store and its manager. The second involved a 'mystery customer', sometimes not an easy one, who visited the stores once a month and assessed the service received.

Acquisitions: A Driving Force for the Firm's Growth and a Source of Motivation for Réal Plourde

> Richard and I also liked the acquisitions because they kept us alive ... Integrating the new stores kept me busy! While Alain and Richard negotiated and set up financing, my job was to figure out how to integrate the stores. We each had a well-defined role, a slice of the cake ... The fact of moving outside Quebec and going into the United States, Europe and Asia was also interesting. Being able to explore the world was a great motivator for me ...

Réal Plourde loved action. Each new acquisition brought its own lot of new learning and challenges. 'Other people's good ideas' were regularly incorporated into the company's general practices. Depending on the size of the acquisition, either the Regional Vice-Presidents or the firm's owners (Alain Bouchard, Jacques D'Amours, Richard Fortin and Réal Plourde were the main shareholders) were responsible for verifying all the information (examining the books, visiting the stores, organizing video-conferences and so on). Réal Plourde even developed a sophisticated grid analysis methodology to assess the return on investment of each store considered for acquisition, including the potential for sales growth in the area where each store was located.

Alain Bouchard kept himself busy 'identifying targets and looking to the future by making new acquisitions'. Réal Plourde kept busy dealing with the constraints inherent to the task of integrating the acquisitions into the group. He decided to set up an integration committee for each new acquisition. As he was quick to point out, an acquisition should create diversity and add value to the firm, not destroy it.

This is how he described the composition of a typical integration committee: 'We combine people from our company – Quebecers, Ontarians, Americans and others– with people from the company we are buying, and they work together. Some people from the acquired companies come into our divisions to get to know us, our company, our stores, our culture and our methods, and vice-versa'.

Innovation, Comparative Analysis, Creativity and Good Practice

To identify changes that could affect the company's environment, Réal Plourde brought his 11 business units together, around a table, and asked them to come up with a list of products for the future. He described the outcome of the brainstorming session as follows: 'Cigarettes were identified as being on the way out, as were soft drinks. As people get older, they're more careful about what they eat. So we had to change our product mix. We started selling sushi in our Western Canadian stores, and hotdogs in the American Midwest. It worked because it was new'.

Not only was he attentive to the suggestions made by his store managers, and to the new products proposed by his suppliers, but he was also familiar with the changing tastes of the customers, who were more concerned about their health and well-being. One of the new trends to emerge was *fresh take away food*: not just any fast food, but tasty, pre-cooked, microwave-ready meals to take home. However, this required a change in the appearance of the stores. He explained what was done:

> If you think back to the 1980s and 1990s, consumers tended to think of convenience stores as places that were badly organized, with products piled on top of one another and not particularly clean ... To be able to offer a fresh food product, we applied what we referred to as the 'Impact' concept (Innovation-Marketing-People-Alimentation-Couche-Tard).[13] We began by renovating and cleaning our stores. Now, we sell coffee, sandwiches and other fresh products and people have confidence in the quality of those foods.

By stimulating creativity and good practices in all the divisions, Réal Plourde was able to encourage his people to learn from each other's successes. He

[13]The slogan used as a basis for the store renovations came from a network-wide competition. The winning store manager proposed: '*Innovation-Marketing*-People-*Alimentation-Couche-Tard*' on the basis that people were needed if the initiative was to be successful. The term '*Impact*' was quickly adopted by the entire network.

published regular comparative tables to facilitate communications between store managers, who were able to call one another on the telephone and talk about what they were doing. 'During major development phases, all our strengths were focused on integration, whereas during calmer periods we were able to polish the system'.

As the group acquired more stores, his work 'had to be adjusted to reflect the size of the company'. For example, instead of analysing individual store results every month, as he used to do in the early days, he examined the general monthly results of each division instead. However, this did not prevent him from travelling throughout North America once a month, with his executives, for a more in-depth analysis.

In the decade 2000–2010, in the wake of these many innovations and changes, Réal Plourde's inner engineer came up with an idea for a centralized distribution centre near the company's main office in the Montreal area. The concept was simple: improve and integrate the computer system while maximizing the fleet of delivery trucks. Everything was automated, and the system was able to display a permanent inventory of all products in each store. Monitoring could be done in real time, making it easier to adjust marketing strategies to individual markets. Réal Plourde described the project, of which he was very proud:

> It all came out of one simple observation, namely that our stores were receiving up to 50 truck deliveries per week. I thought it was crazy for a truck to deliver three boxes each to a bunch of small stores. It made more sense to send them all to a distribution centre, so that the same truck could deliver two or three times a week instead.
>
> The distribution centre idea was designed to improve the system and integrate the computer network. When we first began to manage our stores, the manager would walk around the shelves, and when he found an empty space he wrote down the number of product units he needed and sent the paper to us. Today, it's all automatic. All the manager has to do is ask the machine to process an order, and then validate it. The order is prepared and delivered, and the manager accepts it. The system displays a permanent inventory for each store. Yes, there's a bit of engineering in there!

Réal Plourde used to work up to 60 hours a week and travelled a lot. He needed a healthy lifestyle: exercise every morning, a virtually meat-free diet, very little wine and no cigarettes. And his weekends were spent with his family.

The Next Generation

> We're still working on a very important step, our succession plan. I've appointed regional vice-presidents and two senior

> vice-presidents, each with six markets. There are also successors for store management and several store coordinator positions. Human resource planning and succession plans are part of the company's formal system at all levels.

Réal Plourde had an intense career with Couche-Tard/Circle K. He joined the enterprise in 1985 as its Technical Services Manager, then went to Sales and Operations. He was then Executive Vice-President and Chief Operating Officer, heading operations from 1988 until he retired in 2011. After he retired, he was no longer present in the company on a daily basis. From 2011 to 2014, he was Chairman of the Board and he stayed on as a director afterwards. In 2020, he is still involved in strategic planning and the monthly review of operations. The four original partners all stayed on the board for a period of time after they retired.

In 2020, of the four partners, only Alain Bouchard remains active in the enterprise, at the helm of the company as Founder and Executive Chairman of the Board, a position he has held since he retired as President and CEO at the end of 2014. Richard Fortin, who was the Finance V.P., retired in October 2008, but remained Chairman of the Board until 2011. Jacques D'Amours retired in 2014.

Brian Hannasch was identified to succeed Réal Plourde. They worked closely together for almost 10 years before Brian replaced Réal as head of operations in 2011. Brian became President and CEO after Alain Bouchard retired from that position at the end of 2014. He is now regarded as the fifth partner.

Where next?

> Unlike other entrepreneurs that I've met, Alain is someone who shares. He is a dreamer and a builder, and he needs people to help him. Jacques was already there. Richard came in because Alain wanted a banker . . . As for me, I came in quite by chance. I started out in technical services, and ended up in a very different role. It all came about naturally.

Alain Bouchard often looked elsewhere for the skills he himself did not have. He was always enthusiastic about sharing his dreams with his partners. Over the years, Alimentation Couche-Tard/Circle K became a huge enterprise, not as flexible as the small firm of the 1980s, but much more stable during difficult periods.[14] This was especially evident during the COVID-19 crisis of 2020.

During the 2008–2009 recession, the company was able to correct some practices that might have been misunderstood during periods of prosperity. It was also able to save several million dollars simply by moving from conventional telephone lines to an Internet-based telephone system, reassigning overheads to

---

[14]In 2020, the firm operates more than 16,000 stores and employs more than 133,000 people in 30 countries.

commercial spaces and maximizing work schedules in the stores using a specialized software application.

In April 2010, the company moved to new office premises, still located in Laval and equipped with the latest technology. As a result, it was able to become virtually paper-free; documents are now scanned and digitized.

Réal Plourde's retirement plan had been ready since 2005. When he left his position as Head of Operations in 2011, he did not need a head-hunter to find his replacement because his successor, Brian Hannasch, Senior Vice-President of United States Operations, had been working alongside him for several years. Nevertheless, he noted that as the partners became less involved in everyday operations, the company gradually shifted into the hands of professional managers.

How does he now view his contribution to Couche-Tard? His response is unequivocal: 'I think my contribution was a human one. I was the guy who was there to listen to my partners and provide cohesion when necessary. I think I also played a role, along with the rest of the team, in ensuring the effectiveness of our operational system'.

His greatest satisfaction has been to design projects and see the results they produced. Although his work as a facilitator meant that he was often in the background, he knew very well what was expected of him, because his role, although constantly evolving, 'was clearly defined'.

What advice would he give to would-be facilitators who are expected to assist entrepreneurs with the design and implementation of innovative processes? In his opinion, the three main qualities they need are humility, honesty and integrity. Having said that, a good facilitator should be able to say what needs to be said to his or her boss – not necessarily at a meeting in front of 20 other people, but alone, face-to-face. And of course, there is the question of ethics, something he is unlikely to forget, given his time in Africa.

Réal Plourde also ascribes a great deal of importance to teamwork. He is quick to remark on and appreciate the efforts of his team, without whom most of his projects would never have come to fruition. During their trips to different parts of the company network, Alain Bouchard and Réal Plourde were able to develop a sense of belonging, a great deal of cohesion, and respect not only for senior management but also for the other employees.

While staff turnover rates are high in the stores, especially among the part-time employees, they are very low among full-time employees, a situation of which the partners have always been proud. In spite of differences often expressed between the partners about how they viewed situations and problems, they always maintained a good relationship among themselves. On two occasions, the four of them even agreed to cut their own salaries when the company ran into difficult times.

Réal also notes that it is important to be passionate and to express that passion. In his own case, he had no problem whatsoever in conveying his vision and methods. He looked carefully at the internal and external environment, and never tried to minimize the impact that a decision (customers' need) or choice (new store location) would have for the company. He always worked with the employees to find solutions, identify improvements or implement cutbacks in times of crisis.

After his official retirement from Couche-Tard in 2011, he remained active on the boards of several organizations and became involved in philanthropy, among other activities by creating his own foundation (see the Appendix A).

The Last Words ...

> Our sector changed a lot in my last 20 years with the company. In the 1980s, there was a trend towards standardization of stores. In the second decade of the 21st century, 30 years later, we developed an approach in which every store manager functioned as if he or she owned the store by adjusting to the characteristics of its customers and market.
>
> But that's not all. The notion of time changed as well. People had less time available, and more customers were starting to use convenience stores to save time. If there were three customers waiting in line at the cash desk, we would open another cash desk if we could, so they didn't have to wait long.
>
> We also created training courses to help our managers become more independent, innovative and effective. Alain Bouchard's passion for development always drove the company towards greater levels of growth. As his partners, we were happy to be working in such an intense environment.
>
> I'm lucky to have worked with a company president who was willing to listen to me! Some entrepreneurs don't listen and just do their own thing ... Alain liked to test his ideas. If Richard didn't like it, he'd come to me to see what I thought. If we both disagreed, he accepted that. But if we both agreed with his idea, he'd go ahead with it. The four of us always made our decisions unanimously, although not necessarily formally. We always got on ... It had nothing to do with the number of shares we held! During the 25 years we worked together, we created a great culture. It's a wonderful, exceptional and outstanding story.

Case Discussion

Réal Plourde

(1) Is Réal Plourde an entrepreneur, an intrapreneur, an innovative manager, a facilitator or another category of agent of innovation? Explain the differences between these various roles and justify your answer.

(2) Was it a good idea to refuse to work for Alain Bouchard unless he was paid in shares? List some advantages and disadvantages.

(3) (A) What is Réal Plourde's relationship with innovation? Before he began work with Alain Bouchard, what experience did he have with innovation and with entrepreneurship?
(B) Was Réal Plourde an innovationist (i.e. a person with an interest in innovation)? Or was he beyond that stage, i.e. was he looking for potential opportunities to improve, invent or contribute something new and become an agent of innovation? Explain your answer.

(4) Réal Plourde is an engineer and an MBA. Which of these backgrounds seems to be the most relevant in what he subsequently accomplished? Why? How do you explain the fact that most facilitators are better-educated than the entrepreneurs for whom they work?

(5) Is Réal Plourde a leader? Explain your answer.

(6) Is it possible for a leader to work for another leader? Explain your answer.

(7) (A) How does a facilitator learn what to do in order to add value to the entrepreneur's innovative pattern?
(B) Some facilitators work hard to understand the entrepreneur's vision and may even help the entrepreneur to clarify their vision. What potential inputs do you think a facilitator could make to help an entrepreneur renew his or her vision or improve the organization's performance?

(8) Alain Bouchard is a product developer and uses acquisitions as a means of developing his organization. Réal Plourde seems to be a process innovator. How well do you think they are matched? How do they fit together? What could be improved?

(9) What kind of effects can a facilitator have on the design, development and construction of an organization? Where do you situate Réal Plourde with respect to these elements?

(10) (A) What are the different forms of innovations that a facilitator could contribute to an organization?
(B) What is an appropriate way of preparing to become a facilitator?

Acknowledgements

An initial version of a case study about Réal Plourde (in French) was filed with the HEC Montreal Case Centre in 2010 (9 40 2010 063): *Réal Plourde: facilitateur et généraliste aux multiples talents*. This case study was never published. A copy is available at the HEC Montreal Case Centre (http://www.hec.ca/en/case_centre).

Unless otherwise indicated, the citations in this 2023 version of the case study were taken from an interview conducted by the authors with Réal Plourde on 22 February 2010, in the company's offices in Laval. All citations are free translations from the original French. This case study includes most of the material from the previous case study produced by the authors in 2010. An additional interview was held with Réal Plourde on 21 February 2020.

This case study will be easier to understand if the following case study, telling the story of the enterprise, is read first: *Alain Bouchard, Couche-Tard and Circle K: Conquering the World, Step by Step.*

Information is also available from the company's websites: Couche-Tard/Circle K. Additional information about Couche-Tard/Circle K is available in the following book: Guy Gendron (2016) *Daring to Succeed. How Alain Bouchard built the Couche-Tard and Circle K convenience store empire.* Montreal: Juniper Publishing.

Reference

Gendron, G. (2016). *Daring to succeed. How Alain Bouchard built the Couche-Tard and Circle K convenience store empire* (p. 87). Juniper Publishing.

Appendix

Awards Received

- TOP COO - Canadian Business –2005
- Dunamis Award of Merit 'for his professional and personal success during his remarkable career, and for his social commitment to the community of the City of Laval' – 2009
- Medal - Lieutenant-Governor of Québec – for seniors - 2018.

Social Contributions

Volunteer Work

Moisson Laval 2000–2016, director and chair of the board.
Laval Palliative Care Centre 2004–2017, director and chair of the board.
Ariane Riou & Réal Plourde Foundation: The foundation supports financially palliative care homes and other causes.

Other Activities

* Member of the advisory committees of three SMEs.
* CIMA+ - Engineering firm - 2,300 employees – head office located in Montreal – director and chair of the board.
* Couche-Tard/Circle K - Member of the Board, involved in strategic planning, the business plan and the monthly review of operations.

Chapter 4

From Softimage to Microsoft and Then to Inno-Centre: Pierre Nelis and Entrepreneurial Facilitation

Joëlle Hafsi and Louis Jacques Filion

Abstract

Pierre Nelis joined a small group of artists working for a creative entrepreneur who had invented software to produce movies. He brought a great deal of marketing expertise to a team of technology creators, and it was this that ultimately allowed the firm to sell its software to movie industry leaders throughout the world. The firm – Softimage – was bought by Microsoft, which hired Pierre Nelis to oversee the integration process, and later to develop new communications products. Nelis has an outstanding ability to identify the elements needed by a firm to become more effective, and this led him to set up a one-of-a-kind external facilitation programme that went on to become a model for many business growth support organizations throughout the world, but especially in North America and Europe.

Keywords: Facilitator; facilitation; marketing; external facilitator; business development; international

This chapter has been developed from the publication, Piffault, J. and Filion, L. J. (2007) Pierre Nelis: Facilitator. WACRA *International Journal of Case Method Research & Application*, XIX, 4.

Case
From Softimage to Microsoft and Then to Inno-centre: Pierre Nelis and Entrepreneurial Facilitation[1]

[1]Case written by Joëlle Hafsi and Louis Jacques Filion.

Agents of Innovation, 111–139

Published under exclusive licence by Emerald Publishing Limited
doi:10.1108/978-1-83797-012-420231004

Part 1
Youth and Education

Early Days: Across Continents

Pierre Nelis does not remember his paternal grandparents, who were imprisoned by the Germans and sent to a concentration camp, where they were executed. It was almost a miracle that their son, Marc-Michel, survived. Pierre describes his father's extraordinary odyssey:

> In 1943 my father escaped from a German camp by hiding in a garbage can, and crossed half of Germany to get back to Belgium! My mother's parents hid him in their loft. My mother would take him food, and they fell in love.

After the war, life returned more or less to normal in the Belgian capital of Brussels. Pierre's mother, Louise Baude, went to school and qualified as a nurse, while Marc-Michel Nelis studied psychology, theology and chemistry. They married and moved to Congo, then a Belgian colony, where they built schools and churches and taught their protestant faith. Two of their five children were born there including Pierre. However, shortly after his birth in 1959, civil war broke out and they went back to Belgium in the early 1960s. The move was as quick and brutal as their experience two decades earlier in World War Two.

Pierre has only vague memories of the family's hasty departure from the Congo and the year he spent at a Belgian boarding school before the family packed their bags once again, this time moving to Canada in 1962, where Pierre's father Marc-Michel, a pastor with the United Church, had accepted an appointment as a teacher and chaplain at the Church's French Evangelical Institute of the United Church in Montreal. Marc-Michel, his wife and their five children, of whom Pierre was the youngest, decided to settle in the quiet Province of Québec to start a new life for the second time.

A Peaceful Life in Canada

After moving to Canada, the family quickly settled into its new home. Marc-Michel worked hard, while his wife stayed home to look after the children. Although their new home town of Montreal was predominantly Catholic, Pierre was raised in the Protestant faith. He went to elementary school at an institution governed by the Protestant School Board where his father worked. At high school, his grades were modest; he was much more interested in the theatre and sport, at which he excelled. During the summer vacation, the children went to summer camps to learn English.

Pierre was proud of his father's intellectual abilities, but his older brother, Luc, became his model. Luc introduced him to the Cadets. Pierre applied and was accepted. He was an average student at high school; he did not enjoy it, was not motivated and did not work hard. On the other hand, he enjoyed public speaking and theatre. And he had the cadets, which he loved.

At school, he also admired two of his teachers, one who taught history and the other French. His favourite activity was to read or write stories. Looking back, he now thinks he was more rational than most of his fellow students. The only subject that really interested him was history. Although he was comfortable speaking to groups or acting on a stage, Pierre never considered a career as a teacher or actor. 'I never thought much about what I was going to do. I never went through any major identity crisis – at least, not until I was 40 years old!'

The Canadian Armed Forces: Discipline and a Few Life Lessons

Pierre's activities with the cadets led him to develop an interest in the army. Having graduated from high school, joining the army seemed to be a natural step for him. He joined with the rank of Second Lieutenant. If he had had a bachelor's degree or studied at a military college, he would have been a Lieutenant. Even without a degree, however, he still had an opportunity to become a Lieutenant: what he had to do was to take a basic 3-month officer training course.

He received the required training at the Chilliwack Officers' School, located near north-east of Vancouver 'a beautiful region of British Columbia'. He took the *Aviation 1* course, which he enjoyed because he was alone in a small aircraft. He never considered going on to take *Aviation 2* because to do this, he would have had to sign a 5-year contract and pay back the $125,000 course fee if he dropped out.[2]

Instead, he chose the infantry because he did not have to sign a contract. This involved leaving Chilliwack and moving thousands of kilometres 'to the Army's largest base at the time, in Gagetown, New Brunswick, in Eastern Canada'. Although he enjoyed the infantry at first, because it reminded him of his time in the cadets and at the officers' training school, he found it involved a lot of 'waiting around' and he began to lose his enthusiasm.

He eventually left the army with a diploma and an honourable discharge in 1976, 2 years after joining up. In those 2 years, he had discovered his leadership abilities and had learned that he functioned better as part of a team, rather than alone. Two years in the Canadian Armed Forces taught him discipline, organization and rigour. He learned to adapt quickly to all kinds of new contexts. This would serve him well throughout his life, since he lived and worked in a variety of different environments.

---

[2]All figures are in Canadian dollars unless otherwise indicated.

Apprenticeships in the World of Organizations

First Work Experiences: Applied Learning in a Variety of Fields

Pierre came back to Montreal with his Army diploma in hand and moved back in with his parents. Employers were keen to hire former Army recruits, but before finding a job, Pierre decided to 'try my hand at education'. He quickly came to the conclusion that studying was not for him.[3] However, he realized that he needed a stable, well-paid job:

> I read in the newspaper that Canadian Bonded Credit (CBC) was looking for someone who was bilingual, with good organizational skills and discipline, but not necessarily with experience. I went for an interview and we 'clicked'. So they hired me.[4]

Pierre started out as a clerk and went on to work at virtually every level of the company, gaining experience with everything from paralegal work to court cases and accounting. He also worked one or two evenings a week with lawyer Sheldon Price in his Montreal downtown office, organizing his outstanding commercial accounts. He soon knew everything there was to know about bad debts:

> My starting salary was $9,000 a year, but it had gone up to $12,000 three years later. A five-figure salary was really great at the time. I was a very hard worker. The company was pan-Canadian and employed about fifty people in Montreal. I have no idea what its turnover was – I never even asked myself the question. You have to remember the context. I had zero knowledge of the business world and zero understanding of how a company operated. Today, the first thing I look at is stock market value and the turnover.

After five years at CBC, he felt it was time to move onwards and upwards.

Keeping Growing

Other jobs followed, with additional opportunities to learn. Groves Construction, for example, was a general contractor working 90% of the time for the Grand

---

[3]Pierre Nelis would not go back to school until 1995, when he took the Executive Development Course offered by McGill University, a kind of mini-MBA with the same teachers but without the status, offering practical, short-term training in management, marketing, finance, ethics, human resources and other subjects. Since he was working at Softimage at the time, he took courses in the evenings and on weekends, and in 1996 went on to take the advanced course.

[4]Canadian Bonded Credit (CBC), whose offices were located in Montreal, was a commercial debt recovery company that also offered high-risk financing to clients who were unable to obtain bank loans. Because of the risk, interest rates were high and endorsements were required.

Council of the Crees in the James Bay region, in Northern Québec.[5] With its virtual monopoly over contracts with the Crees, Groves Construction employed between 20 and 500 people, depending on the season, and up to 700 in peak periods. Most of its employees worked in Canada's Great North.

As a jack-of-all-trades, Pierre negotiated with suppliers, bought equipment, recruited workers, took care of accounting for new projects and monitored budgets. Versatility was something Pierre had cultivated since his childhood, and he was able to change jobs easily because every new experience brought new challenges, new knowledge and new skills. With Groves, he learned to take initiatives and explore intrapreneurial behaviour. This was part of the commitment to his job.

Eventually, he answered an advertisement placed by Beauchemin, Beaton, Lapointe (BBL), and was hired as its Operations Manager, to be responsible for administrative support – in other words, everything not connected with engineering.[6]

A Headhunter Changed His Career Path

Although not 'actively' looking for a new job, Pierre was nevertheless recruited by a headhunter, and became Human Resources and Training Manager for Squibb Canada.[7] At the time, his new appointment raised a few smiles among his acquaintances:

> Several people asked me how I'd managed to become a recruitment and training manager when all my experience was in general operations administration. They all thought I didn't have the right experience – it was crazy! However, I just 'clicked' with the guy who hired me – Guy Darcy, the Human Resources and Administration Vice-President. In reality, he was looking for a generalist who he could train as a replacement for himself, since he was about to retire, but there wasn't a suitable vacancy in the company.

As the new Human Resources and Training Manager, Pierre was responsible for preparing job descriptions in collaboration with the division vice-presidents, and recruiting clinical research specialists throughout Canada and Europe. He also put together training courses for medical representatives, and technical courses for office staff.

---

[5]Groves Construction's civil engineers built ice bridges so that, in winter, 24-wheel trucks could carry all the materials required to build airports, villages and infrastructures on Cree territory.

[6]Beauchemin, Beaton, Lapointe (BBL), one of Québec's largest engineering consulting firm in the 1980s, was specialized in environment, transportation and energy. It employed around 200 people, including 180 engineers. Tecsult, also an engineering firm, would later take a shareholding in BBL.

[7]Squibb Canada was a pharmaceutical company located in Montreal. It was one of the industry's major players, due to its research and products in the field of infectious diseases.

In 1989, Squibb was taken over by Bristol Myers. During the transition, one of Pierre's tasks was to analyse the jobs affected by the merger – for example, some regions suddenly found themselves with two representatives. Furthermore, Bristol Myers wanted to take over and bring in its own people. Pierre still considered Guy Darcy to be his boss and intended to remain loyal to the man who had been loyal to him. There were clashes, as the following anecdote shows:

> When Bristol Myers bought Squibb, the new Human Resources and Administration Vice-President organized a meeting the following June with the 18 employees from our department and our boss, Guy Darcy. He started telling us what we should be doing, and I stood up and said 'Excuse me, but as long as Guy Darcy is my boss, I'll be reporting to him'! Ten or fifteen years ago I was still very impulsive and direct. I wasn't in awe of anyone, even the Prime Minister himself! I've always said what I thought. Today, though, I tend to say it differently.

Two weeks later, the entire department, including Guy Darcy, was laid off. 'In any case, the experience brought me some maturity and allowed me to find another job that was twice as interesting, at least at first', he says.

Moving Upwards With Noranda

Noranda Technology was the Noranda Group's research and development centre.[8] The centre was managed by an 'extraordinary guy', Frank Lederman, who was straight out of one of the best management schools in the world, General Electric. His mission was to put the centre back on its feet. Pierre, again the only manager without a PhD, describes the centre's situation and goals:

> The goal was to bring the centre back to world-class level. At the time, it was doing research for the sake of it, with no specific goal that could be measured in terms of quality or time, and no performance evaluation. We had to change the culture, eliminate the dead wood, set up a performance evaluation procedure, give training, modernize the computer infrastructure and implement a project management process.

With Guy Darcy, who became a friend over the years, and Frank Lederman, who raised him to a new level, Pierre had his first experience with sophisticated management concepts and their applications. And yet, his early enthusiasm was

---

[8]Noranda Technology's huge laboratory was located in a warehouse complex containing small-scale reproductions of mines and mini oil refineries. Of the 250 or so people who worked there, approximately 200 were specialist researchers in the mineral, metal and energy sectors, recreating experiments for implementation in the Group's companies.

soon tempered by routine. It was at this point that he experienced his first major identity crisis, the one that led him to Softimage.

Looking for Challenges: The Softimage Adventure

Discovering the World of Technological Creators

Pierre needs action. At Noranda, his last employer before Softimage, his early enthusiasm for the challenges of his job soon waned. As a member of the Association of World Research Centres attending international conferences throughout the world, he often came into contact with:

> . . . high-level grey matter! An enriching and eye-opening experience. So I had a serious talk with myself. 'What do you want to do? Who with? Where? What do you really like? What are your strengths and weaknesses? What do you want to become? Where might you be put to best use?' I looked everywhere. Then I heard of Daniel Langlois, who was something of a tearaway in the high-tech field.

There were pictures of Langlois all over in the media after he won an award for a 'special software application' he had designed. A quick look confirmed that his young organization, Softimage, with just 14 employees at the time, was growing quickly. Daniel Langlois needed someone like Pierre 'to organize it all. There were people, processes and a versatile, highly effective and creative leader stuck in a disorganized environment'. It was a situation that offered a wonderful opportunity for a military-minded and highly structured person like Pierre.

However, to meet with Daniel Langlois and offer his services, Pierre first had to climb over the 'Great Wall of China' in the form of a secretary and a vice-president who were fiercely protective of Langlois, as he was overworked and bombarded by telephone calls, especially from the media.

It was 1992 when Pierre eventually managed to meet Daniel Langlois, an animation software writer who had just become famous for an original application he had designed, which was used to produce films. Langlois was surrounded by a group of creators and artists who, like himself, were highly creative but not organized enough to take advantage of the market for their futuristic technology.[9]

---

[9]After obtaining a Bachelor's degree in design, Daniel Langlois worked in the film industry and computer graphics, creating 3-D computer animations. He launched Softimage in 1986. The firm was specialized in the creation of software that generated 3-D effects. They were used by the media, for instance for weather forecasts, but also in films such as Star Wars, The Matrix, Titanic, Men in Black, Twister, Jurassic Park, The Mash and many others, in numerous countries. After selling Softimage to Microsoft in 1994 ($200 million), Langlois became director of tool design for advanced technologies at Microsoft (1994–1998). He later set up additional enterprises in art sectors and creative industries. He received many awards, and his foundation has made numerous targeted donations to support the arts.

This was the beginning of an adventure in which the combined creativity of Langlois, supported by Pierre's team management and other skills, would propel Softimage onto the world stage.

Pierre eventually managed to bypass 'the Wall', and his first meeting with Daniel Langlois lasted just over an hour. Although very different in terms of appearance – Pierre was dressed like any classic executive, wearing a 'nice suit and tie', while Langlois was dressed in 'a t-shirt and two mismatched training shoes, one orange and one green' – their contact was instantaneous and easy. 'We just clicked', said Pierre:

> From my point of view, he was exactly what I was looking for: disorganized, a victim of his own creativity and growth, an award winner who didn't know how to organize what he had. The office was a boiling pot. I said to myself, *'it's now or never'*. I was happy in my marriage but bored with my work. I'm very serious and structured at work, very intense, a bit like a Ferrari on a racetrack. There's a time to kick back and a time to work. The bigger the challenge, the more intense I am. So I was perfect for the firm. From Daniel's point of view, I think he was attracted by my broad experience and the fact that I enjoyed my work so much.

Pierre joined Softimage shortly after that first interview, in 1992. Appointed Vice-President, Human Resources and Administration, he became the 19th employee in a firm that would have a workforce of 500 by the time it was sold to Microsoft 2 years later, in 1994. Used to operating in structured environments, he began by drawing up his own employment contract, which offered a basic salary along with several stock options. The contract was presented to Daniel Langlois by Julien Blanchard, Softimage's Vice-President for Finance. Langlois signed it.

Although his salary at Softimage was well below what he had earned at Noranda, Pierre did not care. He had never had a luxury lifestyle. 'My car was paid for and I had no debts', he said. His wife Linda was also still employed in the Marketing Department of Beauchemin, Beaton and Lapointe – it was there that the two first met.

Several 'Firsts' at Softimage, Including Market and Organizational Efficiency

Pierre discovered that the total lack of structure was not without its problems for Softimage, as sales began to increase both locally and internationally. One of his early tasks was to draw up employment contracts for all the personnel, containing confidentiality and non-competition agreements. It was a 'first' for the small company.

The founding employees were somewhat put out, since they saw this as a profound change in the organizational culture. Although it was difficult for him, Pierre was patient:

> I had no problems with new employees – they signed the agreements right away. Softimage was the darling of the world animation industry and everyone was desperate to work there. But it took me two years to get the early employees to sign.

Employment contracts meant recruitment. As the company had no recruitment policy, Pierre instituted a rigorous recruitment process designed to identify the best software developers. In 1992, Softimage was growing rapidly, hence the need for new R&D people. In those early days, three people, namely Daniel Langlois, Claude Cajolet (Vice-President, R&D) and Pierre, were responsible for determining the basic requirements for all positions advertised in the media.

Pierre would select between five to ten potential candidates from the applications received, and then refer the best three to Claude Cajolet, who interviewed them along with three or four other people from his team. Each interviewer submitted an assessment report, but regardless of the team's recommendation, the final decision was entirely his, and everyone else simply had to live with it. This meant that every new candidate had seen about ten people before being offered a position at Softimage.

The vacation policy was another 'first' introduced by Pierre:

> I introduced a policy of one month's vacation for Vice-Presidents and three weeks for employees. In reality, though, everyone worked all the time. If we'd been working non-stop for five or six days, we took a bit of extra time in Las Vegas or Amsterdam, for example. But we didn't watch the clock. I was always available by phone, even on Christmas Day and New Year's Day. Softimage was making a lot of money and playing in the major leagues. When you're being paid the amount we were earning, you don't tell your boss you won't be answering the phone one day.

Learning to Be an Entrepreneurial Facilitator

In addition to recruiting 80 new employees, 1992 was an extremely busy year. Pierre travelled extensively. Among several other activities, he opened new offices in Paris and Singapore. Why in those cities? Because the animation market is concentrated in three main regions, all of which are worth about the same in terms of sales volume:

> One-third of our sales were in Pacific Asia, with Japan and South Korea being the leading markets. Another third of our sales were in the United States, to production houses in Texas, the Boston region and California. The other one-third were scattered throughout the world.

In Asia, Singapore was a natural choice. For Pierre, it offered several advantages including the quality and cost of infrastructure and telecommunications, an educated workforce, proximity to an airport and a stable environment.

Pierre recruited and helped select more than four hundred employees over 2 years. The firm's fast growth generated a constant stream of new tasks in addition to the many for which he was already responsible, until in the end he was virtually living at the office. When not physically present, he was always available via the Internet:

> Somewhat naively, I always believed you could be successful in life just by being competent. I didn't think you had to cultivate relationships with people inside and outside the company. The purpose determined the means. I scored. Everything I touched turned to gold. It was wonderful. I was really focused on the task... Everyone benefited.

In 1993, Pierre oversaw four phases of a new construction project on the corner of Saint-Laurent Boulevard and Milton Street, in downtown Montreal, extending the Softimage offices to accommodate its 500 employees. He also computerized the accounting system: Softimage, now a world leader in computer animation, had been using manual systems until then! And he set up a customer service department that was able to respond immediately, 24 hours a day, to customer requests and solve problems all over the world regardless of time differences.

'Building' is what Pierre enjoys the most. When he has nothing to build, he finds his work boring. At Softimage, he did not have time to be bored – the responsibilities and challenges were constant and plentiful.

Individual Responsibility and Accountability Were at the Core of the Enterprise Culture

> Daniel was a great boss! He gave me operational goals and wanted to be kept in the loop, but otherwise he left me alone. Often he didn't know how to achieve the goals himself. And he

> didn't care, he just wanted results. He wasn't interested in operations.

Who, then, was responsible for decisions such as opening up a new market or adding a new application? In most cases, a customer would express a specific need, and then all subsequent decisions were made by the Management Committee, composed of Daniel Langlois, Claude Cajolet (R & D), Dave McCray (Sales) and Pierre (Operations). The Committee met every week and set up the *modus operandi* to respond to the customer's request.

To add elements to existing applications, the V.P. R & D, Claude Cajolet, would look at his team, and if he did not have the right person to develop the application, Pierre would recruit someone for him. As the firm became better known, the demand quickly increased – for instance, once it became known that the blockbuster film *Jurassic Park* had used an innovative software application produced by Softimage, or when the company began to produce software that could be used by television weather forecasters to show moving clouds.

On the other hand, when the Committee was looking for a new market, Pierre would call on his marketing team and ask them to compare the different markets and their specifications. Every decision was made jointly:

> The ideas weren't mine. I had become a facilitator, a kind of semi-entrepreneur who worked to maintain the super-entrepreneur's greatness. Tell me what you want and leave it to me! I'm the one who'll wake up at night, thinking about what to do and how to do it. And Daniel quickly realized that I delivered the goods. I was always ahead of deadlines. I always got organized. I brought structure. My philosophy is 'hire the right people then get them to establish and apply a strategy'. If you have the right pilots, they'll learn to fly whatever plane you give them.

Pierre proved to be an excellent conceiver and producer of complementary visions, because he understood how Langlois' main vision was developing. During his time at Softimage he became a vital element in the realization of his employer's overall vision. The relationship between Daniel Langlois and his right-hand man was remarkably close, but always remained essentially a working relationship.

When it came to organizing the company, the chemistry between the two men was strong – they understood one another quickly and completely. They both worked on complementary processes to make innovations happen: Langlois, the leading entrepreneur, on product creation, and Nelis, the facilitator, on marketing. He created, designed and implemented innovative processes to harvest financial rewards from this intensive creative dynamism.

Family Life vs Business Life

In 1994, the Nelis family landscape changed with the birth of a daughter. For Daniel Langlois, whose child was Softimage, it was almost a betrayal:

> Daniel thought Claude and I would abandon the company.[10] We changed our working hours. We might have been less present in the workplace, but we still worked far more than average, from home when necessary. For example, we'd organize a video-conference rather than a trip to California. The arrival of e-mail certainly helped us. I had dinner at home more often. Linda quit her job to look after our daughter. The two of them travelled with me all over the world. While I worked, they'd visit whatever city we were in. It was a good arrangement all around.

Adaptation to Microsoft: Rigour, Discipline and Business Warfare Education

Discovering the Culture of a Major International Corporation

The year 1994 saw another major event, namely the sale of Softimage to Microsoft. The sale brought a new 3-year contract for Pierre as the leading representative of the Softimage activities within the Microsoft giant organization. It was an important commitment for him. He felt highly motivated to maintain the movement of market development he had initiated within Softimage.

'I was motivated more by the idea of building a company and learning, than by money', he says – although he was careful not to neglect his financial interests. If he left the firm before the end of the 3-year period, he would lose all his stock options. And that meant losing certain wealth: every Softimage share entitled him to 0.458 of a Microsoft share, and Microsoft's shares were divided ten times between 1994 and 1998.

Moshe Litchman, Microsoft's Joint President, was sent to Montreal to head Softimage. Litchman, a software engineer who graduated from MIT, did his military service in Israel and piloted F4 fighter planes. A disciplined individual, he was one of the 20 most important people in Microsoft's succession planning pipeline. Moshe Litchman became Pierre's mentor:

> He taught me about Microsoft's culture, philosophy and know-how, including its rigour and discipline in the production and delivery of products and the entire marketing machine. In the past, we'd delivered our products

[10]Claude Cajolet, Vice-President, R&D, and Pierre Nelis both had their first child at about the same time.

> in typically Québec style, based on what I like to call the *pleasure cruise* philosophy. At Microsoft's Seattle office they gave me the firm's one-month intensive *Business Warfare* course. It was an extraordinary brainwashing experience!

As the Softimage officer responsible for the merger, Pierre became joint manager of the newly merged company, along with Microsoft's Susan Voeller. Although Softimage was owned by Microsoft, it remained 100% Canadian. From 1996 onwards, Pierre wore two hats:

- He was Business Unit Vice-President, responsible for public and governmental affairs at Softimage. His job involved managing the firm's technological infrastructure, meaning that he could abandon his previous duties in the areas of finance, operations and customer service, which had become routine and lacking in challenge for him.
- Now a Microsoft employee, he also oversaw an Internet company project known as *Microsoft Sidewalk*, an Internet publication aimed at a young audience and covering a wide variety of subjects. *Microsoft Sidewalk* was an element of Microsoft's business plan for the creation of virtual companies in different cities – Paris, London, Moscow, New York and Montreal – to establish trends throughout the world. However, the Montreal component had lagged far behind the other four.

As the person responsible for the *Microsoft Sidewalk* website, Pierre recruited 20 people, designers and journalists, from the Montreal region. The site's editorial content was aimed at the 18–35 age group and included restaurant reviews as well as various 'Lifestyle' columns. However, the venture proved unprofitable due to poor web penetration, and Microsoft sold the entire operation, including the Montreal component, to Ticketmaster, its main competitor.

In an attempt to keep Pierre on the payroll, Microsoft offered him the position of general manager at its Seattle, or Washington or Singapore office (his choice). All three cities were important centres for the company:

> After visiting Singapore with Linda and my daughter, I turned them down. My wife is an athlete – she competed in pre-Olympic races and still runs every day. In Québec, you can run anywhere. In Singapore, you must run on a track out in the suburbs, about ten miles from where we would have been living. I also wanted another child and a calmer lifestyle that would allow me to get back into shape. My three-year contract was over, and I was free to do what I wanted. In 1998, I decided to leave Microsoft to

> become a *coach* or *mentor* for other entrepreneurs. I decided I'd rather choose my projects and stay in Montreal.

And so an important chapter in Pierre's life came to a close.

A Five-Year Transition: 1998–2003

From Operations to a Support Resource for Entrepreneurs and CEOs

At every stage of his life, Pierre Nelis has been a facilitator, sometimes without realizing it. At Tecsult, Noranda and Bristol Myers Squibb, he always did something to contribute to the firm's success. He commits to everything he does, and his brand image has been that of a developer. And yet, it was at Softimage that he took entrepreneurial facilitation to the next level, helping to transform a young small enterprise into an international flagship company.

After he left Microsoft, Pierre dreamed of taking a year off to relax, rebuild his health, put his personal life in order and do some thinking about what he would do next. And yet, all he got was one summer with his wife and their daughter, because when he returned to Montreal, the telephone began to ring. Now financially secure, he was able to pick and choose the activities in which he would get involved, but his main aim was to work less intensely and have a less stressful life.

He was known in the Montreal area as one of the leading stars of Softimage, and was seen as an exceptional business developer. In addition to that, the expertise he had gained at Microsoft enhanced his reputation as an expert in business structuring. Many of Montreal's entrepreneurs and CEOs wanted to meet him for advice.

For instance, he worked on a special project (an internet lifestyle platform – BHVR) for Richard Szalwinski, one of Softimage's former programmers who created Discreet Logic. He also contributed to a series of community and volunteer projects. Occasionally he would help a start-up or young firm that had encountered problems. He was also a coach, mentor and advisor at the local *Community and Entrepreneurship Centre* near his home in Montreal.

However, he soon realized that he needed challenges to thrive, and that action was his fuel, the thing that gave him the greatest satisfaction. He was not the kind of person who could live off his wealth and do nothing. He gained satisfaction and motivation from being involved in the venture creation and development process, but did not feel he would like to start a business himself.

Through his involvement as an *internal facilitator*, then as a mentor and a coach in a variety of projects and enterprises, he learned a new trade: that of *external facilitator*. It was a transition that gradually led him to a new career with Inno-centre.

Joining Inno-centre[11]

A Home Port That Allowed Him to Do What He Loved – Using External Facilitation as a Mean to Help Firms Grow

> In 2003, I met with Claude Martel, the President, CEO and creator of Inno-centre. He asked me to help two young students from Mc Gill University who were in the process of launching an enterprise (SimActive). I became an advisor for their project. These two entrepreneurs had developed an application that could identify the differences between two images in real time. I'm still a member of their board.
>
> After I'd completed three assignments for Inno-centre, Claude Martel asked me if I'd join the organization as an advisor. Subsequently, in 2006, I became VP and *General Director*. I've stayed there ever since and have helped with Inno-centre's transformation and development.
>
> I've been a member of the board of directors since I first joined the organization. Inno-Centre has grown a lot in the last 15 years. In 2013, I became *Vice-President and Operations Manager,* as we developed a structure that included two Managing Directors, one in Montreal and one in Quebec City, each covering a vast territory. I've also been involved in a few projects outside the organization.
>
> Our president, Claude Martel, is a political virtuoso, and he's really educated me in all things political. That includes us, our clients, and governments. He's great at navigating all these waters and knowing what to do or what not to do.

At Inno-centre, Pierre was involved in a wide variety of sectors, including agri-food, clean technology, software applications, medical equipment, new media, industrial technologies and several others. His job, which he attacked with gusto, was to set up external facilitation processes to support the growth of mid-sized firms. Gradually, over the 10 years that followed, he recruited and coordinated more than 100 experienced practitioners, many of whom were entrepreneurs and owner-managers of SMEs, to act as advisors to innovative, high growth companies. He loved the fact that every new assignment was a new challenge.

What exactly did he do at Inno-centre? What services did he provide? How did his external facilitation services help firms to attain new levels of development? How was he able to match firms with the expertise they needed to support or

---

[11]https://www.inno-centre.com/en

speed up their growth? What were the innovations he helped to improve through the external facilitation process? These latter aspects were his main challenges. Over the years, his thinking became more complex. He describes Softimage as his 'appetizer', Microsoft as his 'main course' and Inno-centre as his 'dessert'.

Right from the beginning, Claude Martel gave Pierre the flexibility and space he needed to decide how he wanted to work and to structure the intervention process. He quickly developed a more complex intervention structure that included a combination of expertise needed for each assignment. Instead of continuing to act as an external facilitator, he designed an approach where he structured interventions implemented by a team of external facilitators who were themselves entrepreneurs and practitioners: a one-of-a-kind approach.

He quickly realized that understanding the entrepreneur/CEO was more important than understanding the product or the problems faced by the firm he was helping. In fact, understanding a multiplicity of issues, including the entrepreneur's aspirations, was what enabled him to help position their firm.

Inno-centre: Channelling Entrepreneurial Energy and Expertise

Inno-centre is an independent non-profit organization in the broader public sector, funded by a variety of Government programs, which provides consulting services for innovative SMEs. Claude Martel has headed Inno-centre since he founded it in 1987. At the beginning, he positioned it as an incubator to help start-ups but as its activities evolved, it became more of an accelerator that helps firms to grow. Its strength lies in the expertise of its advisors, especially in technological innovation. Most of these advisors are experienced entrepreneurs able to communicate what they have learnt to other entrepreneurs, so that they can make improvements or prepare successful innovations and developments.

Over the years, Claude Martel has built a strong culture of innovation to address the far-reaching technological and other changes occurring in the global entrepreneurial environment. The result has been an avant-gardist organization able to work on different forms of innovation, not only on products and processes but also in different areas of management, including human resources, marketing and finance. His aim over the past 30 years has always been to help create a movement that would allow Montreal to maintain its ranking as one of the most creative cities in the world.[12]

People now refer to the 'Inno-centre model' as an effective learning transfer model that speeds up innovation in the firms that use its services. The model has been applied in other cities in Canada, Mexico and several countries of Europe.

Inno-centre's board of directors includes entrepreneurs from different business sectors and well-known university researchers. As an organization, it is both flexible and agile. The management team, composed of only six people, each with a clear role is supported by an administrative team of five people, three of whom

[12]Richard Florida, Martin Prosperity Institute.

work exclusively on client programs and services. It may be small, but its operations are among the largest in Canada.[13,14]

From Internal Facilitator to External Facilitation Matchmaker

Effective External Facilitation: Matching Coaches to Clients

Pierre was able to build on the original system put in place by the founder of Inno-centre, developing an approach to offer external facilitation activities and answer the needs of client firms, rather like a tailor producing made-to-measure clothing.

He has perfected his role as an external facilitator by supervising the implementation of hundreds of external facilitation interventions. In addition, he has continued to learn how to identify the most appropriate methods and structures to answer the needs of fast-growing entrepreneurs and their firms. His entrepreneurial facilitation approach continues to evolve, as does his method of supervising its application by the entrepreneur-advisors he identifies, selects and coordinates. As a result, and over the years, he has become a kind of *matchmaker*: a conductor who oversees an army of 100 external facilitators that he 'connects' with entrepreneurs.

His own experience as an internal and external facilitator, combined with his extensive knowledge of the entrepreneurial, organizational and business worlds, allows him to quickly diagnose the needs of entrepreneurs and firms referred by partner investors or financial institutions. Here is how he describes his role:

> I am what is referred to as a *Chief Operating Officer*. I manage more than 100 people. In reality, I also manage the relationships with our clients. I meet with potential clients, and after diagnosing their needs, I structure the remainder of the process before drafting and signing service agreements.
>
> A service agreement is a contract for 200 hours of support, described in an intervention plan. It may focus on strategy, marketing tactics or other aspects of management, each requiring 25 or 50 hours or more, depending on needs. It may also include 100 hours of plant re-engineering or other advisory activities.
>
> Next, I identify a senior advisor, who becomes a coordinator assigned to the firm for the duration of the project. The senior advisor will then choose the resources and expertise he or she needs, from my team of more than 100 people, to carry out the 200-hour mandate.

---

[13]https://www.inno-centre.com/en/equipes/categorie/management-team/

[14]https://www.inno-centre.com/en/equipes/categorie/administrative-team/

Pierre needs a two-hour meeting – often it is a lunch – with an entrepreneur 'to identify his or her needs, understand the *modus operandi* and gain an overview of his or her personality'. Back at the office, he identifies the best team for the job – in other words, he assesses the best fit between the senior advisor/coordinator on the one hand and the client on the other. He considers two, three or even four potential scenarios that may help the team to function smoothly and effectively. His intuition, developed from many years of experience, plays an important role in this process. He uses both his imaginative and analytical skills to consider different possibilities for a project. He acknowledges that this is always a challenge and is never easy.

Once the diagnosis has been made and the various scenarios have been considered, what he refers to as the 'matchmaking process' can begin. Which one of the 100 or so advisors is best qualified to lead this type of assignment? Which two or three others have the right combination of complementary knowledge, skills, expertise and characteristics to operate in the project and support the senior advisor? Do they have enough time to devote to the assignment? What are their motivations? What factors will encourage them to become involved in the project?

He then organizes exploratory meetings to make sure the people he has chosen are compatible. Once these steps have been completed, he begins to build a potential process, defining a mandate, obtaining signatures on the service contract and then monitoring its application to make sure it is carried out as agreed. The contract signed with the client firm is a service agreement between Inno-centre, represented by Pierre, and the entrepreneur owner-manager of the client firm. It identifies the needs of the entrepreneur and the firm, and lays down the terms of a 200-hour assignment to be carried out in no more than 6 months.

A strategic aspect of Pierre's work is to use his external facilitation expertise to identify the people who are most likely to work well together. The choice of the senior advisor who will lead the process requires particular care. It involves diagnosing the situation accurately and then selecting a person with the skills to address every aspect of the assignment. Pierre likens it to 'project management matchmaking'. He must then sell the potential results to the client entrepreneur. As he points out:

> The most difficult aspect is to make sure the 200 hours are used evenly over the six-month period, so that we don't end up, after five and a half months, in a situation where we've only used 150 hours. Why? Because everyone is busy. The entrepreneurs are running their firms and we tag onto the internal team. Why the six-month stipulation? Because everything that has to be done must be done within that period. Contexts develop quickly. If we let things slide, it may have an impact on the firm's other projects, as well as on our own projects. I have to assign appropriate resources in the best possible way, according to the needs of each project, and the project has to be completed within a specific number of hours in a given timeframe.

Once the project is underway, Pierre is not usually involved again unless the coordinator asks him for advice. The Managing Director of the region concerned is then in charge of monitoring and supervising the project. When Pierre does become involved, his time is not counted in the 200 hours, because he is an Inno-centre employee, not an advisor. The example below details one of his recent interventions:

> A senior advisor might call me to talk about a specific situation with an entrepreneur. The last time this happened, it was with a highly profitable company that makes silicone sealants for windows. The firm in question is a North American leader in its field. The entrepreneur wanted to review its governance structure and was thinking of setting up a board of directors. I spent three hours with him, sharing my experience, discussing the pros and cons. I gave him some advice that he could subsequently work on with the project coordinator. I really did this to help him and share my experience, because I don't work on specific projects. In this particular case, I recommended setting up an advisory board. I told him it had the same benefits as a board of directors, without all the legal constraints.

Firms Undergoing Growth or Restructuring

What happens before a contract is signed? There is a lot of behind-the-scenes work to be done. All the firms served by Inno-centre have their head offices in the Province of Québec. Many of them export or have operations abroad. Some work in several sectors at once, sometimes in different regions or countries. They are always referred by private investors, partners or financial lending institutions, banks or sometimes by a city or other public agency with a financial stake in the firm. A referral is essential to obtain Inno-centre's services, but it is not the only acceptance criterion.

Pierre makes it a point always to do his due diligence on every referral, so that he can offer a customized response and identify advisors able to meet the firm's needs. It is very rare that a firm asks for a different coordinator or different advisors or cancels the contract before the end of the assignment.

As for the firms that are referred to Inno-centre, most (80%) are SMEs, but some (20%) are start-ups. The SMEs are usually medium-sized firms with a turnover of around $40 million or more. The turnover of smaller client firms ranges from $0 to $2 million. There are some exceptions, larger firms with a turnover of up to $500 million. However, they all have one thing in common: innovation. According to Pierre, some of these firms are 'very promising'. They are leaders in their respective sectors and are generally highly innovative gazelles (fast growing firms).

The Challenges of Project Management

The Future

In addition to signing up clients and developing business, Pierre works on strategy with his boss, Inno-centre CEO Claude Martel:

> Ideally, the advisors end up knowing one another well. They work together on a first assignment, and they come across one another again, during other assignments. Teams form, and they meld and become effective. However, as we grow, new players join us constantly. They have to integrate the group. It's an ongoing task.
>
> Ideally, I'd freeze things in time, I'd take a snapshot, I'd use the same teams and I'd assign them to new projects. It would be perfect if things always stayed the same. But they don't – they change. The organization evolves continually. It's our biggest problem and challenge. Obtaining clients, signing contracts, all that is fine. Meeting with entrepreneurs and convincing them to work with us, that's fine too. But maintaining a high level of performance is extremely demanding. Things have to be restructured constantly.

Living in the Age of Technology

When technology is used properly, it makes life easier for companies. Pierre gives some examples:

> A small business entrepreneur has a smartphone and people throughout the firm have them too. The salespeople on the road all have smartphones, they have GPS systems in their cars, everything is automated, information is everywhere, everyone sends e-mails, and people talk to each other less. Life is fast. I think it's a positive thing.
>
> In factories, we refer to this as 4.0: machines have sensors, so they're referenced to settings, meaning that if something goes wrong, the supervisor receives an alert on his or her phone. So, it's extremely efficient and quick, and everything is automated. Call it artificial intelligence if you want, but it's still part of the automation process. In some countries they've banned tablets in classrooms. I think that's a huge mistake. When tablets are used properly, they're very effective.

A Major Concern for the Future

The labour shortage in northern countries is a growing daily concern for Pierre and his client firms. The situation is becoming critical in some sectors in Canada.

There are many reasons for this, including the fact that families have fewer children, but two reasons in particular are important: first, Canadians no longer want to work in certain sectors, and second, as Pierre points out, 'you can't convert easily a summer season worker into a winter season worker because the skill set isn't the same'. And yet, some service sector entrepreneurs have been extremely imaginative.

His Succession

Naturally, Pierre has spoken to Claude Martel about his own succession. He has given himself at least another 10 years (until 2030) before he hands over the reins. He hopes to take full advantage of this time to step back and reflect on his career.

Epilogue
Pierre Nelis, the Man: Evangelist or Philanthropist

Some Thoughts and Lessons Learned and Shared by Pierre Nelis

> Microsoft is recognized for its best practices. All I've done is to adapt Microsoft's recruitment process to our advisors and employees: job descriptions, multiple interviews with the people who will be working directly or indirectly with the person who is hired, and with the hiring manager. Each person gives their verdict: hire or no hire. The hiring manager decides. He can hire a person even if everyone else says no hire, but he will have to live with the new employee and provide a development plan for the aspects that need to be improved.

When he comes in class, Pierre shares with the students some personal thoughts: questioning who he is, what he does, his strengths and weaknesses, his future potential, what he is really able to do, achieve, undertake and complete successfully. Is he a manager? Or is he an entrepreneur? Or is he a semi-entrepreneur? Or someone who smooths the way for entrepreneurs and others?

Although he was extremely effective at designing and structuring activity processes, he did not regard himself as an entrepreneur who could design and market a new product or a new firm. But when it came to helping someone else, he could always be counted on to roll up his sleeves and get the job done.

> Don't ask me to design a vision but count on me to understand the fuzzy vision of an entrepreneur and help make it happen. I'm totally incapable of creating something out of nothing.

> When it comes to generating an idea for something that doesn't exist, I don't know how to do that, and I don't want to know. I don't even want to try because I know I'd fail. I only go to war when I know I can win!

Pierre is quick to acknowledge that, if his life had unfolded differently, he may have become a tradesperson ... 'What I actually wanted was to fulfil my potential', and he knew he could not do this by going into business for himself. He hates the 'blank sheet' concept and the thought of having to devise a project for himself. However, he needs a cause. He knows he is neither a manager nor an entrepreneur. He knows he needs action and can make things happen when working with someone else, especially if that someone is a demanding entrepreneur.

He has often visited classrooms and talked to MBA students. Sometimes he appears to be an evangelist, preaching his gospel. At other times, he comes across as a very structured military officer. When students ask him how he defines himself (who is Pierre Nelis?), he says he has never been able to do so clearly. 'I don't fit any of the typical terms you use in business schools, such as manager or entrepreneur'. But perhaps the most accurate description is that of an 'imaginative facilitator, someone who can design activities that make a difference for an entrepreneur, someone who is a designer of processes to help innovative products become successful on the market'.

Working with SMEs, Pierre has found that they are not usually enthusiastic about consultancy because they are worried about involving outsiders in their businesses. However, by setting up an advisory board, they can access advice and expertise. As he points out:

> When investors buy equity, they require a board of directors. They don't have a choice. But I think entrepreneurs have the same level of resistance to anything that resembles a board or a committee, whether it's a board of directors or an advisory board. I offer them a gateway that's less onerous: an advisory board.

Having been an internal facilitator in his previous jobs, and an external facilitator and facilitation matchmaker at Inno-centre, he has developed some interesting views on the differences between these roles:

> Internal and external facilitators are both catalysts, but internal facilitators are more involved as stakeholders because they benefit directly from the added value they help to generate. If what they do helps the firm to grow and to become more profitable, they benefit. Also, as facilitators, they are usually in key positions with management, as influencers. Of necessity, an internal facilitator is part of the inner circle. The role of an external facilitator is very different because he or she isn't part of the internal movement generated by the entrepreneur.

Transparency, Rigour and Generosity

When he was younger, Pierre did not always put all his cards on the table, perhaps because he was not really aware of his strengths and weaknesses. More recently, however, he has begun 'being straight with people', so that the rules of the game are clear.

Pierre has always preferred teamwork over working alone, and has always made sure his team-mates understand the importance of setting goals, drawing up action plans and being prepared to step away from the beaten path.

Despite this mindset, it is not always easy for him to work with entrepreneurs – for example, it is often difficult to make entrepreneurs understand a different point of view at odds with their preconceived ideas. Pierre overcomes this by managing his working relationships and helping entrepreneurs to realize that a different point of view is not necessarily a contradiction but can be an attempt to see the problem from another perspective. It involves learning that could benefit the company's interests.

Rigour is as important as transparency in any company. A certain amount of tact is needed to maintain a balance between an adventurous entrepreneur who does not like to be pressured and the other members of the team who may sometimes feel pressured by the entrepreneur's methods. Pierre has learned a great deal about human nature, organizational development, environmental complexity, tensions within organizations and competition within societies.

He would like to be able to apply all this learning in environments that are more stable than those he has known so far. 'Is there some way of living a normal life, one in which there's a balance between work and family, and yet still have a job that's stimulating and exciting? The answer is "yes" if you're an entrepreneur because you have the control over what is to be done and what you are going to do to make things happen. But what if you're not an entrepreneur, if you're not a person who can decide what is to be done and who will do it? There must be something!'

Generous by nature since he was a child, Pierre has identified a certain number of activities that interest and stimulate him. He is involved in some of them:

> Everyone works as part of a team and lives in a society. Once you've understood that and feel comfortable with it, it's easy to be generous. You have to be disciplined, of course. I've always given whenever I've had the time. I've been involved in all kinds of things – beauty products, fashion design, travel agencies. It's fascinating, you really learn a lot.

Projective Thinking, Learning and the Importance of Clear Psychological Contracts

To realize a vision, entrepreneurs need to surround themselves with key people. Daniel Langlois, for example, had his wife, who was his Vice-President of Visual

Research, as well as Dave McCray, who was his sales representative in the United States, Claude Cajolet, his R&D Vice-President, and Pierre, his right-hand man.

Entrepreneurs need the additional skills of people around them. They must forge relationships based on trust and communication, because an entrepreneur 'who works in a vacuum is bound to fail'. They also need to draw up 'psychological contracts' so that everyone concerned knows what to expect of the others. Having collaborators who will become efficient facilitators can make a big difference for an entrepreneur. In most cases it will make a difference between growth and no growth, and between profit and stagnation.

Based on his experience, Pierre has come to understand that entrepreneurs do not work easily in structures that are organized mechanically. They need an organic human resources system that is highly flexible and adaptable. Their key people therefore need to be open-minded, amenable and also versatile, in terms of both their skills and their personality.

Whoever the entrepreneur may be, the working relationship must be built on generalist foundations, because otherwise 'nobody is comfortable, even if the generalist is highly competent and versatile. How, then, does this attitude translate into everyday terms? The answer may be primarily through an open mindset and open-minded behaviour, and through an amenable personality that is able to respond to the entrepreneur's bursts of spontaneity'.

In an entrepreneurial situation, managers' lives are often difficult. They must be able to adjust to the pace and speed of their leader. Being familiar with the management field, managers may sometimes find it hard to adjust to entrepreneurial contingencies. Entrepreneurs, for their part, are never totally satisfied with their own specialty field, but are often drawn to other subjects, sectors or novelties. In contrast, they tend to regard their specialty field as their own personal domain – sometimes you enter it at your own risk and peril! Pierre talks about how he was able to gain access to Softimage's R&D committee meetings:

> It's a real dilemma. You need to learn all about the entrepreneur's personal domain, but the entrepreneur doesn't always want you to! At Softimage, Daniel didn't understand why I wanted to know all about the firm's intrinsic core. It knocked him off balance. All I wanted was to understand the secret recipe – how they used computer code to create realistic hair on a movie screen. At the same time, the entrepreneur mustn't feel as if you're stepping on his toes. You really have to explain the whys and wherefores to him. But how can you do your work properly if you don't understand the roots of the business?

After weeks of sitting in on R&D committee meetings, Pierre was able to understand the 'ins and outs' of Softimage. He questioned his R&D colleagues and asked them about their ideas, because he felt this was the only way of achieving excellence and identifying the elements required to develop and market products.

Regardless of their qualifications and education, an entrepreneur's key people must be able to adjust to different situations – 'they need to be open minded, willing to step away from the beaten path, and leave established paradigms aside'. At Microsoft, he observed the creativity of the facilitators working with and around Bill Gates. This is the basic definition of a 'facilitator' – someone whose role lies between true management and true entrepreneurship.

How, though, can facilitators learn to adjust to different entrepreneurial styles? Pierre does not really have an answer to this question. Things like this are not taught in management schools. He suggests that students should 'go and work with founding owner-managers, in cooperative-type arrangements'. He also suggests keeping abreast of world trends, because 'these days you can't make do with the local news, you have to visit websites and follow news from around the world'.

His main advice to entrepreneurs is never to burn their bridges, because 'life goes on. People move on to other things and turn to other people'. A rational person, he does not believe in astrology, although he does recognize the importance of luck in his own life and the lives of all the entrepreneurs he has met in the course of his career:

> It's as if all the pieces fall into place at some point. Rather like a game of chess: you make two moves, and the third becomes inevitable. You have to organize things so that your basic blueprint is conducive to what you want, but then you almost have to cross your fingers and hope! Is luck a random thing, or can you influence it?

Pierre does not have an answer but, on the other hand, he has this to say: 'I like to choose what I do and the people with whom I do it'. With family roots across three continents and a varied career path, Pierre has travelled many different roads, 'working with some great entrepreneurs and getting to know many others along the way'. For the last stage of his career, he has chosen to work with entrepreneurs 'because they keep feeding my learning needs'. And he can use what he learns to improve the innovative and entrepreneurial processes that support company development.

Pierre Nelis, the Man and His Values: An Evangelist of Facilitation

Pierre's time at Softimage was an intense period that allowed him, without realizing it, to develop his own facilitation skills and pattern of activities moulded around an entrepreneur's vision, culture and products. Later at Inno-centre, he behaved in the same pattern and became again an internal facilitator for the CEO in the same way he had done it at Softimage. However, to understand why he had this need to 'evangelize' this pattern on a larger scale in the practice of external facilitation, we need to go back several years. He has often been asked if his father's work as a pastor has influenced him in this respect.[15] As Pierre points out:

> I often tell people: 'When you believe in something, when you have a mission, you have to evangelize it'. I use the term 'evangelize'. And it works well in business. People understand what it means. There may be an unconscious or conscious connection with my father, I don't know, but in business, people understand the term. So if you have a mission and a strategy and you believe in it, you have to evangelize it to everyone, at every level of the firm. You have to have conviction, to communicate it and reinforce it. You need to keep your inner fire lit and never stop sharing it. That's what I mean by 'evangelize'.

Building High-Growth SMEs: Learning to Live With Strong Cycles

His high-flying Softimage/Microsoft years, when Pierre almost divorced three or four times and nearly destroyed his health (for example, he put on more than 50 lbs. in a single year – 1993), marked his life. Too much stress, too much travel, always waiting for a flight somewhere in the world: eventually, he felt the need to slow down. At the end of his 3-year contract with Microsoft, although he had enjoyed his work, he felt somewhat relieved to be free again. However, he is quick to acknowledge that those years shaped the man he is today:

> Everything I've done in the past has made me able to do what I do now, and led me to a point where I have a balanced lifestyle and don't need to travel the world. I've found a level of stability that allows me to do incredibly interesting things and still spend quality time with my family. I couldn't have done this if I hadn't worked for some of the best companies in the world and earned a financial cushion that leaves me free to do what I want.
>
> Since I joined Inno-centre, the fact of working with so many entrepreneurs in so many different sectors has certainly allowed me to grow. My work is varied, to say the least.

His health has improved considerably through cardiovascular exercise, jogging and cycling – lots of cycling, throughout the world. He is especially fond of

---

[15]The term 'evangelize' was part of the culture of his father who was a missionary and a pastor.

Europe. Summer and winter alike (on his exercise bike in winter, when Montreal's weather prevents him from cycling outdoors) he pedals at least 5,000 km per year. As he points out:

> When I pedal my bike, after half an hour or so my heart is beating hard, I can feel the blood flowing through my body, and I feel wonderful, almost euphoric. Obviously, my wife and I still cycle outdoors when it's cold, and we often take cycling holidays.

As for his family life, Pierre and his wife had a second daughter, to their joy, and not only has he been able to spend more time with his family, but he also became more involved in his children's lives, eating breakfast with them before they went to school and helping them with their homework in the evening – not to mention the months of vacation time and the dozen or so statutory holidays throughout the year.

Sharing and Volunteering

Pierre has always remained involved in the entrepreneurial community as a mentor, coach, facilitator or investor. He has slowed down a lot, but still sits on five boards of directors. One of these boards – the foundation of a large hospital with more than 700 beds, whose investment committee manages $50 million per year – takes up one full day per week. Pierre describes it as 'big business'. His tasks include recruiting new, younger people to build a succession. He has this to say about his volunteer activities:

> It's easy to say it's because I have the means to do it. But even at the beginning of my career, when I was just a lowly employee, I still did charity work, although to a lesser extent. When I was in my 20s, for example, I was on the Centraide committee. I organized spaghetti dinners to raise funds – it was all I could do at the time.[16] However, the gratification was the same, even when I was a 9 to 5 employee like everyone else.

How does Pierre explain this need to be involved with different causes? Did the inspiration come from his father, pastor Marc-Michel Nelis? Does Pierre regard his career as an internal and external facilitator, as a kind of continuation of the family culture in which he grew up? His answer is interesting:

> I'm one of five children, but I'm the one who's most involved in charitable causes. The others aren't involved. Yet, they were brought up in the same context as me. I don't think I had as

[16]A charitable organization that raises funds to finance community organizations in the Montreal region: http://www.centraide-mtl.org/en/giving/

close a relationship with my father as the others, because I'm the youngest.[17] My father was exhausted when I was born. And I was also the most active. My mother was exhausted too. They'd given all they had to give. They'd raised four children before me. I was the baby of the family. Obviously, I had an intense personality, and I was very committed to my projects. I remember my father used to donate what he could to two or three organizations. I noticed that. Maybe it inspired me to do the same. But I do more than that. I get involved, I also give my time. I gave it then, and I give it now.

Case Discussion

Pierre Nelis

(1) Pierre Nelis's parents were immigrants. What are the advantages and the disadvantages of being immigrant, as far as innovation is concerned?

(2) What impact do you think previous army training has for someone who goes on to become an innovationist or an agent of innovation?

(3) Identify some of the lessons Pierre Nelis learned from the jobs he held before joining Softimage, and rate each lesson with a score of 1–10 for its relevance in preparing him to become an innovationist and subsequently an agent of innovation. Give reasons for your answer.

(4) (A) How do you assess his determination and the way he approached Softimage's owner? What arguments could he use to sell himself and his capacity to perform?

(B) How would you negotiate a job with someone who may become your boss? List some of the key arguments in your sales pitch.

(5) (A) Is it a good idea to join a firm where you will be the only person with a specific skill, and where the other employees are all specialised in the sector concerned? Why?

(B) How do you transition from employee to facilitator? How does this happen? Is it because of particular circumstances? Is it as a result of a request from the entrepreneur? Or is it because of the instincts you developed as an innovationist, or your leadership culture, or your commitment to obtaining results? Can you think of other possibilities? Explain and justify your answers.

(6) (A) Pierre Nelis had little exposure to sales before he went to work at Softimage. He did not know anything about the sector, which was still at the emergent stage. How is it possible to do something you have not done before, in a sector where people are still trying to understand potential markets and customers?

[17]There are about 6 years between the oldest and the youngest Nelis children.

(B) Perhaps Pierre Nelis was desperate for action in his bureaucratic job as a well-paid executive working for a big corporation. Was he simply lucky to find his new job? Or did he search methodically for a challenge?

(7) Would you have stayed with a large multinational corporation such as Microsoft, and would you have worked abroad even if your spouse did not want to move? Explain how you might have dealt with this type of situation.

(8) (A) What do you think are the advantages and disadvantages of the innovative external facilitation network approach applied by Pierre Nelis at Inno-Centre?

(B) In your opinion, what are the main difficulties that must be overcome in order to operate a network of special advisors to small business CEOs?

(9) In person, Pierre Nelis is very humble. His main motivators in life seem to be his need to learn and help others (his father was an evangelical pastor and his mother was a nurse). How important are these criteria when selecting a professional activity?

(10) Identify five lessons from the story of Pierre Nelis that may help you to improve your innovative capabilities.

Acknowledgements

Pierre Nelis was a frequent speaker in the entrepreneurship courses given by one of the authors at HEC Montréal in the early 2000s. A lot of the information used in this case was gathered from his stimulating discussions with students.

An initial case study was produced following a long interview conducted by the authors on 12 May 2004: Piffault, J. and L. J. Filion (2007) Pierre Nelis: Facilitator. *WACRA, Twenty-fourth International Conference*, Instituto Technológico de Monterrey, Campus de Guadalajara, Zapopán, Jalisco, México, July. Published in the Conference proceedings. Also published in: *International Journal of Case Method Research & Application (IJCRA)*: Issue 4, 2007, Electronic Journal: WACRA website (www.wacra.org). NB The co-authors of both cases are Joëlle Piffault-Hafsi and Louis Jacques Filion.

This case includes parts of this early version. However, other sections are based mostly on a three-hour interview conducted with the authors on 3 December 2018. This case study was completed in 2020 and includes most of the material from the previous case study written in 2007.

Section 3
Life Stories of Intrapreneurs

Intrapreneurs are employees who are extremely committed to what they do and are willing to circumvent the rules in order to implement improvements that will better serve the organization's clients.

Intrapreneurship is an ideal way to learn about innovative practice, especially as the risk is lower than for entrepreneurship. However, it is not risk-free. Many intrapreneurs define themselves as 'employees who go to work knowing they could be fired at any time'.

Intrapreneurs can benefit from the resources, support and advice of experienced people who work in the same organization.

I have studied many intrapreneurs over the years and have identified five main characteristics.

First, intrapreneurs are usually highly competent in their respective trades or professions to such an extent that they are prepared to break through the barriers of what is normally done and open up new paths.

Second, they are usually more familiar than other employees with the resources of the organization for which they work. They know about the production facilities and may have identified equipment or materials that could be put to better use. They have spoken to people outside their own department and have identified others both inside and outside the organization who have expertise that could potentially be useful to the enterprise. Their internal and external relations networks are usually more highly developed than those of other employees in similar positions.

Third, they have spoken in depth with the people who have been with the organization the longest, to see what is or is not possible. A typical comment would be: 'I need to know how far I can stretch things. I do this by consulting people with many years of experience in the firm'.

Fourth, the intrapreneur's work is often made possible by the support of someone in a senior position, be it a manager or a vice president, or sometimes the CEO. The two intrapreneurs whose life stories are presented in this book owe their survival to the leaders of their respective firms, whose support became a key element in carrying the success of their projects.

Fifth, intrapreneurs are people who perform innovative tasks within organizations but have no control over the resources. Some go on to become entrepreneurs – in other words, they become self-employed extrapreneurs and continue to do what they used to do as intrapreneurs, this time for themselves.

Innovative practice is similar in many respects regardless of which agent of innovation applies it. For example, many entrepreneurs started out as intrapreneurs or facilitators, while others, after selling their firms or retiring, become external facilitators or even intrapreneurs. Both the intrapreneurs presented in the following pages have played all these roles.

Many intrapreneurs carry out incremental innovations. However, some go further and engage in radical innovation. This is the case for the two intrapreneurs whose stories are presented here. Each in their own way became the instigators of veritable revolutions in their respective sectors.

Elmar Mock

Elmar Mock often visited my classes in Canada and in Switzerland, where he was kind enough to host students in his company on several occasions. Each time, he was able to convey his enthusiasm for innovation. When you meet him, you quickly realize that nothing will ever be the same after he has worked on it.

He started out as an inventor and intrapreneur, and ultimately became an entrepreneur, launching an external facilitation business to support the creation and application of radical innovations. He has given countless inspiring speeches at international forums and serves as a real-life example of everything that is best about creative thinking.

Emerson de Almeida

Emerson de Almeida is an idealist who has always wanted to change the world. As a young journalist, he worked hard to raise social awareness, a path that almost cost him his life when the military junta running his country placed strict controls on the media.

He found a way to support the development of his country by setting up a business education organization that helped thousands of Brazilian enterprise leaders to manage more innovatively so that their firms would perform better in Brazil and on international markets. The management institution he founded is now classified among the best in its field.

Chapter 5

Elmar Mock, From the Swatch to Creaholic: Inventor, Intrapreneur and Entrepreneur

Louis Jacques Filion and Rico J. Baldegger

Abstract

Elmar Mock's extraordinary story began in a small village in Switzerland. Born in 1954, he was the son of an Austrian immigrant and a Swiss mother. School was difficult, as he struggled with dyslexia. Nevertheless, he graduated from engineering school, obtained a job with a Swiss manufacturer, ETA. By the age of 26, he had co-invented the Swatch. Following the accidental death of his brother, Stéphane, in 1985, he decided to leave his job and launch his own creativity and innovation consulting company, Creaholic, in 1986.

In 2014, Elmar retired from Creaholic and created with his second wife Hélène Mock née Kett, a second company: 'Mock-Kett'. He has created more than 80 families of patents in various industries and has been involved in more than 600 projects. He is also a member of the advisory boards of some of the spin-offs incubated by Creaholic. He remains active as a speaker and international consultant with 'Mock-Kett', which promotes the motivational side of invention. He has received numerous awards and his book 'The Innovation Factory' has been published in three languages.

The case depicts a one-of-a-kind creative mindset and offers in-depth reflections on the concepts of creativity, innovation and intrapreneurship and their applications in organizations.[1]

Keywords: Intrapreneur; intrapreneurship; inventor; entrepreneur; external facilitator; consultant

[1]Intrapreneurship is defined as the capacity for employees to create, design and implement innovations; in other words, to act as entrepreneurs within the organization where they work.

Agents of Innovation, 143–167

Published under exclusive licence by Emerald Publishing Limited
doi:10.1108/978-1-83797-012-420231005

Case
Elmar Mock, From the Swatch to Creaholic: Inventor, Intrapreneur and Entrepreneur[2]

Elmar Mock's extraordinary story began in a small village in Switzerland. Born in 1954, he was the son of an Austrian immigrant and a Swiss mother. The family moved several times during his childhood, and he found it hard at first to make friends. School was difficult too, as he struggled with dyslexia. Nevertheless, he graduated from engineering school, obtained a job with Swiss movement manufacturer ETA, and had co-invented the Swatch by the age of 26. Following the accidental death of his brother, Stéphane, in 1985, he decided to leave his job and launch his own creativity and innovation consulting company, Creaholic, in 1986.

After founding a second company, 'Mock-Kett', with his wife Hélène Mock née Kett in 2014, Elmar Mock retired from Creaholic but was invited to stay on as Honorary President of the board. He has created more than 80 families of patents in various industries and has been involved in more than 600 projects. He is also a member of the advisory boards of some of the spin-offs incubated by Creaholic. He remains active as a speaker and international consultant with 'Mock-Kett', which promotes the motivational side of invention. He has received numerous awards and his book 'The Innovation Factory' has been published in three languages.

The case depicts a one-of-a-kind creative mindset and offers in-depth reflections on the concepts of creativity, innovation and intrapreneurship and their applications in organizations.[3]

An Unusual Family Background and Childhood

The name 'Mock' is a Swiss-German word which, literally translated, means 'piece or block'. It is used to denote a small, compact, muscular person in good physical condition. Elmar's family can be traced back to the 11th century, to the Herisau/Appenzell region of Switzerland. His ancestors were farmers. Two were burned at the stake for witchcraft, and his paternal grandfather worked as a station inspector in Austria's federal state of Vorarlberg.

Elmar's father, Herbert Mock, was of Austrian nationality. Herbert's life was marked by a tragic accident with a gun that occurred when he was just 17 years old. During the Second World War he was charged with the task of killing birds to stop them from eating crops in the fields. However, he accidentally shot himself and was so seriously injured that he had to be taken to hospital in Vienna.

His life changed once again when his girlfriend became pregnant. He quickly realized he did not love her and had no wish to marry her. With the support of his

---

[2]Case written by Louis Jacques Filion and Rico J. Baldegger.

[3]Intrapreneurship is defined as the capacity for employees to create, design and implement innovations; in other words, to act as entrepreneurs within the organization where they work.

own father, who offered to take care of the child, he left his village in Austria and moved to Brig, in Switzerland, to start a new life. Physically weakened by the gunshot injury, Herbert decided to train as a watchmaker.

Herbert eventually married a French-speaking Swiss girl, Marianne Delaloye. They had three children, one girl (the oldest) and two boys, the elder being Elmar, born in 1954. Life was not easy for the young family. Not being of Swiss nationality, Herbert was not allowed to work as a watchmaker in Switzerland and was forced to accept an unskilled position in the watch-making industry. He eventually obtained Swiss nationality in 1958 and obtained recognition as a watchmaker.

At Herbert's insistence, the family, although bilingual (French and German), spoke only French at home, with the result that Elmar was unable to communicate with his German-speaking grandparents and half-brother in Austria. In addition, Herbert had to send monthly child support payments to Austria, placing an additional burden on the family's limited means.

An Atypical Child and a Stranger in His Own Milieu

Elmar describes himself as a 'rather difficult child' with a tendency to destroy things. He remembers being forced to wear leather pants, which was unusual in French-speaking Switzerland and set him apart from the other children. In the difficult aftermath of the Second World War, he also found it hard to deal with the fact that his father shared the same nationality as Hitler. In addition, he lived as a Catholic in a Protestant community, and was fairly short in stature, the kind of child others made fun of. He says he learned to deal with the challenges of this relative isolation by developing a sense of humour.

Religion played a dominant role in the family's everyday life. Together with a sub-community of foreign workers, mostly from Italy, Spain and Portugal, they attended the local Catholic church, and Elmar was confirmed when he was just 8 years old. After his confirmation, feeling 'energised by the Holy Spirit', he beat up one of the much larger boys who had bullied him in the past, and although his parents were shocked at the incident, he himself felt empowered and self-confident as a result.

Winters in the Swiss Jura were harsh and cold. Unable to make friends, Elmar remembers spending a lot of time alone, outside, staring into space, dreaming, feeling the cold air on his skin. Time passed slowly, and he began to devise ways to amuse himself. One Sunday, he stole 50 cents from the church collection plate and then claimed to have found it in the grass. He did the same thing for several consecutive weeks, until his father challenged his story. After that, he did not dare to steal from the church again.

Elmar's mother had never been happy in the village of La-Chaux-de-Fonds, where the family lived, and when Elmar was 8 years old they moved to Lausanne, where Elmar became friends with their landlord's son. Two years later, Herbert lost his job. Elmar, of course, told his best friend, who in turn told his own father, the landlord. Worried about the family's ability to pay the rent, the landlord approached Herbert, who was embarrassed and humiliated. Ten-year-old Elmar earned a beating for his 'loose tongue'. The family moved once again, this time to Biel/Bienne, where Elmar lived for 30 years. Although the frequent moves were not easy, they provided the young Elmar with enough material to entertain his classmates with stories, and eventually to make new friends.

In Biel/Bienne, Elmar devised a plan to make some pocket money. The local milkman would deliver milk to people's doorsteps and collect the money they had left out for him, leaving change where necessary. Elmar began to follow him on his round, stealing one or two cents from each house, hoping people would not notice. His plan seemed to work at first.

At the same time, however, he got into trouble at school for forging his parents' signatures on failed tests. The teacher contacted his parents directly, and Elmar was sent home to face the music. As he pulled out his handkerchief to dry his tears, all his stolen money tumbled to the floor. His father administered a punishment he would remember for the rest of his life, forcing Elmar to knock on the door of every house from which he had stolen, to confess what he had done and apologise. Although most people took the attitude that 'boys will be boys', Elmar never forgot the embarrassment and never stole again.

A Troublemaker at Home and at School

Elmar describes himself as a 'terrible' student who was always in trouble. He was forced to repeat Grade 3 when the family moved to Biel/Bienne and he entered a different school system. Later, he had to repeat Grade 6 because of a skiing accident that kept him in bed for 6 months. He was also dyslexic, and he struggled with subjects such as German and French, although he was able to perform fairly well in maths and physics.

While the skiing accident had a negative impact on his academic performance, he regards it as a positive turning point in his life, since it gave him time to read and think. Confined to bed, he quickly realized that his 'friends', the ones with whom he always got into trouble, had not bothered to visit him. With plenty of time to reflect, he decided to make new friends when he eventually left the hospital. His performance at school improved, but he continued to misbehave and spent many free afternoons working with the school janitor as punishment.

The situation was not helped by the fact that Elmar's older sister was an outstanding student and an excellent competitive swimmer. She won the Swiss National Championship several times and ranked among the five best swimmers in Europe, receiving lots of attention from the media. Compared to her, Elmar felt unaccomplished and was regarded as the family's troublemaker, a 'black sheep' with no prospects.

All this changed when his sister was short-listed for Switzerland's 1968 Olympic swimming team. Her trainer wanted to take her to California, where she could study and train at the same time, free of charge, but her parents refused to let her go. Upset at their decision, she over-trained and eventually sustained an injury that cost her the chance to qualify for the Olympics. Devastated, she rebelled and left home.

For Elmar, the change was a radical one. Suddenly he became the good boy; it was his chance finally to be 'number one' in his family. He turned to religion, always an important part of family life, and became so enthusiastic that he considered becoming a monk and living in a monastery.

University, Marriage and the Work Market: Taking His Place in Society

When he eventually left high school, however, Elmar applied instead to Biel/Bienne's College of Technology and was accepted into an engineering programme. He loved engineering, and his academic success gradually helped restore his self-confidence. It was a time when he began to forge a stronger sense of self, along with the desire to commit to something in life. Although he still dreamt of becoming a monk and devoting himself to God, and although he was fascinated by the Benedictine way of life, he soon realized his interest in girls in general, and one girl in particular, would make life in a monastery impossible.

His girlfriend was studying to become a teacher. The two developed a very close relationship, and when she finished her studies, she proposed to Elmar. The pair married when he was 21 and she was just 20, starting her new career as a teacher. They went on to have three children, two boys and a girl. Elmar notes that it was not marriage itself but the fact of having children which had the greatest impact on his life, since it changed his perception of responsibility. Before, he had never worn a helmet when riding his motorcycle, but he began to do so when his first son was born.

A Standard Job in the Swiss Watch-Making Industry

In 1975, when Elmar got married, the Swiss watch-making industry was in crisis. The following year, Elmar was the only one of the 16 students in his engineering class to find a job. He had produced an outstanding diploma thesis in technology that earned him the best grade of the group.[4] ETA, the area's largest micro-technology employer, decided to support the university's engineering programme by offering employment for at least one of its graduates. Because of the exceptional quality of his thesis, Elmar was the one who was chosen. At 22 years old, he had a Bachelor's degree in micro-technology engineering from a recognized institution, and a job in a big corporation.

ETA was the country's leading producer of watch movements. However, the industry was shifting from mechanical movements to quartz and electronic movements, which required plastic components. ETA had no experience with plastic moulding, and entrusted Elmar with the task of producing the new parts.

[4]Title: Influence of injection settings on component quality (*Influence des paramètres d'injection sur la qualité des pièces produites*).

With the help of a colleague, and by reading books, he began work on a plastic injection procedure, but had the impression that he understood 'nothing at all' about what he was trying to do.

In addition, his job, an office-based position, was not what he had wanted or expected. He struggled hard to function and to fit into a big structure. It was something he felt did not suit his more inventive and creative nature.

He decided to leave the company and go back to school to study plastic polymers. The firm's CEO, hearing this, offered to pay for his studies if he would commit to ETA for 2 years afterwards. Elmar accepted and embarked on a 1-year postgraduate programme with his full salary.

Three Swiss institutions offered programs of interest to him. He chose the one in Brugg Windisch, in the German-speaking part of Switzerland, because it would allow him to live at home and commute to school by train each day. The language was potentially a problem for Elmar, who spoke only French, but he found it fairly easy to learn the field's specialized terminology and was functional in Swiss German after only 3 months. During his summer vacation, he continued to go into school every day to write his thesis and he received his diploma as planned within the year.[5]

Industrial Watches and Polymer Engineering at ETA: A Technological Creator Moves away From the Norm

The Swiss watch industry had changed considerably since the mid-1920s. Modern civilization demanded efficient structures, meetings, schedules, and fixed working hours. Time had become a key issue for organizations throughout the world. This had major impacts for the industrialised United States of America. The demand for watches triggered the development of the American watch-making industry, and the Swiss, who already dominated the upper market segments, reacted by forming cartels to produce cheap watches. The cartels were well-organised, splitting the work among the country's major watch-making companies. Thanks to this strategy, Switzerland had gained 85% of the world watch market by the end of the 1960s.

The 1970s proved to be difficult, however, and the watch industry struggled due to a combination of economic crisis, stagnating sales of cheap watches and the emergence of new competitors such as Seiko from Japan. Despite Switzerland's achievements – including the invention of the digital watch, liquid crystal and the quartz principle – Switzerland's global market share plummeted to less than 20% in the space of 10 years. Part of this was due to its refusal to use anything other than mechanical movements in its high-end products. The culture of the Swiss watch industry was fairly rigid: 'real' watches were the ones that had mechanical movements; digital and quartz were suitable only for cheaper and second-rate products intended for markets in Africa and some parts of Asia.

---

[5]Master's degree in plastic-technology engineering (Brugg-Windisch, CH).

The Swatch

In 1970, Switzerland totally dominated global watch production with 85% of the market. However, by 1978, when Elmar Mock completed his Master's programme, the country's market share had plummeted to 22%. Companies like ETA were laying off hundreds of watchmakers every month. A few months before the end of Elmar Mock's postgraduate studies, ETA's CEO had been replaced by a newcomer to the watch industry. This was a very rare event in the sector but an indication that the sector needed major transformations.

The new CEO, Ernst Thomke, began his career as a mechanic in the watch industry, but went back to school to study science and medicine. He also trained in management and marketing at INSEAD, in France, and became a successful marketing specialist in the pharmaceutical industry. This young, aggressive, 38-year-old CEO was hired in 1978 to save ETA, at a time when the Swiss watch industry was going through an extremely difficult phase. He had been looking for innovations, and in particular for a way to produce cheap watches and enter the low-cost watch segment. This was a significant challenge that required a major shift in the culture of the sector in Switzerland.

When Elmar Mock graduated in polymer engineering, he received several job offers and approached ETA's CEO to ask if the company really needed him as an employee. If not, he had offers from companies willing to reimburse the expenses and salary he had received during his studies. ETA's response was unequivocal: they wanted to keep him. So Elmar used the opportunity to renegotiate his salary, which was considerably less than his wife's, who was a teacher. He was also glad to be able to keep his promise to the company.

A Conservative Industry Is Shaken Up: The Birth of the Swatch

Upon his return to ETA, Elmar Mock enjoyed considerable freedom within the company, testing and experimenting in plastic engineering. In 1979, along with a colleague, Jacques Müller, he was sent to Germany to study a new plastic technology. During their trip, the two men got on well, and over their evening beers they had fun making plans to 'revolutionize' the conservative watch-making industry.

In 1980, two years after completing his postgraduate studies, and without realising it at the time, Elmar began working with Jacques Müller on what would eventually become the Swatch (1980–1984).[6] One day, he decided he needed more sophisticated equipment to go further in his experiments, and he submitted an order for a brand-new plastic injection moulding machine at a cost of 500,000 Swiss Francs. Clearly, even in a company employing more than 2,000 people, an order of this magnitude needed several signatures, and it eventually found its way to CEO Thomke's desk.

[6] Nicolas Hayek was 'officially' considered to be the father of the Swatch. However, by the time he was appointed to head the firm's parent holding company, the Swatch had already been in existence for more than 2 years.

The result was an uproar. Not only was the watch-making industry undergoing extensive restructuring and downsizing to increase profitability, but ETA itself was in a critical situation. In recent years, it had laid off more than 4,000 employees. 27 March 1980, is a date Elmar Mock will remember forever. At 11:00 a.m. he was summoned by Mr Thomke's secretary to a meeting with the CEO himself at 1:00 p.m. to justify his request. He immediately rushed to the office of his friend Jacques Müller, and within two hours the two of them had produced a sketch of what might become a plastic watch. There had been no market surveys, no cost estimates, no study of any kind, and no plans.

Breaking all the Rules and Expecting to Be Fired

When Elmar arrived at the CEO's office, Mr Thomke was furious. He was known as a hard-liner and the two delinquents were to suffer his toughness. He berated Elmar for his thoughtlessness, lack of maturity and lack of realism for ordering a 'new toy' at a cost of half a million Swiss Francs, at a time when the company was on its knees and laying off staff by the hundreds. Then, after half an hour of harsh criticism, Ernst Thomke asked: 'What exactly do you think you're going to do with this machine?' Elmar was unable to answer most of the questions asked by the CEO. However, he showed him the elementary sketch that he and Jacques Müller had just produced and said timidly in a low voice: 'Sir, we want to make a cheap plastic watch like this'.

Elmar explained that their idea was to use a new injection moulding technique to produce an inexpensive plastic watch. Intrigued, Thomke sat back, looked at the drawing carefully and asked if he could keep it. He looked at it again and again, from different angles, as though he could not believe what he was seeing. It was as if someone had given him a drawing by someone from another planet. Then, reining in his temper, looking somewhat shell-shocked, he said: 'I've been searching for a new project like this for two years. This is exactly the kind of thing I've been saying I wanted. I don't understand why none of the company's experienced watchmakers has ever been able to produce something like this'.

From that remark, Elmar and Jacques Müller deduced that some of the firm's watchmakers were in fact working on new product development. Still, they left the CEO's office absolutely convinced there would be an internal hurricane and they would be fired the next day. Many people had been fired for less.

Later that day, Elmar was summoned by the head of R & D, who was also angry because he had never heard about the project before and had not been consulted. Elmar's sketch was rudimentary, even childish according to the firm's R & D division, and certainly not at the level of what would be expected from an experienced watchmaker. In addition, it had not been approved by any of Elmar's superiors, who were completely in the dark about the project. Moreover, the design had not been produced according to internal procedures, and even worse, it had not been assigned a number, an unforgivable sin in what was a strictly bureaucratic corporation. As a result, nobody dared to approve it.

The R & D manager's fury stemmed mainly from the fact that, because the project had been developed outside the system and was contrary to the rules, he would receive no credit for it. Worse, he could be blamed, and perhaps even fired, for having allowed someone in his division to work on something that did not comply with the rules and was not based on the traditional watchmaking expertise that had made earned the company its excellent reputation.

He therefore viewed the drawing as a catastrophe for him, something that might destroy his reputation and perhaps jeopardise his career. Even if the rules had been followed, the project would never have been approved and therefore would never have made its way to the CEO's desk. The R & D manager asked the same question as the CEO: 'How is it that I've been asking for something like this for the last year, and nobody responded?' Again, after the meeting with the R & D manager, Elmar was sure he would be fired, but he soon discovered that his superiors were angry not only at him and his colleague, but also at the organization's inaction.

Developing a Revolutionary Product in a Hostile Environment

Elmar's colleague, Jacques Müller, was a mechanical watchmaker, and Elmar was a novice in plastic engineering. The two had discussed their ideas and had discovered that they complemented one another in terms of their skills, knowledge and creative ideas. In addition, both were low-level employees, at the very bottom of the hierarchy, and had nothing to lose within the company. In spite of a stream of negative reactions from most of the senior hierarchy except for the R&D manager, ETA's CEO decided to support the idea and move forward with the project.

The pair were hugely relieved: they would not be fired after all, and the machine they had ordered would be bought so they could play with their 'toy' and work on their experiments. Most of the experienced watchmakers who were consulted felt it was impossible to produce a 'plastic' watch that would work. They thought the company was wasting precious resources. However, the CEO was supportive and decided to help the dissidents swim against the current.

Within a few weeks, the wind had changed. Elmar and his partner were no longer pariahs within the company, or the 'class jokers'. They had become project creators, respected by senior management. They were released from all their other responsibilities and given the freedom to focus exclusively on their project, with the expectation that they would produce drawings and models within 6 months.

In the highly conservative watch-making industry, people were wary of paradigm-breakers who tried to move away from the beaten path. However, ETA was on its knees, and the CEO was desperate for a revolutionary product that would haul the company back from the brink of failure. The initiative proposed by Elmar Mock and Jacques Müller turned out to be one of the most innovative projects the watch industry had ever seen.[7]

Not only that, but it was also one of the most significant revolutions ever to take place in the watch industry and, paradoxically, one of the least costly in watch-making history, carried out by a team of just two people who had the courage of their convictions and dared to work outside the established norms. Mock and Müller continued to receive negative feedback from most of the company's departments; their only real support came from CEO Thomke himself, who was a newcomer with no background in watch industry management and had therefore not been 'indoctrinated' by the industry's traditional, conservative culture. As a newcomer, he also did not have many personal links with the sector's traditional leaders within this enterprise.

The first designs were submitted after 6 months, and the project was extended for some additional months. Near the end of 1980, the pair had produced just one watch, whose hands turned in the wrong direction. It had taken almost a year to obtain an initial 'working' prototype that did not in fact work properly. All this served to cement their reputation as failures within the company. But the CEO was determined to proceed and progress was considered sufficient enough for the initiative to continue.

The name 'Swatch' was assigned to the product in September 1981. On 23 December 1981, the first five functional Swatches were produced and were sent as a Christmas gift to the CEO. But they only worked for a few days and then stopped. Elmar remembers another special date: 'Ernst Thomke called us on December 26, 1981, during the Christmas holidays, and we went to his office. He said: 'If the watches were able to work for a few days, we must be close to making them work all the time'.

'My father, who was an experienced watchmaker, was very useful. He helped to break down all the pieces. He was very attentive to the details and examined each and every component carefully, under the microscope, making sure they connected properly with the others. He told me: 'Listen, the space is too narrow here, and too wide here, and the component isn't polished enough here, there's a problem with this, etc.' While he didn't build the product, he was very helpful in diagnosing its problems. We had to find solutions to all the problems he had identified. It took us several months, but the watch worked well as a result'.

---

[7]It took 30 years for the watch industry to recognize the outstanding work of these two inventors. On 16 September 2010, Elmar Mock and Jacques Müller received one of the watch-making industry's most prestigious awards: *The Gaïa Award*. Ernst Thomke received the same award on 19 September 2013. In 2017, in addition to numerous recognitions, Elmar Mock was the only Swiss representative of the 14 finalists from eight different countries for the *European Patent Office* (EPO) *Life Achievement, Inventor Award*. The following year he was invited to be part of the jury.

The final adjustments were made and a patent was filed on 12 August 1982, for a plastic watch, the first product of its kind, to be known as the Swatch. It may have been born out of controversy, but it went on to become a major turning point in the watch-making industry, a radical innovation that would allow the industry to reinvent itself.

However, the problems were by no means over. In the fall of 1982, 10,000 freshly minted Swatches were sent to Texas to be sold alongside other watches in jewellers' stores. However, the venture was a fiasco. The Swatches did not sell and were returned to Switzerland at the end of the year. Clearly, if a product was different, it would have to be marketed in a different way: in other words, a radical product innovation would require a similarly radical marketing innovation. In the spring of 1983, the watches were placed in general stores instead of specialised jewellers' stores. They became, and are still today, a resounding success.

An Innovation in Product Concept and Design: The Swatch Conquers the Planet

Ernst Thomke believed the only way for the watch industry to diversify was by making new types of watches. If the company was to survive, it had to find a way of making cheaper watches. His aim was to win the cheap watch segment and refocus the company to face growing international competition in that sector. This was completely contrary to the strategy adopted by the rest of the Swiss watch industry, which was interested mainly in producing expensive watches for the high-end segment.

Elmar Mock's challenge was to find a creative solution and design cheap models that would be easy to market. The watch he was working on had fewer parts than the classic models produced by other Swiss manufacturers. The case was made from plastic but was nevertheless robust. The expensive machine he had ordered was used to produce plastic components for the Swatch. Through trial and error, the team was able to reduce the number of components from 91 in a standard watch, to just 51 in the Swatch.[8] Metal was used for the internal movement, but the entire casing was made of plastic. At one point, the decision was made to produce a non-repairable watch, once again moving away from standard practice in the Swiss watch industry.

The original target markets for the new product were Africa, India and South America. It was Mr Franz Sprecher, a visionary marketing consultant who came up with the idea of creating a fashionable watch – a kind of Rolex for ordinary people – that could be sold on the European and North American markets.[9] The project's design phase, when the chic appearance and look of the new Swatch was influenced to a large extent by designers and marketing people, was very difficult

---

[8]150 pieces for a traditional mechanical watch.

[9]During the product development phase, Elmar Mock humorously referred to the new watch as the 'Prolex' (proletarian Rolex).

for Elmar to accept. He felt they were 'killing' his project and turning his product into something else. He was upset that the designers had added complex printing, surfaces and tiles that were four times as expensive as the plastic parts he had designed.

In the end, however, the influence of the designers and marketing team proved to be a key element in launching 'Fashion that Ticks', which went on to become a huge success. The Swatch had a huge impact throughout the globe. It changed the world's perception of the Swiss watch industry, showing that it was capable of being innovative and stepping away from the beaten path. The Swatch entered the European market on 1 March 1983.

The name 'Swatch' was originally a combination of two words, 'Swiss' and 'Watch'.[10] It could not be protected as a trademark in Switzerland because every watch produced in that country is a 'Swiss Watch'. Fortunately for the team, however, 'swatch' is also a general term used in the fashion industry to refer to a bolt or sample of fabric. It was on this basis that the company was able to protect the name 'Swatch' worldwide.

The Swatch conquered the planet at a speed that was virtually unheard-of for a single product. In 2020, more than 550 million Swatches had been sold, generating revenues of US$ 6.6 billion (see Table 1, *Chronology of the Swatch*).

From Inventor to Bureaucratic Clerk

During the creative process, Elmar Mock enjoyed a considerable amount of freedom. He was the product inventor and designer, he designed the tools required to produce the watch and he was in charge of the injection process, being the company's only polymer engineer. For 4 years, he managed the development of the entire engineering process, right up to final production. He served as the product's 'living memory', monitoring everything that was done to avoid repetition and to maintain a certain level of consistency. In 1982–1983, six patents prepared by Mock and Müller were filed by ETA.

But as the organization grew, Elmar became increasingly frustrated. As the new watch became a success, it also became subject to ISO 9000, product planning, SAP and other bureaucratic constraints. New people were brought in, all with the authority to tell him what he could or could not do. He began to feel he did not belong in such an environment, because it no longer allowed him to express his creativity.

[10]The first name chosen was Vulgaris, the second Popularis, the third Calibre 500, and the fourth and final was Swatch. Jacques Müller, Bernard Müller and Maryse Schmidt were the creators of the final Swatch design. Franz Sprecher was the marketing leader and the person who finalized the name in September 1981, working with an American consulting firm in New York.

Table 1. Chronology of the Swatch.

Dates	**Events**
1976	Elmar Mock (EM) is hired by ETA.
1977–1978	EM takes an intensive 1-year programme in the emerging field of plastic polymers.
1978	Ernst Thomke is hired by ETA as the new CEO, tasked with turning the company around.
1979	EM and Jacques Müller (JM) study new plastics technologies in Germany.
1979–1980	After exploring the field, EM and JM start work on using plastic in watch manufacturing, and then on creating a new, entirely plastic watch.
1980	EM and JM ask the company to purchase an injection moulding machine to continue their experiments.
27 March 1980	Tipping point: Meeting with Ernst Thomke for permission to continue their experiments leading to the production of a plastic watch. Draft of the first Swatch design.
December 1980	First technical drawings completed. EM and JM submit their first five plastic watch prototypes.
26 December 1980	Major meeting with CEO Ernst Thomke. Joint decision to continue with product development.
April 1981	The marketing team becomes involved in the project.
September 1981	Invention of the name *Swatch* for the first-ever plastic watch.
23 December 1981	The first five plastic watches function normally.
November 1982	*Sale of the first Swatch collection in the United States (Dallas, Texas).*
March 1983	*The Swatch is launched on the European market.*
1983	Nicolas Georges Hayek suggests a merger and integration of several Swiss watchmaking companies, and SMH (acronym for Société suisse de microélectronique et d'horlogerie SA) is created. Nicolas G. Hayek becomes its CEO. ETA joins the group.
1986	EM leaves ETA.
1998	SMH becomes the Swatch Group.

From Swatch to RockWatch

The revenues from the Swatch were invested in ETA's other watch brands, including Omega, Tissot, Longines and Breguet. The Tissot brand was largely unknown at the time. Elmar Mock was asked to work on a new project, the RockWatch (1985), which was intended to launch Tissot on the United States market. The new watch was to be made of granite. It would have a leather strap and a chrome-steel back. The plan was to produce 1,000 units.

Elmar was asked to study the materials required for the new project, in conjunction with the other people involved, including his younger brother Stéphane, who was also employed by ETA. The team planned to fly to Stuttgart for the study, but at the last minute Elmar, under pressure from his wife to celebrate their 10th wedding anniversary, went with her to Rome, on vacation, instead.

The company's plane crashed on the way to Stuttgart, and four of the five passengers, including Elmar's brother, died. The only survivor was Jacques Müller, who was hospitalised for almost a year.

The death of his brother, to whom he was close, destroyed any remaining interest Elmar may have had in ETA. He resigned his position and left. Two months later, at the request of Mr Thomke, he came back to finish the RockWatch project, producing the required 1,000 units. The product was a success, and generated sales of more than 100 million Swiss francs.

In addition to being unsure of his purpose at ETA now that the Swatch and RockWatch had both been launched, Elmar was upset that he was paid a bonus of only 700 Swiss Francs for his contribution to the Swatch project. Now aged 28, he was among the 30 best-paid managers at ETA, but had lost confidence in the company's capacity to support creative projects. In addition, he was morally and emotionally exhausted.

His main frustration with the Swatch was that it had become, to use his own term, 'boring'. His original concept had been transformed into what he described as 'just another watch', and he believed it had lost its appeal. And so, he completed the RockWatch project and left the company definitively in 1986, at the age of 32, believing the world was 'out there waiting for him', as the inventor of the Swatch.

After the Swatch and the RockWatch, the Creator's Blues: From Intrapreneur to Extrapreneur[11]

When Elmar Mock left ETA, he was emotionally drained and upset about his brother's death. He was also sad about the condition of his working partner Jacques Müller, who was fighting to recover from the plane crash, and was exhausted after completing two major projects. He felt the company would never

[11]Extrapreneurs are people who become entrepreneurs and work on what they used to do for others as intrapreneurs.

be the same again. It had lost the spirit and the 'temporary culture' that had allowed for the creation of the Swatch. Elmar became convinced it would never again allow initiatives that would lead to real innovations. He no longer trusted the management's ability to authorise any kind of innovative new project. Mr Thomke, whose entrepreneurial approach had allowed the enterprise to reinvent itself, and the only senior executive Elmar had ever really appreciated, had left ETA to lead ASUAG-SSIH, a holding created by finance consultant Nicolas Hayek, of which ETA was now a part.

The holding later went on to become the Swatch Group and Nicolas Hayek, who also became a business restructuring consultant, became its board chair. Ernst Thomke had been replaced at ETA by a conventional manager, and Elmar no longer enjoyed his work, a situation that troubled him because he was only 32 years old.[12] Creating his own company seemed like the only avenue open to him, if he was to become creative again. In 1986, he launched a company that he called Createc, and that subsequently became Creaholic.[13]

Why did he choose to create a new company instead of working for another employer? 'I was convinced there was a market for innovation, in the form of saleable new products. Innovation wasn't as important then as it is today but I could see that organizations were starting to be interested in it, and that the interest would grow'.

Elmar Mock believed small companies could not afford the expensive experts and professionals they needed to be really innovative and came up with the idea of setting up his own team of experts, qualified people who could be leased out to small companies for specific periods of time to help innovate and develop new products and projects. Once a project was up and running, the experts could move on to their next task.

When Createc was first launched, it did not enjoy the success he had hoped for. At ETA, he had lived in a cocoon, and admits he had no concept of what the world was really like. Forced out of his comfort zone, he reacted emotionally and became frustrated. Times were difficult, and after 3 years the new Swatch Group president, Nicolas Hayek, asked him if he would like to return to the company, offering him several alternatives, including leadership of one of the group's firms (to be chosen by Elmar).[14]

Elmar almost accepted the offer, which would have quadrupled his salary, but in the end, after consulting his wife, he decided he would rather persevere alone than work for someone he did not respect.

---

[12]As President of the Swatch Group, Ernst Thomke did not get on with his boss, board chair Nicolas Hayek, and left the group.

[13]Elmar Mock changed the name of his company because he did not want it to become identified solely with the technology sector.

[14]Elmar Mock did not get on with Nicolas Hayek. The two men first met in 1984, a year after the Swatch was first launched, when Hayek had not yet joined the company. Eventually the media would baptise Hayek 'the father of the Swatch'. Although Hayek never claimed the title for himself, he never denied it either. See Table 1, p. 160.

One of his friends sent more contracts his way, to help him through the difficult period. At the same time, one of his former teachers at the Engineering School asked him to cover for him during a 6-month sabbatical. Elmar agreed, and taught classes for between 8 and 15 hours a week, to feed his family, spending the rest of his time looking for clients and working on their projects.

Creaholic: An Original and Unique Concept

Introducing Creativity to Organizations

Elmar knew something was wrong with his business model, and he struggled to understand what it was. This 3-year process of reflection led him to reconsider what was truly important for him, and he began to understand what he wanted to do with his life. In 1986, the creativity model he prepared as a result of this formed the basis for a new business model and a new company, which he eventually named 'Creaholic'. It had taken 3 years of profound self-examination to reach this new starting point, which took him from self-employment to the construction of a real enterprise. He began to hire people, and together they went on to develop a company that would leave its mark in the field of creativity and innovation support.

Creaholic is a team of innovative experts from a variety of different fields: science, design, engineering, electronics, economics, etc. 'In the early days we were mainly engineers, then came the designers, then the economists, then the lawyers, and nowadays the newcomers are mainly from the social sciences. Now, we work mostly on *human-centred design* and coaching'.

Creaholic works on a wide range of products, from hearing aids to ski gear, from packaging to flavours, from software to micromechanical devices, and collaborates at various points in the innovation journey, from idea to implementation – exploring, conceptualizing, designing, building, testing, refining and to some extent selling. Creaholic helps its clients to turn dreams into real products, giving them a timely business advantage.

In 2020, Creaholic employs roughly 60 people from different backgrounds. They work with between 200 and 300 clients, but mostly with 50–60 main clients. They have produced over 800 innovations and 200 families of patents. They focus on creativity and innovation, not following the usual boundaries between disciplines, and where necessary hiring outside specialists to assist them. They offer perspectives that used to be unheard of and earn between 9 and 10 million Swiss francs per year in consulting fees.

As a consulting firm in the area of creativity, Creaholic has several original and unique organizational principles. For example:[15]

(1) No production or market sales of its design results.
(2) Never work with a client's competitors.

---

[15]Gilles Garel and Elmar Mock (2016a). For additional information on the internal organization and functioning of Creaholic, see: Chapter 5, The Metaphor of the Matriarch, pp. 125–139.

(3) Multidisciplinary teams that avoid specialties and constantly explore new fields of activities.
(4) A sort of capitalist kolkhoz characterized by transparency. The decision process is deliberative – everyone can speak out.
(5) A kind of incubator transforming some of its main ideas into start-ups.

The firm's internal organization is unique. Every person who works at Creaholic is a partner, and any partner can become a shareholder, depending on their level of merit. So far, about one-third of the partners have become shareholders. Only the people who work at Creaholic can become shareholders. The plus value is derived solely from creative activities. Governance is egalitarian: one person, one vote. Shareholders can also create spin-offs (eight start-ups have been created so far). Fewer than 10 people have left the firm since it was created in 1986.

The partners are professional inventors. They operate along the same lines as they suggest to their clients: if you want to innovate, you need to be ambidextrous: *exploitation* supported by improvements that lead to incremental innovation and/or *exploration* supported by increased creativity that leads to radical innovation.

'We're not farmers like most of our clients, who have structures that sow, produce and store. That's not what we do. Fundamentally, we're hunter-gatherers who have to live in harmony and adapt permanently to the world around us. We don't plant things and we don't own things. The two systems coexist alongside one another. There will always be farming systems and there will always be hunter-gatherer systems. Everyone finds the path that best suits them'.

'The more organizations need to become and remain innovative and reinvent themselves, the more they will need support. In fact, since the firm was created, the need for support has grown steadily over time. However, our development hasn't been based on a classical strategic planning process. In other words, growth hasn't resulted from our strategic choices, it's been determined by market demand. I never imagined that Creaholic would become what it is today, with 60 people (in 2020). And like many of our clients, Creaholic will always have to redefine and reinvent itself, or it will disappear.'

Elmar Mock's Concept of Creativity

Elmar Mock spent most of his life working on radical innovations. He has created more than 80 families of patents in various industries and has experience with more than 600 projects. He speaks of the three energies in human beings: *technosophy, creativity, and exploration*, and adds *curiosity* as the common denominator applicable to all three elements. In his view, true entrepreneurs are explorers. *Technosophy* is the technical know-how, experience and information generally acquired at school – in other words, a field of expertise, something a person either has or is in the process of acquiring.

Creativity, the second energy, is directly opposed to all this. As for *exploration* and *curiosity*, it encompasses the need to investigate, observe, question and explore (e.g. an entrepreneur who explores a new territory). These three energies are interdependent. In other words, *creativity* cannot flourish without a certain amount of *technosophy* (education and learning) and *curiosity*.

Elmar Mock defines *creativity* as a set of mental phases, which he classifies as the 'gas', 'liquid' and 'crystal' phases.

The 'GAS' phase is defined by terms such as liberty, movement, fantasy, utopia, illusion and chaos. It is during this phase that free-floating elements collide to produce new ideas, generally when the person comes into contact with an unexpected disturbance. Elmar Mock associates the 'GAS' phase with childhood.

The next phase, 'LIQUID', marks the period when the 'GAS' phase evolves and condenses to liquid form. Elmar Mock associates this phase with education and development, and notes that it usually takes place during the school years. He uses terms such as beauty, grace and evolution, as well as density, desperation and tears, to describe it.

The third phase, 'CRYSTAL' or 'solid', is when creativity takes on a tangible or solid form. Elmar Mock describes it as the 'success' of creativity and the achievement of stability. Humankind, he believes, needs the illusion of stability in order to function. Humans make plans, organise their lives, get married, have children and save for retirement. In other words, they strive for the illusion of stability. Religion used to offer the after-life as a target for eternal stability, but in the modern age, stability has evolved into the 'day after tomorrow', in other words, the illusion of forthcoming future success.

Elmar Mock believes 'solids' will always win over 'gases' and 'liquids', precisely because human beings and societies strive collectively for stability, not change. 'Solids' are essential to success but cannot be created without 'gases' and 'liquids', which, paradoxically, are rejected by 'solids' because they destroy what people see as being stable. The human perception of stability is often an illusion, as environments continue to change at a faster pace. Elmar Mock feels this is one of the important challenges facing organizations: they need to find a way to manage creativity and achieve a balance between 'gases', 'liquids' and 'solids'.

Becoming a Consultant in Creativity and Innovation: Crossing the Desert

Elmar Mock's company Creaholic focuses mainly on the 'gas' and 'liquid' phases to produce 'solids' in organizations, since it is the 'solids' that will generate the company's success. For humanity, success can only ever be 'solid'. In the 'gas' and 'liquid' phases, creativity is regarded as being outside the norm; the elements produced by creative people are often rejected by organizations – a contradiction in terms, since without them, the organization cannot produce 'solids' and achieve long-term stability. The task of managing 'gases', 'liquids' and 'solids' under one roof can be extremely challenging, since the logic underlying each phase is so different.

Creaholic is a technical consulting firm whose aim is to foster creativity. It was set up to help organizations develop inventions, products, processes and concepts. In the early days, Elmar Mock worked alone. After leaving ETA, his greatest challenge was to deal with the freedom he obtained as a result. Not only did he travel extensively, but he also worked on weekends and in the evenings and continued to teach several hours a week to earn extra income. It was 4 years before the company generated enough revenue to allow him to provide a basic living for his family. It was around that time that Elmar Mock met the man who would become his first partner in the business. Marcel Aeschlimann was one of his students and agreed to come on board without pay until the company could afford to give him a salary.

The market for services such as those offered by Creaholic was extremely difficult at the time. The company's first two clients – now regular customers – were recruited quite by chance. In one case, Swatch's marketing manager mentioned Elmar Mock's name to the CEO of a Swatch supplier, Tetra Pak, a food packaging firm, which subsequently signed a 3-month contract with Creaholic and went on to generate more than 20% of the company's turnover in the next 15 years. Today, it still accounts for between 5% and 10% of Creaholic's total sales.

According to Elmar Mock, the issue generally faced by businesses is that they lack fresh, new ideas. They simply duplicate things that already exist and are not radically innovative. Innovation cannot be integrated forcibly into a business. To innovate, the business must combine its own 'internal genetics' with 'free genetics' from outside. Its own genetics play a key role in accepting the final outcome. If there is no original business DNA built into the innovation, it will never be accepted.

In the 2020s, it is estimated that Creaholic will generate annual revenues of more than four billion Swiss Francs for its clients, purely with its ideas. All the employees are partners, except for 10 who are shareholders. Creaholic has two business models: the mercenary business model, under which it works for clients such as Tetra Pak, and the spinoff business model, under which it creates new businesses.

The mercenary model generates revenue that allows the company to pay its employees' salaries. Profits are shared at the end of the year. The goal is to keep as little money as possible in the company. Surpluses are used to fuel the spinoff business model. Creaholic develops one start-up roughly every 2 years. These newly founded companies are owned not by Creaholic itself, but by its employees.

Elmar Mock describes Creaholic as a 'capitalistic kolkhoz', or capitalistic contradiction, since it generates profits but then gives them away. He feels this dual model maintains motivation, since all value generated is distributed to the organization's members. Creaholic has no external shareholders. If someone leaves the company or dies, their shares are automatically returned to the company at a nominal cost.

In the early years, the company had three major shareholders: founder Elmar Mock (30%), his original partner Marcel Aeschlimann (30%), and a third partner, André Klopfenstein (20%). However, these percentages changed as the company handed over power to its second and now third generations.

As for the start-ups, they remain initially in the Creaholic family, but over time the employees concerned are allowed to keep their shares even if they leave the company. This structure provides some compensation for the loss of dividends from the money Creaholic invests in its start-ups instead of distributing it to its partners. Creaholic's salary structure is highly transparent. Everyone knows what every other person earns, and end-of-year profit shares are calculated using a mathematical formula known by everyone concerned.

In 2020, marketing remains a challenge, since the company cannot work with industry competitors of its existing clients. Each time it wants to attract a new customer, it must find a new field of activity. It acquires between four and six new customers per year, and up to 10 in good years. However, its primary goal is to develop expandable activities with its existing clients.

Elmar Mock does not believe in 'creative systems'. He believes an organization cannot change, but the humans who work for it can change and adapt. Paradoxically, humans are also the biggest hurdles to creativity. He compares creativity in humans to pearls in oysters. A lucky oyster will not develop a pearl but will simply enjoy life in the ocean. Pearls are only developed when oysters are exposed to a disturbing element.

In other words, if a person is to become creative, he or she must be exposed to a disturbance. It is human nature to adapt to situations like a chameleon, because this is what we learn at school: listen to the teacher, obey the rules, and be kind to others. Real innovations are therefore innovations that simplify life, and real innovators focus on the disturbance factor.

Elmar Mock does not associate 'innovation' with 'development'. In his mind, the term 'develop' refers to the constant evolution of a system or organization, which is precisely what is not wanted in creativity. Instead, he prefers the German term 'entwerfen', which, roughly translated, means 'outline'. A designer outlines an idea, and an engineer develops it. The concept comes before the product.

In addition, he has identified two types of business models: the 'onion' model and the 'innovation' model. The 'onion' model is based on job descriptions, departments, structures and organization. Roughly 95% of companies use this model. Their goal is to slightly modify existing ideas (changing the shape, colour or size of a product, for example), based on the logic that if an idea has worked once, it should work again. The 'onion' model allows them to be fast, cost-efficient and successful, without the need to make major changes. It is a model that allows companies to survive. However, for long-term success, it is not enough. Success requires 'innovation', not renovation. 'The difference is small but key'. In Elmar Mock's opinion, innovation is a question of habit and training. It is a way of thinking and reacting that can be learned.

Creaholic works on *radical innovation* as opposed to *incremental innovation*, offering consulting services to help its clients with specific projects and training them to deal with creativity. Its goal is to change mental models, not organizations. It also aims to educate.

The company has grown significantly in recent years, and Elmar Mock is aware that with growth comes the need to foster creativity within its own ranks. For example, once a fortnight it hosts a creative breakfast, where the whole workforce meets at 7 a.m. to pool their creative ideas and approaches. Every day for the next 2 weeks, one of these ideas is tested to see if it works.

In addition to working with the company, Elmar Mock has continued to teach creativity at university. He has developed a 1-year, three-phase programme based on his concept of creativity (disturbance, invention and concept), and has been pleasantly surprized by his students' achievements. His teaching experience has confirmed his assumption that creativity is not an unusual phenomenon but is a skill that can be learned and trained by changing a person's mental model.

Retirement and Succession

Elmar Mock is not sure he will ever really retire. 'I am and will always be a free electron', he says! He first retired from Creaholic in 2014, becoming its 'Honorary President', and then retired more permanently in 2019. However, this has not prevented him from going into work regularly, almost on a daily basis. He no longer wants to be involved in internal decisions. 'I'm there when they need me, but I'm like an old monkey. I'm no longer the guy who makes decisions'.

'If you stay in place for too long, the next generation doesn't get a chance to develop. Transmission is absolutely key. I've been preparing for it for almost 20 years. As far back as 1995, I knew I was going to convert my colleagues gradually into co-shareholders and partners'.

Of everything he has done, he considers Creaholic to be his greatest achievement. 'It's the chicken that lays eggs! I needed to find a system capable of doing what it does. An egg is very nice, but if you don't produce chickens, you won't have other eggs'.

Life After Retirement

When he first retired in 2014, he and his second wife, Hélène (they were married in 2003), created a new firm, Mock-Kett, which organizes workshops and keynotes. It was born out of the realization that for a product or a concept to succeed in the modern world, it needs three things: 'An Idea, a Story and Finance. A great idea for a good product without a story is just a great idea. A good story without a product is just a good story. A good story about a great idea for a good product with the right financing is a success in the making'.

The company has enabled them to travel and to continue to do the things they had gradually begun to do together over the years. They are currently preparing a new book of fables on the art of innovating. They spend their time between their cottage in Scotland, their chalet in Switzerland and visiting their children who are based in Paris, Hong Kong, Melbourne and Zürich.

Elmar Mock became a popular public speaker. He likes to share ideas, often in a colourful way. A few examples are presented in Appendix A below.

Case Discussion

Elmar Mock

(1) What differentiates Elmar Mock from other people? What are his main added values?
(2) Is he a creator, an artist, an inventor, an innovator, a dreamer, a free thinker, an intrapreneur, a facilitator or an entrepreneur? What kind of agent of innovation is he?
(3) What do you think about his unconventional approaches to innovation?
(4) (A) Would you like to work with Elmar Mock? Why?
(B) Did his life story change your view of what it means to innovate? Give reasons for your answer.
(5) (A) What do you think about how he expresses his creative potential?
(B) Do you think his decision to swim against the current was courageous or foolhardy?
(6) Was it a good idea for a watchmaker working in a traditional watchmaking factory to study in an emerging sector such as plastics?
(7) Elmar has played all kinds of roles as an agent of innovation. Where do you think he fits best? As an intrapreneur? As an inventor? As an entrepreneur inspiring a younger generation of agents of innovation? As an external facilitator supporting inventors and other agents of innovation? Or as an international speaker encouraging audiences to be more creative?
(8) (A) Would you hire him as an external facilitator or consultant? Why? What would you expect from him?
(B) What did you learn from his life story? How did it help to improve your own interest in innovation? Did his story make you want become an agent of innovation?
(9) What do you think about how he dealt with the product development process, moving from fuzzy, to liquid to solid? How would you apply this approach?
(10) (A) Would you like to join Creaholic and become an external consultant working on the introduction, design and implementation of innovations? Why? What additional input would you bring to the firm?
(B) If you look at the different roles played by Elmar Mock as an agent of innovation, which do you think would best fit you? Why?

Acknowledgements

This case study was written using information gathered from several sources. It began when we visited and spent time with Elmar Mock at Creaholic with groups of students, to talk about innovation. These sessions were followed by Elmar's inspiring presentations in class and at Creaholic's headquarter in Bienne (CH) in addition to the ensuing discussions with students from an MBA course in entrepreneurship at the HEG-FR (Haute École de Gestion – Fribourg School of Management – affiliated to the University of Applied Sciences and Arts Western Switzerland HES-SO) (2008–2020).

An eight-hour interview with Elmar Mock was later conducted in his office in Biel/Bienne, Switzerland, on 16 June 2011, by Louis Jacques Filion, Rico Baldegger and Verena Huber, who was, at the time, a student in the Master's Program in Entrepreneurship at HEG-FR. The authors extend their particular appreciation to Verena, who produced the written transcript of this eight-hour taped interview.

Additional information included a two hour PowerPoint presentation made by Elmar Mock at HEC Montreal on 3 October 2011; a one-day meeting with Elmar Mock and students from the Master's Program in Entrepreneurship at HEG-FR, held at the Creaholic offices in Biel/Bienne on 12 June 2012; speeches presented by Elmar Mock at the World Entrepreneurship Forum and elsewhere that were attended by one of the authors; several magazine articles about Elmar Mock; and lastly, a four-hour working session with Elmar Mock on 6 May 2014 and additional meetings over the following years to revise and finalize this case study. A two-hour interview was also conducted with Elmar Mock by Rico Baldegger and Louis Jacques Filion at the HEG-FR on 14 January 2020, and second one on ZOOM on 2 May 2020. The first case study was produced in 2012. It was followed by several versions over a decade.

Elmar Mock presents his creativity concepts in conferences abroad. His concepts are also described alongside those of an innovation specialist in a book they co-authored: Gilles Garel & Elmar Mock (2016) *The Innovation Factory. Taking the Plunge*. CRC Press (Taylor & Francis). Original French edition: *La fabrique de l'innovation* (Paris: Dunod; first edition, 2012, second edition, 2016).

References

Garel, G., & Mock, E. (2016a). *The Innovation Factory. Taking the Plunge* (pp. 125–129). CRC Press (Taylor & Francis).

Garel, G., & Mock, E. (2016b). *The Innovation Factory*. CRC Press.

Appendix: Sharing Some Thoughts

The Future of the Watch

Elmar is always delighted to talk about the disruption that connectivity has injected into the watchmaking sector: '*Watches used to be the metronomes that paced our days. Nowadays, we schedule our lives differently. Time still matters to us, but we will see a change in the way we use watches and a departure from the usual way in which they are worn. In future, our wrists will no longer be the only body part on which we keep time. So we can no longer define watches on the basis of the way we wear them, and they will have many more functions than simply keeping time*'.

Success

The problem with success – the contradiction, if you will – is that to create a good idea, you need a very open mind, but to be successful with a product, you need to close your mind and focus on productivity, profitability and efficiency. Curiously, the art of invention is openness, while the art of starting an innovative project or launching a start-up involves reducing the number of options and choosing the one in which you believe. In short, it's the ability to sacrifice good ideas for the benefit of the ideas we think have the most potential. These are two very different mindsets!

Swatch

The Swatch was the revelation that enabled me to believe in myself and to understand that I could create things. Before the Swatch experience, I didn't know if I was an inventor. I think a lot of people aren't aware of what they can do. They're afraid. As humans, we're our own limitations. The pleasure of creativity lies in the joy of discovering that it really works, sometimes at a time when you don't expect it. You have to learn to trust yourself and believe that things are possible, even if you're not absolutely certain that they're possible.

Organizations of the Future

I really believe in the ability of teams to create. I believe less and less in the individual ability of a single leader. I think no inventor ever truly works alone, and no society depends on a single person. It's always groups, teams, packs. I prefer to use the term 'pack' rather than 'group of individuals'. I believe in packs because there's a certain level of complicity, but I also believe in groups too, in all kinds of groups. But you have to know how to manage them. Group management shouldn't be hierarchical, it should be natural and organic.

The Young Generation

'The new generation wants to give meaning to life. That's something which is truly interesting. It's a new politicisation. Growing numbers of young people tell me: Look, it's not necessarily what I'm going to earn that interests me the most. I want what I do to have some meaning. And that's a change about which I'm passionate'.

The Metaphor of the Matriarch

One of Elmar Mock's subjects of reflection in recent years has been the Metaphor of the Matriach. No case study about him would be complete if it did not include some of his views on this subject, which is very important to him.

> *The Metaphor of the Matriarch was a revelation that came to me fairly late in life. It took many years for me to understand it properly. Human societies have been dominated by a patriarchal model, whereas the way firms are managed, especially today, is more matriarchal. Most bosses behave more like mothers than like men.*
>
> *A mother is always in conflict between her short-term survival instinct and her long-term conservation instinct...She has to live and eat every day and still prepare for future generations...You have to exploit and explore. This tension is a well-known fact in innovation management and is referred to as 'ambidexterity'.*[16]

[16]Gilles Garel and Elmar Mock (2016b). Chapter 5: The Metaphor of the Matriarch, pp. 125–139.

Chapter 6

Emerson de Almeida and the Creation of Fundação Dom Cabral: Leading a Brazilian Revolution in Executive Education

Cândido Borges, Fernando Dolabela and Louis Jacques Filion

Abstract

As of 2020, London's *Financial Times* had ranked *Fundação Dom Cabral* (FDC) as one of the world's leading executive education institutions and the top such institution in Latin America for 15 consecutive years. In 2011, FDC was also ranked fifth on the *Financial Times*' list of the 40 most respected business schools in the world. For FDC itself and for its co-founder, Emerson de Almeida, this recognition was a wonderful way of celebrating the 35th anniversary of an institution that has become a leader in applied management education in Brazil.

How did this young Brazilian institution achieve this? As is the case for any great undertaking, many people played crucial roles in its creation and consolidation. However, its history is closely tied to the life of its co-founder, Emerson de Almeida.

Emerson was FDC's Chief Executive from its foundation in 1976 until 2012, when he became President of its Board of Governance.[1] He is primarily an innovator and drew his inspiration from visits to world-renowned business schools. Once he understood the needs arising from executive thinking processes, he was able to adapt these schools' best practices to suit the Brazilian culture and context.

'You must always try the impossible', he says. This case study presents the story of an exceptional institutional intrapreneur who championed and led the transformation of executive education in Brazil.

[1]The Board of Governance is responsible for FDC's governance. It ensures compliance with the institution's mission, principles, values and longevity.

Agents of Innovation, 169–192

Published under exclusive licence by Emerald Publishing Limited
doi:10.1108/978-1-83797-012-420231006

Keywords: Intrapreneur; intrapreneurship; business education; economic development; social leader; social consciousness

Case

Emerson de Almeida and the Creation of Fundação Dom Cabral: Leading a Brazilian Revolution in Executive Education[2]

As of 2020, London's *Financial Times* had ranked *Fundação Dom Cabral* (FDC) as one of the world's leading executive education institutions and the top such institution in Latin America for 15 consecutive years. In 2011, FDC was also ranked fifth on the Financial Times' list of the 40 most respected business schools in the world. For FDC itself and for its co-founder, Emerson de Almeida, this recognition was a wonderful way of celebrating the 35th anniversary of an institution that has become a leader in applied management education in Brazil.

How did this young Brazilian institution achieve this? As is the case for any great undertaking, many people played crucial roles in its creation and consolidation. However, its history is closely tied to the life of its co-founder, Emerson de Almeida.

Emerson was FDC's Chief Executive from its foundation in 1976 until 2012, when he became President of its Board of Governance.[3] He is primarily an innovator and drew his inspiration from visits to world-renowned business schools. Once he understood the needs arising from executive thinking processes, he was able to adapt these schools' best practices to suit the Brazilian culture and context.

'You must always try the impossible', he says. This case study presents the story of an exceptional institutional intrapreneur who championed and led the transformation of executive education in Brazil.

Introduction to Entrepreneurial Practice: Operating a Stall in a Public Market

In the late 1940s, Emerson's father, Geraldino José de Almeida, left his position as train station master in Mateus Leme, a small town of roughly 10,000 inhabitants in Minas Gerais, Brazil, and was unable to find another stable job. After 3 years of informal jobs and poor meals, the family moved to the state capital, Belo Horizonte. Emerson, born in 1941, was the second of the family's six children. Although he was only 8 years old at the time, he clearly remembers the move as being a crucial event in his life.

When the family settled in Belo Horizonte, Geraldino bought a stall in the Feira dos Produtores, a public market located in the neighbourhood of Lagoinha.[4] He sold everything (fruit, cereals, hats, and so on) and was able to

---

[2]Case written by Cândido Borges, Fernando Dolabela and Louis Jacques Filion.

[3]The Board of Governance is responsible for FDC's governance. It ensures compliance with the institution's mission, principles, values and longevity.

[4]Commonly called 'barraca' by Brazilians.

make enough money to cover the family's basic needs. However, he had to work 7 days a week, every day of the year except Good Friday. The whole family helped out, even Emerson's mother, Geralda Braz de Almeida, whenever she had time.

It was here, at the family's market stall, that Emerson discovered the world of business. His job was to talk to customers and sell. He quickly learned to balance school and work. When he came home from school at midday, his mother gave him lunch and he then took a lunch box to his father, who spent the whole day at the market. Emerson would stay for the afternoon, helping out as much as he could.

His older brother, Geraldo, who also worked on the market stall, showed early signs of being an entrepreneur. This is what Emerson had to say about him:

> My brother, who was 11 years old at the time, borrowed money from one of our mother's sisters – Aunt Zezé – to buy balloons that he could resell to people in the Carnival parades on the city's main streets. He earned a considerable amount of money, paid back the loan and gave me a share. We used the money to make a wooden stand on which we could hang small items that we wanted to sell in the market.
>
> This had nothing to do with my father's stall. My brother became an entrepreneur at age 11, and me, at age 9. I used to earn a bit of money selling combs, razor blades, trays, hair nets and other odds and ends. My most constant customers were the prostitutes who lived near the market. They were especially kind to me and treated me as if I were their own child. With the money we earned from our sales, my brother bought his own market stall. Years later, he bought a second one and became a respected trader.

Feeding on Dreams – Big Dreams

By the time Emerson was 17 years old, he already had 8 years of work experience with his father and brother, and got a job with a company that imported German car parts, thanks to another of his mother's sisters – Aunt Lydia. He became a 'jack of all trades', cleaning offices, running errands, photocopying documents, serving water and coffee. The office opened at 8 a.m. but Emerson always arrived early.

> I used to arrive at 7 a.m. for two reasons: first to clean the office, and second, to do what I liked best, namely typing out my dreams on a piece of paper. I used to write things like 'I'm going to make millions of boats, ships and planes and show the Brazilian flag to the whole world!' I loved to dream.

Emerson dreamt big. However, his dreams were not for himself – he never dreamt of becoming a millionaire – they were for his country. For example, he dreamt of an economically vibrant Brazil, a world power with a major industrial park. He dreamt of a country where poverty had been eradicated, one that would become a model of development for the world. He had a very fertile imagination and certainly did not lack ambition.

Emerson worked all day and went to public school in the evenings. When he was 18 years old, he left his job, the family market stall and the partnership with his brother to do his 1-year compulsory military service. While in the armed forces, he became involved in sports and physical activity and learned the importance of discipline (something he realized, years later, he had inherited from his father) while continuing to study at night. With his deeply-held pacifist convictions, he knew he would be unable to go to war and kill people. At the end of his military service, he left the armed forces and bought a stall at the same market as his father and brother.

Left-Wing Student Leader and Socially Committed Revolutionary Journalist

In Brazil, in the early 1960s, tensions between the left and right were high. In 1963, against this high-pressure background, Emerson decided to run for the presidency of his school's student union.

> Most students were left-wing and against the military. I was one of two candidates, and there was a lot of propaganda, not to mention an all-out political war, to decide which of us would be elected. I did everything I could to win, and ended up with 1,700 votes compared to my opponent's 200. And so I became president of the student union.

The issues taken up by Emerson and his student union colleagues went beyond the realms of academia; for example, he defended structural changes in the country. However, he quickly came into conflict with the school board. The school's principal, a military sympathizer, turned some of the students and teachers against the union, and by the end of Emerson's first year as student union president, he was facing strong opposition.

Brazil's President João Goulart was overthrown in a military coup on March 31, 1964, and the army took control of the country's government (they would hold power for the next 21 years). Emerson's situation worsened after the military take-over, and without the support of the school's teachers and student body, he resigned his position as student union president and left the school.

During his time as student union president, he had begun to work as a journalist with *Diário Católico*, Belo Horizonte's second-largest newspaper. He worked in the market in the mornings, for the newspaper in the afternoons, and studied at night.

He earned nothing from the newspaper during his first 6 months as a journalist, but worked for the sheer pleasure of writing, meeting people and listening to their stories. He only began to receive a small salary when he left school, sold his market stall and took a full-time job with the newspaper. At the same time, he enrolled in the undergraduate degree programme in Economics at Universidade Federal de Minas Gerais – UFMG (Federal University of Minas Gerais) in Belo Horizonte. He did not want to become an economist, but chose that particular programme because of his work as a journalist, which required him to write about politics and economics.

He went on to work for three other newspapers, two of which had national circulation (*Jornal do Brazil* and *Correio da Manhã*), and also for TV Belo Horizonte, known today as TV Globo.[5–7]

Inspired by a Perfectionist Father, the Search for Challenge

> When I think about what I've done in my life, I always revisit my fourth birthday. My maternal grandfather and others had been invited to my birthday party. I was playing with a hammer and broke the doorstep just as the guests arrived. My father, who was a lovely man but also very strict, scolded me in front of the guests.
>
> I don't remember holding a grudge or having a problem with him because of that. But recently, when I began to write a book about entrepreneurship among people in vulnerable situations, I suddenly felt the effect of that scolding in front of other people. I think it was the impulse that made me become an entrepreneur!
>
> I lived my life to show my father that I was capable of doing things that deserved praise, not just reprimands. And they would have to be extraordinary things, like the ones I typed out when I was an office boy. If I'd continued to work with my father, I wouldn't have had a chance to prove that I was capable of doing something out of the ordinary.

---

[5]Jornal do Brazil was one of the most respected newspaper in Brazil. Founded in 1891, it circulated until 2010, when it made the transition to online-only.

[6]Correio da Manhã started to circulate in 1901 and opposed almost all Brazil's presidents over the years, which is why it was persecuted and closed on several occasions. It closed down definitively in 1974.

[7]TV Globo is a Brazilian free-to-air television network. It is the second largest commercial television network in the world, viewed by more than 200 million people daily.

> In 2001, when we inaugurated the FDC campus in Nova Lima, Minas Gerais, at a prestigious ceremony attended by the President of the Republic, Ministers of State and dozens of executives, businessmen and public sector representatives, I caught a glimpse of my father and thought: 'Do you see, Dad? I deserve recognition and applause.'

In 1968, Emerson accepted an invitation to set up the communications office of Pontifícia Universidade Católica de Minas Gerais (Pontifical Catholic University of Minas Gerais), known today as *PUC Minas*, while still working part-time at *Correio da Manhã*. He reported directly to the University's President, Dom Serafim Fernandes de Araújo, whom he had invited as a speaker when he was president of the student union. Dom Serafim was a religious leader closely involved in the life of the community. He played a vital role in Belo Horizonte life, interceding for political prisoners and helping to prevent the University itself from being closed down by the military junta.

Emerson set up a simple structure for the University's new communications office, composed of a part-time advisor and a secretary. His aim was to establish a good relationship between the University and the press. To facilitate contact with journalists, he organized a weekly conference on communications to which he invited Brazilian personalities in the fields of advertising and journalism, as well as students, journalists and teachers. The event was a real success, and not only helped establish conditions for the creation of a School of Communications that would come into operation years later, but also stifled a separatist movement in the University's School of Engineering.

At the time, however, life was far from easy for journalists. After the military coup, press censorship became increasingly severe, especially after 1968, as the regime became tougher. Journalists were forbidden from publishing anything against the regime. Emerson lost his job with two newspapers because of his political stance. Several of his fellow journalists were also fired, others were arrested and some disappeared, never to be seen again.

When Emerson obtained his Economics degree in 1969, censorship had intensified and persecution of the press had become more widespread. He therefore decided to take a postgraduate degree course abroad. Now age 28, he applied for and obtained a grant from the French government and left for France with his wife, Nilda Lúcia Santos de Almeida, whom he had married in 1966. They spent 2 years in Paris, where he obtained a Master's degree in journalism, at the *Institut français de presse* and the *Institut d'études économiques et sociales*. During their vacations, the couple travelled through Soviet-dominated countries and were deeply disillusioned by the poverty they saw and by communism's lack of perspective.

You Find Your Path by Walking: Looking to the Future

Emerson went back to Brazil and to the University in 1972, and was invited by Dom Serafim to become a professor and deputy director in the newly-established School of Communications. Months later, he represented the University at a seminar held in Southern Brazil by the Ministry of Education on the organization of 'university extension' services.[8] As he always did after a work trip, he wrote a report on the seminar and sent it to the President. It would soon produce results.

> I presented a report on the seminar, and a few days later the President and the Secretary General of the University proposed that I should set up the Extension Center (CEX). I was appointed its director and established its structure, which consisted in two small rooms and five part-time employees. We began by organizing short courses in different fields, as well as cultural events, research workshops and so on. We tried to organize the extension in a professional way.

The Brazilian economy grew annually by 12% between 1972 and 1974. A Fiat car factory and a large steel works were built in the Belo Horizonte region, creating thousands of jobs. The University also expanded considerably. Emerson and his team were active and enthusiastic. They quickly identified an unmet demand in the field of management and structured a set of programs for company employees, since the demand far outstripped the number of places already available.

The topics covered in management and executive training were new to the team members who needed to learn about their client group quickly. Emerson pointed out:

> We wanted in-depth knowledge of the profiles of our course participants. We realized that they were very different from the University's traditional students. They were between 30 and 50 years of age and were mainly interested in learning things they could practice and apply in their companies. We prepared our courses accordingly. Major changes were introduced to make the content more practical. To teach it, we chose not only professors from the University but also professionals from companies who had more practical experience than the professors.

The Extension Center expanded quickly, attracting the attention of the University's senior management. Emerson and his team then suggested constructing a

[8]The term 'university extension' refers to ongoing educational activities in different fields not covered by regular academic programs: culture, human rights, environment, health, poverty, etc. These activities help establish other forms of connection between universities and the environment in which they operate.

building specifically for extension activities on the University campus. Dom Serafim supported the proposal and made preparations for it, identifying the site, the building architecture and the budget. However, an obstacle arose that threw the whole project into doubt.

Entrepreneurs and Intrapreneurs Are Tenacious: Obstacles Can Be Opportunities

In 1975, Emerson had an unpleasant surprise: the scale model of the future CEX building, proudly displayed in the President's waiting room, had disappeared. When asked where it was, the Secretary General replied: 'We've decided that it won't be built after all'. 'But what about the resources we were promised?' asked Emerson. 'We're going to invest them in another sector', was the answer. Emerson could not believe his ears. Unfortunately, it was true: the head of the University had decided to discontinue the project.

The Extension Center's fast growth had generated a lot of jealousy that had, in turn, sparked a movement against the construction of the new building. Part of the University had taken a stand against what it perceived as the preferential treatment given to extension programme participants: for example, the chairs were more comfortable than those offered to regular undergraduate students, and the lecturers had more practical expertise.

The challenge was a considerable one, but Emerson was determined not to let the project die. He turned to Dom Serafim, the President who had always been so supportive of the Center's work. Dom Serafim promised to do what he could, and asked two of his collaborators to find a solution to the problem.

During the impasse, while a solution was being sought, Emerson continued to work at the Extension Center and, with permission from his superiors, he also began to work part-time for another institution, *Fundação João Pinheiro*, a State of Minas Gerais Institute that had set up the Centro de Desenvolvimento em Administração (Center for Development in Administration, or CDA) with the mission of improving the managerial skills of senior employees in the public and private sectors. Its main focus was executive education. Emerson quickly learned a lot about executive training and was able to expand his network of contacts.[9]

> Fundação João Pinheiro had connections with New York's Columbia University. American professors came to teach courses and CDA people went to Columbia to do their MBAs. The CDA organized seminars for high-level executives. I worked in the marketing department, promoting the programs, for about six months. It taught me a great deal about how to organize these courses.

---

[9]In English: Center for Development in Administration.

A New Challenge: Setting Up Fundação Dom Cabral

The University eventually found a solution for the Extension Center. The Law School had an old association known as Dom Cabral, whose role was to award scholarships to law students in need.[10] However, it was inactive and only existed on paper. The President decided to abolish this association, set up *Fundação Dom Cabral* instead, and transfer all courses and activities involving companies from the Extension Center to the new foundation. The Extension Center continued to exist but was responsible for cultural and social activities only.

Emerson left *Fundação João Pinheiro* and returned to work full-time for the Catholic University. He admitted, however, that he had considered the possibility of moving permanently to *Fundação João Pinheiro*'s CDA because of the doubts about the Extension Center's future.

> CDA had actually considered the possibility of becoming a business school. If the opposition to the creation of Fundação Dom Cabral had intensified to the point where the President no longer supported it, I think I would have left the University and worked full-time for CDA. When I realized that Dom Serafim wholeheartedly supported the creation of Fundação Dom Cabral, I left CDA and went back to the Catholic University full-time.

Fundação Dom Cabral was created on 9 August 1976. Dom Serafim, as President of the University, was appointed to chair its board. Emerson continued to run the Extension Center on a part-time basis while getting FDC up and running. His initial position was that of superintendent of the new organization, which was legally independent of the University.[11] 'From the beginning, Dom Serafim supported us 100%', he said. FDC gained its independence but did not have University resources. 'Go ahead, it's your project, I have confidence in you', he said.

A Dreamer Becomes a Visionary Leader

Emerson took the President's advice and was happy to be able to work on the development of the education centre he had dreamed about. Three courses from the former Extension Center – Corporate Law, Economic Engineering and Occupational Safety Engineering – were transferred to FDC, guaranteeing its survival in the early months.

[10]Dom Cabral (Dom Antônio dos Santos Cabral) was the first bishop of Belo Horizonte. He was very popular and recognized in the community as a great entrepreneur – he set up the *Diário Católico* and other newspapers and founded the Catholic University of Minas Gerais. Born in 1884, in Propriá (Sergipe), he was (arch) bishop of Belo Horizonte from 1922 until his death in 1967.

[11]At the time, the title of the position was 'Superintendent' and not 'Dean', as is the case today.

At the time of the transfer, the Extension Center had 18 full-time employees. Emerson invited some of them to work at FDC. Moving from the University-run Extension Center to the independent FDC meant leaving a stable job for an uncertain position in a new organization. However, only one of the invited employees chose not to move. FDC began with eight employees, leaving 10 at the Extension Center. One of the employees who transferred to the newly-established FDC was Paulo Roberto Garcia Lemos, who became Emerson's right-hand man and worked tirelessly over the next 15 years to achieve his visionary leader's goals.

> I was not really interested in management from a technical or operational point of view. He and I formed a perfect, complementary pair right from the beginning. He was pragmatic, rational and highly organized. He had his feet firmly on the ground. He was the one who made the whole thing work. He managed the finances and the organization. I was more of a development dreamer, a visionary.

By January 1977, FDC had acquired four or five more employees and had moved to a rented building owned by the Catholic Church in the Santo Agostinho neighbourhood of Belo Horizonte.[12] Now fully independent of the University, FDC began to operate on its own beyond the University's walls and circuit. Emerson left his position as director of the Extension Center and became the full-time Dean of FDC. In the early days, FDC team planned their programs and carried out enough activities to survive, under the guidance of Paulo Lemos. It required a certain amount of tenacity which was fuelled by the team's dream of transforming FDC into something great, an organization that would become a point of reference in its field of expertise.

> The whole team took on the task of building on the dream to form something different and non-traditional (...). Our dream was quite diffuse. Like the story of the three masons: the first saw himself laying bricks, the second saw himself building a wall and the third saw himself building a cathedral. We also wanted to build a cathedral instead of just laying bricks (...). We had a dream that motivated us, but we didn't have a clear vision of what FDC should become in reality. It took us 20 years to formulate the vision we have today: a center to develop executives and companies, not simply a traditional academic business school.

About a year after it was created, FDC sent the occupational safety specialty courses back to the University along with other technology projects that it had

---

[12]Rua Bernardo Guimarães, 3071 Santo Agostinho. This is where FDC was first based in Belo Horizonte. In August 2001, FDC's second campus was inaugurated, along a beautiful lake at Princesa Diana Avenue, 760, Alphaville, Lagoa dos Ingleses in Nova Lima, a suburb of Belo Horizonte. The campus in Belo Horizonte is still in operation.

tried and failed to organize successfully. Ten years later, in 1986, Emerson also negotiated the return of the Corporate Law course to the University. 'We had discovered that management was our vocation', he said. 'The vision of an organization focused on applied management gradually became clearer'.

Commitment, Trust and Openness to Change: Drive and Determination to Overcome Difficulty

FDC faced a major crisis in 1981, when Brazil's economic situation had deteriorated rapidly. In the early 1970s the country had experienced the euphoria of fast economic growth but, by the early 1980s, the situation had reversed. In 1981, the country went into a recession and the GDP variation was minus 4.3%. The demand for new FDC courses declined and there were no enrolments at all for some courses.

FDC had invested a lot of energy and resources in a project with a large French business school (CESA, now part of *Groupe HEC*). The project brought notoriety in terms of the institution's image but ended with a financial deficit. FDC found itself without enough resources to pay its employees and was unable to meet its financial obligations in the short and medium terms. Rumours circulated about its imminent closure.

The team took steps to extract FDC from its predicament. The most radical step was the decision by Emerson and his management colleagues to cut their own salaries by 50% for a period of 6 months. They managed to obtain a similar 50% reduction in their rental costs, thanks to Dom Serafim's mediation and negotiations between the FDC and the Catholic Church which owned the building.

In addition to cutting its expenditure, FDC needed liquidity to be able to operate through the crisis. It obtained long-term financing at a reasonable interest rate and was able to survive over time. However, the bank asked for real estate as collateral, something FDC did not have, so Emerson and his wife used their own home as collateral for the loan.

In addition to reorganizing its finances, FDC underwent another change in the sale of its products and the relationship with its customers. In the early years it had focused on offering open programs that needed large investments in communications and marketing. All that was about to change.

Partnerships With Clients and Additional International Alliances

In 1980, FDC introduced a new strategy that not only allowed it to survive but also became a decisive factor in its success: designing bespoke training programs and forming partnerships with companies.

According to Emerson: 'The history of FDC is a history of partnerships with companies on the one hand, and alliances with international schools on the other'. The first partnership was formed in 1980. At the time, the Brazilian government was facing a financial crisis due to high levels of foreign debt and decided to set up programs to promote exports. However, Brazilian companies were not accustomed to exporting.

This is what Emerson had to say about the situation: 'They had neither the information nor the experience in foreign trade to export ... Reading the newspapers and following debates on the economy, we discovered that the need to train executives in export operations was an opportunity. So we proposed an association with companies. We established the Centro de Estudos e de Desenvolvimento para a Exportação – (CEDEX) in collaboration with 14 companies that made significant financial contributions to support the initiative'.[13]

Companies came to CEDEX to learn about new export rules, international markets, international marketing and so on. The programme was introduced at the right time to meet the needs of large numbers of people and organizations with an interest in exporting. The shift towards training executives and companies in the foreign trade sector gradually gained momentum and FDC found itself in the coordinating role. Minas Gerais eventually became the second most important Brazilian state in terms of exports.[14] The country's main foreign trade agents, in both the public and private sectors, began to engage with the State, helping to consolidate a culture focused on exports, thanks mainly to the annual 'Minas Export Award', promoted in partnership with *Diário do Comércio*.

Nine years later, in 1989, the Brazilian economy, which had been closed to foreign products until then, was gradually moving towards a more open structure. This was the year of the country's first direct presidential election since the end of the military regime. The candidate who was favourite in the polls, Fernando Collor de Mello, had promised to open up the Brazilian market and in fact did so after his election and investiture in March 1990. Entrepreneurs were worried that foreign companies might invade the market and feared that the new open market context would be a serious threat to their businesses. Emerson and his team identified this as an opportunity for additional development at the FDC. Here is what he had to say about it:

> Realizing that entrepreneurs were worried, we decided to invite a group of them to talk about the subject. We contacted every Brazilian state to sell our project, which we named the Centro de Tecnologia Empresarial (CTE).[15] Entrepreneurs were interested in our idea of creating a center in conjunction with them, to support them through the transition from closed to open economy. They needed it. We wanted to train high-level executives for a more competitive, open economy. Ten large Brazilian companies or multinational companies based in Brazil joined us and put money into the program.

[13]In English: Center for the Study and Development of Foreign Trade.
[14]Brasil has 26 states.
[15]In English: Management Technology Center.

Imaginative Proposal to Create *With* and not *For* the Client

Why did companies decide to take part? Why did they trust FDC and not another institution to develop their executives? Here is Emerson's answer to the question.

> It met a real need. We suggested setting up a center with the companies, instead of just for them. All CTE's creation, formulation and structuring documents were prepared together, with the participation of the companies, not just by the FDC technical team. The companies became the co-founders and co-owners of the Center. It would become the CTE's fundamental characteristic. At meetings, I never said: 'Let's do this or that.' Instead, I said: 'We have a problem. Let's find a solution together.' The Programa de Gestão Avançada (PGA) was born out of this partnership, in an alliance with INSEAD, an internationally recognized school in France. The directors of the main Brazilian and multinational companies operating in Latin America were involved and are still involved.[16]

Journalists Became Trainers and Broke the Rules of Traditional Managerial Approaches

CTE started its operations in 1988, with 10 large companies. By 2006 this number had grown to 25. Building on the success of the programme, FDC set up new groups of companies working in partnership on specific projects. CTE became a model for new programs with companies. These were not simply isolated programs or training; on the contrary, FDC monitored learning and promoted knowledge sharing and the creation of networks between participants. This is how Emerson explained how the partnerships worked:

> My colleagues and I who set up FDC were all journalists. A reporter's work is to uncover what is happening in society by identifying events that can be turned into news. Our journalistic background was very helpful at both the Extension Center and the FDC. The secret lay in our habit of getting to know and understanding our clients. This meant carefully monitoring the companies' external environment: what was happening in the market, in the economy, in society, in politics, and so on. I always read the daily newspapers, much more than books on management. When we were looking for companies to set up our first partnership, CEDEX and then CTE, we knew what was

[16]In English: Advanced Management Program.

> happening, what worried people and what was of interest to the companies.

Thanks to their journalistic background, FDC's key players had the skills they needed to draft programs in consultation with the client base, and to define learning needs in collaboration with users. This approach minimized the risk of failure, since the involvement of the people concerned meant that the result was more likely to be satisfactory to them. Typical academic activities were replaced or complemented by exchanges of experience and knowledge between participants, enriching the educational process. Relationship networks helped to generate know-how.

In 1992, FDC set up the Parceiros para a Excelência Programme (PAEX) aimed at small and medium-sized companies. Five years later, 190 companies from Brazil, Argentina, Chile, Ecuador and Paraguay were involved in the programme. Ultimately, there were more than 500 companies from all over Brazil.[17]

In 1999, FDC set up the Parceria para o Desenvolvimento do Acionista e da Família Empresária Program (PDA), initially intended for six family businesses.[18] A few years later, the initiative had attracted more than 50 partner companies. In 2003, it set up the Global Players' Project for Brazilian companies wanting to expand their activities beyond Brazil's borders, but subsequently discontinued it. The FDC's most significant partnership came more recently, with the CEOs' Legacy initiative, which brings together an impressive group of company leaders interested in designing ways of transferring their legacy.

Open Innovation in Practice

Until the late 1980s, FDC was still a local and regional organization and most of its clients came from its home state. Later, through the creation of the CTE and additional partnerships with companies, it was able to acquire clients from other Brazilian states and even from abroad. As a result, it became a national organization. Emerson commented:

> Our institution, small and local, still fragile and with little experience, suddenly found itself with large companies, some already multinational, associated with the CTE and expecting our support.[19] We'd had the audacity to recruit them, but then we had to figure out how to support them. I'm talking about companies with the stature of Rhodia, Petrobras, Metal Leve, ABB, Phillips, Xerox, Natura and others, all of which joined the CTE. It was a huge challenge! Fortunately, the director of one of

[17]In English: Partners for Excellence.

[18]In English: Shareholder and Business Family Development Partnership.

[19]In Brazil, the best institutions in the field had, until that time, been concentrated in the cities of São Paulo and Rio de Janeiro.

> the companies advised us to look for an institution with international experience that would agree to help us improve our level of competency.

Cooperation with international institutions was one of the measures used by FDC to create conditions in which it could serve its clients properly. At the time, in 1990, FDC entered into an alliance with INSEAD (the European Institute of Business Administration located in Fontainebleau near Paris, France), which Emerson had visited in 1975 during his time at the Extension Center.

INSEAD is one of more than a hundred institutions Emerson visited throughout the world, even before FDC was created. The visits enabled him to form an international network of alliances, some of which still exist today. He became familiar with the world's main business schools and their Deans and directors, developing his knowledge of executive education programs and approaches.

> From the time the Extension Center was established, I began to travel to see other structures in operation. When I came back from each trip, I used to meet with my colleagues to tell them about what I had seen. Sharing this information has always been a way to generate ideas and discover how to take advantage of them. As a result of this, we formed the first international alliance with Group HEC Paris. We used to send managers and teachers there to perfect their skills, and HEC professors came to work with us. We did case studies and wrote books.

In the 1990s, FDC's early alliances with HEC Paris and INSEAD opened the door to partnerships with the *Kellogg School of Management at Northwestern University* in Evanston (close to Chicago), the *Sauder Business School* – a faculty at the University of British Columbia (UBC) – in Vancouver, Columbia University in New York (Columbia Centre on Sustainable Investment), Fudan University in China, the Skolkovo Management School in Russia and the Indian Business School (IBS).

A network of schools in Argentina, Peru, Chile and Mexico was also set up. At the instigation of the then Dean of the University of Chile's Business School, Emerson also launched the Spanish version of his first book *Plantando Carvalhos – Fundamentos da Empresa Relevante*. The FDC's international incursion peaked with the creation of the International Advisory Council, with the support of Emerson's close friend, Professor Donald P. Jacobs, then Dean of the Kellogg School of Management. The Council has been in operation for 10 years and continues to be an important FDC asset.

The Influence of International Networks: An Emerging Institution Fostering New and Innovative Approaches

Every visit to a foreign business school became an opportunity for Emerson to refine his vision and think about what could be done at FDC. Over the years, thanks to these visits, he was better able to understand how to design an identity for FDC. His vision also evolved and became closely tied to the needs of Brazilian managers and senior executives.

> I was able to clarify our true vocation through my visits to other schools and by attending meetings of the associations of which they were members. As I developed a comparative picture of other schools, I came to realize that FDC was not a traditional business school; it was a center for the development of executives and companies. Our field of action is education. What people conventionally refer to as the teaching of business administration is carried out by a very diverse set of institutions. Some are dependent, part of a university, and offer MBA programs as part of their activities (Kellogg School of Management). Others, besides being part of a university, offer undergraduate courses as the central focus of their activities (Sauder Business School). These schools have a lot of academic professors and research is what predominates. Our characteristics bring us closer to organizations such as IMD (Lausanne – Switzerland) and Ashridge (Hult Ashridge Executive Education – England), both of which are independent institutions with a strong focus on applied knowledge.[20]

Energy, Self-Learning and Vision

Setting up and managing partnerships with companies and alliances with international schools, in addition to the day-to-day operations of FDC, required a great deal of energy, as well as emotional balance and the ability to learn from experience. Emerson notes that, over time, he was able to design a vision of what he hoped to achieve, the place he wanted to occupy on the market, and the type of organization he needed to do this.

> To set up the CTE, we visited roughly 50 large companies. Once the CTE had been established, we brought together between 20 and 25 managers from those companies, every three months for several years. We often visited associate companies to exchange ideas and listen to their concerns, so that we could help them adapt to their needs. I also spent a lot of time observing and learning

[20]International Institute for Management Development (IMD Business School).

> from other schools abroad – I would say nearly 30% of my time was devoted to visits to institutions and seminars with entrepreneurs or colleagues from other institutions throughout the world.

Emerson developed a number of habits to help maintain his emotional balance: for example, he swam 1,000 metres 5 days a week, alternating with Pilates. In addition, he operated a dairy farm where the cows were still milked the old-fashioned way, and he raised birds in the wild, something he learned with the help of a colleague from FDC.

His favourite time of the day has been and still remains the 5 a.m. milking, followed by lively conversation with the farm hands over coffee and dry bread. His days on the farm bring him into contact with nature, which he appreciates. At the same time, he undergoes psychotherapy. 'I've been in therapy with a psychiatrist for many years. It helps me get to know myself and understand other people better'.

A number of people are important and also inspire him, one way or another. On the first page of his book there are three quotations: 'To my father, source of identity', 'To my wife and children, source of warmth' and 'To Dom Serafim Fernandes de Araújo, source of autonomy'. He adds Don Jacobs from the Kellogg School of Management who, in addition to being a friend, was a source of inspiration and helped with the construction of the FDC campus in Nova Lima and the creation of the International Advisory Council.

Emerson mentions the culture of 'a job well done' that he inherited from his father. One day, while they were planting *jabuticaba* seedlings (a typical Brazilian native fruit), he noticed that the holes dug by his father were identical in depth and width.

> My father was my companion, my friend. Together we planted many hundreds of trees, and every time, it was the same level of precision: the holes were 60 centimeters deep and 40 centimeters wide. He liked to work very precisely ... He used a tape measure when digging the holes. They had to be 60 centimeters; 59 or 61 would not do. That's how precise he was.

The Perceptions of Employees and Collaborators

To understand how collaborators and employees viewed Emerson's leadership, the authors of this case study collected information from people who were among the first to be involved in the project. One of them was Afonso Cozzi, who was Associate Dean from 1977 to 1999. He was involved in several phases of the FDC's growth and consolidation in Brazil, and played a role in projects with business schools across North America and Europe. Since then he has been involved with FDC's Center of Entrepreneurship and Innovation, first as Coordinator and more recently as a professor. He had this to say:

> The FDC project was led by Emerson de Almeida from the beginning and throughout. He always insisted on excellence as an integral part of all our activities. Through his decisions he clearly showed his determination to establish international partnerships and position FDC as one of the world's elite executive education schools. His vision was always inspiring and he was never afraid of innovation. In particular, he focused on building a team of executives and professors with a solid academic background and the ability to communicate their practical experience of business management.

Emerson de Almeida Beyond FDC

Emerson had a dream of building an exceptional institution that would be instrumental in constructing a Brazil with the capacity to be an economic power, and he was able to turn it into reality. While he did not manufacture 'a million Brazilian boats, ships and airplanes carrying the Brazilian flag all over the world', as he had dreamt of doing when he was 17 years old, he nevertheless helped to educate Brazilian executives and give them the skills they needed to achieve their dreams.

However, building an economically strong country was not his only dream. He also dreamt of a fairer Brazil, without social inequality. He still has that dream. He knows that Brazil needs social development as well as economic development, and this particular task is far from over. He therefore still wants to expand FDC's agenda to include people in vulnerable situations. He has the support of the Board of Trustees and most of his FDC colleagues for this.

> Brazil has more inequalities than any other country in the world (...). It will take 20 to 30 years to achieve significant, visible, concrete results in reducing the social deficit. For us at FDC, it is not just about developing executives, public and private managers and entrepreneurs, but about building a fairer, more equitable society. This will be my main focus until I leave the institution.

In Emerson's view, FDC must be useful to society. 'If the community does not see it as being useful, it will disappear', he says. 'Being useful to society' is one of FDC's eight principles.

Transferring the Dream: Wisdom and Creativity in Finding a Successor

Emerson knows that other factors, in addition to social utility, are crucial to ensuring the longevity and development of an institution like FDC. One of these factors is the leadership succession process. He knows of several organizations that disappeared after an abrupt succession. In 2007, when he celebrated his 66th birthday, he began to prepare the process of appointing a successor, monitored by the Board of Trustees and with the support of his management colleagues.

He had been FDC's chief executive since the institution was first established in 1976, and his term of office was due to end in 2012. In 2008, he sent an internal memo to all employees, informing them that he considered his current 4-year term to be his last. 'I'm convinced that FDC's longevity requires renewal at all levels and functions, in a timely way'. To prepare the organization for this, and to avoid abruptness, his successor was chosen a year before the end of his term, in 2011.

> Over the past few years, I've spent a lot of time trying to write down the fundamentals of FDC for the next few years. This is a contribution to the future Dean and to the new generation. It led to the publication of a book, entitled 'Plantando Carvalhos – Fundamentos da Empresa Relevante' which, along with the document entitled 'The FDC's Strategy for 2026', approved by the Board of Trustees, would serve as inspiration for the new generation.[21]

The aim of the first FDC succession phase was to transition from a long-standing administration (almost 35 years), one that had shaped the nature and the culture of the organization, to a new reality for the institution. In March 2012, the new Dean, Wagner Furtado Veloso, officially took over a mandate with no defined term (he would remain in the position until the end of 2015) and Emerson became President of the Board of Governance.

Emerson notes that:

> In agreement with the Board of Trustees, the first succession was based on the concept of 'transition', to prepare the organization and myself for a more profound change. I remained at FDC, but only as the guardian of its mission and values, with no direct involvement in operations. Both the organization and I needed to go through a period of learning. The word 'transition' meant a process spread over a certain amount of time (an intermediate phase). The successor had no defined term of office.

[21] In English: Planting Oak Trees – Fundamentals of the relevant company – See the list of publications at the end of this case study.

> The atmosphere was easy throughout the process and I was overwhelmed by a sense of peace and tranquility and of 'mission accomplished'. My father was no longer in the audience, as he had been when the campus was first opened, but I imagined him feeling proud and saying that everything I had led the FDC team to do was worthwhile.

Emerson says the first succession period was governed by the term 'transition' and the second by 'evolution'. The second phase, based on what had been learned from the first, comprised a strategic reflection involving all the employees, on the future positioning of FDC in the global market. The final report emphasized the need for change. Emerson also listened to what was being said internally, an initiative that added to the robustness of the process.

Much was learned from the first change of command and this learning was used to prepare a second change for the longer term.

> Under Wagner Veloso's stewardship, we understood that the transition phase between the first administration and the next had been completed, and that the institution now needed to prepare for a new challenge. While FDC was still under Wagner Veloso's direction, we chose a group of collaborators to carry out a strategic reflection on the FDC's future positioning in the global market (horizon of 2020). As we chose the collaborators and followed the process of reflection, we were able to identify emerging leaders.
>
> The final report indicated a need for change, while preserving the organization's mission, principles and climate. It was also clear that the new Dean's main mission would be to lead the team as it implemented the vision for the proposed new positioning. We therefore instituted a robust internal listening process, meeting with the Board of Trustees committee appointed to monitor the process and obtaining the support of a consultant specialized in succession. During these meetings, questions were raised about behaviour (cultural alignment, influence on colleagues, etc.), governance and leadership (guidance for clients and results, knowledge of the organization, etc.) and emotional quotient, at both the intrapersonal (self-awareness and self-control) and interpersonal (understanding the emotions of colleagues and building social networks) levels.

Emerson goes on:

> I decided to do the interviews with all the personnel myself, but I always reported the results to the other committee members. One of the things I wanted to hear was the employees' opinion

> regarding who should be on the implementation team. I asked everyone: Who do you see leading the team? Obviously it wasn't a question of counting votes in a ballot box, but of identifying the qualifications and attributes people felt the ideal candidate should have.

This information was crucial when deciding who should replace Wagner Veloso. At the same time, a consulting firm specialized in succession processes had been hired to carry out an assessment. Both these processes led to the same conclusion and Antonio Batista da Silva Junior was appointed Dean of the institution in January, 2016.

In his book entitled *A Sucessão como ela é – de sentimentos a jogos políticos nas organizações*, Emerson reports and discusses the experience of leaders and companies during succession processes.[22] He focuses on two aspects, one subjective (the human aspect) and the other objective (the technical issues impacting organizations). When addressing the subjective aspect, he draws on his own experience, describing the contradictory feelings that emerged during the succession and replacement process. When addressing the objective aspect, he highlights the instability that occurs when a succession is too abrupt and the stability that is achieved by a programmed, gradual succession process, when an organization takes the time to develop a foundation from which it can reinvent itself under a new leadership.

After leaving the executive position at FDC, Emerson, the intrapreneur, went back to his roots, to become an entrepreneur again. This time, however, there was no market stall; instead, he developed and operated two small vineyards in Mendoza, Argentina: *Pedacito del Cielo and Gracias a la Vida* (producing a wine of the same name). 'This is the title of a Latin American song that celebrates life among friends and family, and I chose it to be the name of my wine for obvious reasons'.[23] His new life allows him to enjoy nature and work on real products. Some people call this 'entrepreneurial happiness'; others call it 'entrepreneurial wisdom'.

Legacy and Future Prospects

Emerson has always been a dreamer who dares to 'do': in other words, a builder. He has always been true to himself. From a student leader swimming against the tide, he went on to become a journalist fighting injustice. This, in turn, led him to

[22]In English: Succession as it is – from feelings to political games in organizations.

[23]Gracias a la vida is s a popular folk song composed and originally performed by Chilean singer Violeta Parra.

become an intrapreneur who co-created and developed FDC.[24] FDC was Brazil's first-ever higher learning institution to develop a revolutionary method that involved designing executive training *with* companies instead of *for* companies. Throughout his life, he also maintained his interest in farming.

His gradual departure from FDC may have impacted not only FDC itself, but also executive learning in Brazil. He had been one of the leaders responsible for a profound change in Brazil's business culture by transmitting his international culture to senior Brazilian executives. Early in his career, he studied in Europe for 2 years and continued to learn from international institutions throughout his life. As a result, he developed and was able to communicate his own, very particular culture as an entrepreneur, intrapreneur, international learner and innovator. It is difficult to assess the impact of his departure on Brazil's business culture.

Over the decades, FDC has become a hive where people go to learn the practical aspects of business development and international activity. But it has also become the centre of a networking system where people learn by observing and being inspired by successful executives. What can FDC now do to accentuate these aspects?

Emerson always wanted FDC to serve not only Brazil's organizational leaders, but also the country as a whole. Was his dream idealistic or achievable? Might FDC go on to develop social entrepreneurship programs? What about the ecological concerns of the younger generations? What types of programs should be developed to address these emerging aspirations? What kind of profile will the executives of the future need?

Awards

1981 – Inconfidência dos Méritos Cívicos – Medal from the Government of the State of Minas Gerais

1987 – Inconfidência dos Méritos Excepcionais – Great Medal from the Government of the State of Minas Gerais

2001 – Federaminas National Entrepreneur Award (Federation of Commercial, Industrial, Agricultural and Livestock Associations of Minas Gerais), in recognition of his performance as Dean of Fundação Dom Cabral

2006 – President Juscelino Kubistchek Medal – from the Government of Minas Gerais

2006 – Business Leader in the Education Sector, from Gazeta Mercantil Newspaper

[24]Emerson de Almeida considers that FDC was co-founded by himself and Dom Serafim Fernandes de Araújo (1924–2019), then the President of Pontifícia Universidade Católica de Minas Gerais (nowadays PUC Minas), who was the supporting leader without whom Emerson considers the project would not have been possible. Dom Serafim was appointed Cardinal by Pope John Paul II in 1998.

2006 – Economist Maria Regina Nabuco Medal for Excellence in Teaching and Research - Minas Gerais Economic Development Award – ASSEMG/ COMMON MARKET
2009 – Juscelino Kubitschek Order Medal from the Minas Gerais Commercial Association
2010 – Elected as one of the 100 most influential Brazilians by Revista Época
2011 – Consular Merit Medal from the State of Minas Gerais
2013 – Outstanding Economist of Minas Gerais
2013 – Joaquim José Da Silva Xavier – Tiradentes Medal
2016 – Business Merit Medal – Federaminas
2017 – ADCE Minas Award (Association of Christian Business Leaders – MG) for social and corporate responsibility – for his contribution to the reinforcement of ethics and sustainability in business and society, based on Christian values
2018 – Order of Merit Medal – Infraero.

Publications

- Fundamentos da Empresa Relevante - Meu aprendizado na FDC, Campus/ Elsevier, 2006
- Plantando Carvalhos – Fundamentos da Empresa Relevante – Campus/ Elsevier, 2011
- Plantando Robles – Fundamentos de la Empresa Relevante – Campus/ Elsevier, 2013
- A sucessão como ela é – de sentimentos a jogos políticos nas organizações – Saraiva, 2016
- Many articles.

Case Discussion

Emerson de Almeida

(1) Emerson de Almeida operated a stand with his brother in a public market. Was this a good way to prepare for his future career as a journalist, an innovationist and an agent of innovation?
(2) When he was young, Emerson was a big dreamer. He envisioned his country, Brazil, becoming a major industrial state. Was this a realistic way of preparing to become a social leader and an innovationist?
(3) As a student leader, Emerson went against the trends of a dictatorship and took on a controversial role as a journalist denouncing its abuses. How well did this prepare him for his future role as an agent of innovation? Why? Explain your answer.
(4) Emerson developed an organization in the field of management education, but he knew nothing about education or management or management

education. Given this, how do you explain the fact that Fundaçao Dom Cabral became so well-known for the quality of its management education programs and courses?

(5) Is it easier to become an intrapreneur or an entrepreneur? Which role requires a higher level of innovation? Which role involves higher levels of risk? For each role, which aspects are the most difficult to cope with?

(6) Intrapreneurs have often been described as people who go into work every day knowing that they might be fired at any moment. How did Emerson manage to survive? What lessons did you learn from his experience as an intrapreneur?

(7) In your opinion, is it easier to be an intrapreneur in a large organization or a small one? In the private sector or in the public sector?

(8) What advice would you have given to Emerson to make sure the organization he created would continue to be innovative and dynamic after his retirement?

(9) After his retirement, Emerson became an entrepreneur. Why do you think so many intrapreneurs eventually become entrepreneurs?

(10) Identify the three most meaningful and useful lessons you learned from Emerson's life history. Have these lessons changed the way you will approach innovation? Have they changed your thoughts on becoming (or not becoming) an agent of innovation?

Acknowledgements

The authors thank the HEC Montréal Case Center for its support (http://www.hec.ca/en/case_centre). The citations in the current version of the case study, produced in 2020, were taken from several interviews with Emerson de Almeida. The first was conducted on 8 May 2006, by Fernando Dolabela and Louis Jacques Filion at Emerson de Almeida's office on the institution's new campus at Alphaville, Lagoa dos Ingleses, in Nova Lima, a suburb of Belo Horizonte, in the Brazilian state of Minas Gerais. The second was conducted on 1 June 2006, by Cândido Borges and Louis Jacques Filion at HEC Montréal. Both interviews lasted about three hours. They were taped and transcribed. Additional information on Fundação Dom Cabral can be found on the following website: www.fdc.org.br. The authors thank Emerson de Almeida for his gracious collaboration throughout the years.

Section 4

Chapter 7

Lessons for Innovationists and Aspiring Agents of Innovation

Louis Jacques Filion

Keywords: Teamwork; mentor; advisory board; complementary expertise; alliances subcontract

The stories in this book describe the activities of three different categories and six different types of agents of innovation. Despite their widely differing personalities and contexts, their behaviours and actions were nevertheless similar in many respects. For example, they all innovated by creating something new, which they then took to the market. Some agents of innovation are inventors of the product/service they market. Others adapt and add improvements, contributing additional value to an existing product, service or process. This chapter reflects about lessons learned from agents of innovation.

Entrepreneurs take the risk of producing and marketing something that is new, using their own resources. Facilitators and intrapreneurs do the same thing, but they use the resources of the organization that employs them. The level of their innovation may be outstanding but their level of risk is not the same as that of an entrepreneur.

The capacity to communicate internally and externally is increasingly important for all categories of agents of innovation. Markets keep changing and organizations must pivot continually to adjust to changing market conditions. To do this, external communications with users, and often with sub-contractors who are well-informed about what is happening in the sector and related sectors, are needed to remain up-to-date with evolving needs. Information on what competitors are doing is a 'must'. Continuous internal communications with facilitators to share information about market and technology changes are also essential.

Entrepreneurs

Entrepreneurs identify a need and transform it into an opportunity by designing a product or service that they then market as an innovation. The entrepreneur's work has become more sophisticated in recent decades. For example, many

Agents of Innovation, 195–200

doi:10.1108/978-1-83797-012-420231007

entrepreneurs now work in teams, using the expertise of specialists who serve as internal or external facilitators. They seek advice from mentors and set up advisory boards composed of external facilitators with experience. They also tend to make more alliances with other entrepreneurs who contribute complementary expertise to their own.

In addition, the market has become global and is flooded each year by countless new products. Entrepreneurs now subcontract many of their activities, especially manufacturing. In short, they have become not only designers and creators of innovation, but also coordinators of human, manufacturing, financial, marketing and technological resources. As a result, they need to have a clear vision and the ability to communicate and work with many players inside and outside their firms, including specialized facilitators. Many entrepreneurs began as intrapreneurs. This is how they first learned their craft.

In both cases they have understood that the ability to structure a guiding thread, in the form of a vision, allows them to look to the future in a more coherent way. This guiding thread helps them to select the right people, especially facilitators, with whom it will be easier to work in a learning and creative environment. Entrepreneurs are learners and constant innovators. These skills have become more important as the speed of change increases in markets everywhere. The ability to self-renew and communicate impacts the dynamics of the entrepreneur's relationships with the members of his or her team, and especially with the facilitators who also play a role in the ongoing process of learning and renewal.

Agents of innovation require emotional, analytical, imaginative, systemic, relational and practical intelligence. Entrepreneurs are no exception. They must be able to commit deeply and learn about the sector and topic. They need to be creative in inventing new methods and patterns and be organized enough to assess risk. They design and share visions that they use to recruit, assess, develop and manage proper relationships inside the firm. They integrate and develop networks outside the firm (including social networks) and develop judgement with regard to the timing of action.

Facilitators

Many facilitators are highly educated. Often, their knowledge of their own area of responsibility goes far beyond that of most of the organization's other managers, including the entrepreneur. The entrepreneur invents products that do not exist; the facilitator invents processes that do not exist in order to render the entrepreneur's innovations viable. Facilitators must therefore understand the entrepreneur's vision and devise original ways of operationalizing it. They need space to express their creativity. This requires a high level of trust on the part of their entrepreneur.

In small firms where the leaders tend to be more familiar with their close collaborators and employees, it is usually easier for them to identify facilitators who will support their projects. In micro-enterprises, for example, innovations tend to be concentrated around the entrepreneur's projects. This dynamic is a function not only of the entrepreneur's ability to communicate, but also of the potential facilitator's ability to listen, understand and respond creatively.

Facilitation demands emotional intelligence in order to relate closely to the leader and his or her projects. It also requires well-articulated, analytical, imaginative, systemic, relational and practical intelligence. Facilitators need to know the subject inside out, be creative, have a well-organized mind, understand the entrepreneur's vision, use their judgement when interacting with the entrepreneur and other key players, integrate networks inside and outside the firm and accurately evaluate the timing of actions.

Intrapreneurs

Intrapreneurial practice is subject to the same requirements as entrepreneurial practice although the risk is usually lower. As intrapreneurs, people can give free rein to their innovative skills even when the context is not fully conducive. They do the same kinds of things as entrepreneurs – designing and implementing innovations – but they do so in a context where they do not control the resources.

Intrapreneurs usually express a high level of loyalty to their clients. They do what they feel they should do to serve their clients as best they can, often in spite of bureaucratic rules. Eventually, many will launch their own firms and will become successful doing what they were not allowed to do by their former employers.

The life stories of the two intrapreneurs presented in this book are similar in some respects and different in others. For example, Elmar Mock went against the culture of the watch-making company for which he worked. He knew he was risking dismissal by doing so. Emerson de Almeida was in a similar situation. Both Elmar and Emerson survived thanks to the support of strong organizational leaders who stood by them in spite of pressure to make them conform to the culture and customs of the conservative enterprises and sectors in which they worked. These visionary leaders understood that their 'deviant' agents of innovation were giving the organization an opportunity to renew itself through the radical innovation they were proposing.

Intrapreneurs are sometimes regarded as outcasts or even renegades by bureaucratic and rigid employees who see them using the enterprise's resources for their own purposes, not realizing that they are doing so to improve the situation of clients and therefore being useful to the enterprise that is hiring them.

Characteristics of Agents of Innovation

Table 2 summarizes the main characteristics of agents of innovation and presents five key characteristics of each of the three categories of agents of innovation described in this book.

Table 2. Agents of Innovation in Action: Some Characteristics.

Entrepreneurs	Facilitators	Intrapreneurs
Generate innovations	Continually think of ways to improve what the entrepreneur and organization do	Pay particular attention to user/client needs
Design a vision: a space to be occupied on the market	Understand the entrepreneur's vision and designs imaginative ways of realizing it successfully	Design added value for clients and for potential new clients
Assess risks (most of the time)	Ensure that visions are implemented profitably	Generate innovations that may endanger their survival in the organization
Commit with passion	Commit deeply	Commit prudently in contexts where they may not control the organization of work or use of resources
Lead and moderate a team, in an upbeat way	Maintain a strong bond with the entrepreneur	Learn to work in contexts where internal support may be needed to survive and maintain their project alive

Which Role Should I Choose?

As an innovationist, you may be wondering which of these three roles you should choose. The answer depends on many factors associated with whom you are, what expertise and skills you have, where you are, how you are surrounded, what you plan to achieve, the stage you have reached in your career and your level of expertise in the area in which you would like to innovate. The context in which you work can make a difference. Circumstances often play a role in the emergence of agents of innovation. Remember that 'luck comes to those who are prepared'. People become agents of innovation because their minds were already set on it.

Coco Chanel became an entrepreneur at a young age. Her father was self-employed. As a child, she learned sewing with her mother and, as a teenager, with the nuns who educated her. Her lovers helped to trigger her interest in innovation. She then started to design and make hats for women and sold them on beaches in summer. Her lovers went on to become mentors, coaches and facilitators. They played a major supporting role in helping her to establish her business and create her enterprise. Although she often found it difficult to work with facilitators, for example during the creation and marketing of her perfume, she herself went on to become an external facilitator, through her support for artists.

Alain Bouchard was a facilitator for several years, before he went on to become an intrapreneur in the same sector. During all that time, he watched and learnt from the entrepreneurs and top managers who employed him. However, his commitment caused frictions with some employers. Throughout his career, he remained committed to his store managers, helping them to improve their innovative capabilities. Réal Plourde, his main facilitator, designed training programs to prepare store managers to be more efficient, learn to read their environment and become more innovative.

The facilitators and intrapreneurs described in this book all had experience as entrepreneurs, facilitators and intrapreneurs at some point in their careers. They were led by circumstances to adopt one of these roles in the longer term. If you are an innovationist considering a role as an agent of innovation, you may be able to choose the role that interests you the most and prepare for it accordingly, but circumstances may also be your deciding factor. In becoming an innovationist, you have developed fertile ground for many potential career paths. You will be ready to become an agent of innovation when the opportunity arises.

You may be highly creative but unable to live with the uncertainty and risk that entrepreneurs must accept, or you may not have the level of versatility needed to lead a firm. If this is the case, starting out as a facilitator or an intrapreneur may be a better choice. You may intend to remain in your current profession, but becoming an innovationist may open many new potential avenues for you. This often happens to engineers and lawyers who gradually become involved in more innovative activities.

Many entrepreneurs have been able to develop because they knew how to surround themselves with facilitators. Thomas Edison and Steve Jobs, for example, were team leaders and product developers throughout their lives because they were able to work with facilitators, sometimes motivating them but always pushing them to their limits. The phenomenon of team entrepreneurship is growing and has become a way of sharing the pressure of uncertainty. Interactive commitment to a project can be very creative. It is useful to think about the people with whom you will surround yourself, inside and outside the firm.

In recent decades, many different types of agents of innovation have emerged, in established sectors such as technology and manufacturing but also in emerging sectors such as ecology and cooperation, as well as in social, psychological and other human services. Entrepreneurial activity serves as the model for these emerging forms of innovative practice. The fields of innovation and entrepreneurship have always been intertwined, and this is increasingly the case today. More trained people are needed to understand and apply innovation at all levels and across all sectors.

This book is intended to be a celebration of this emerging interest in innovation, and especially in the practice of team innovation. As the speed of change accelerates, growing numbers of people are beginning to think about how they can best prepare for a more innovative life. There is room for everyone. I hope the six agents of innovation presented in this book will serve as inspiration on your own personal journey.

Appendix

From Innovationist to Agent of Innovation

The Seven Exercises

The exercises that follow are meant to be completed after reading the life histories presented in this book. They focus on how people relate to and think about innovation: who agents of innovation are, how they think, what they do, how they do it and the main differences between entrepreneurs, facilitators and intrapreneurs. You should identify three, four or five different characteristics for each of these three categories. The idea is to help you organize your mind so that you can situate yourself more clearly with respect to the category you think suits you best. The exercises will prepare you to become more innovative, and to make better use of yourself and of your capabilities.

Exercise 1: Preliminary Self-Assessment

(1) What is your favourite category of agent of innovation? Why? Did one of the case studies present a more appropriate role model for you? If so, why?
(2) Which sectors are more attractive to you? Name three and indicate the one you prefer. Why do you prefer it? Give at least three reasons.
(3) What kinds of partners would you like to work with? What are your criteria when identifying and selecting potential partners or collaborators?
(4) What makes you potentially attractive as an agent of innovation for an enterprise?
(5) What value will you add to society? What will you do to support sustainable development?

Exercise 2: Defining Your Own Creative Model for Innovation

Like many people, you may be unsure of your own innovative potential. Is your creative culture developed enough to support the creation of innovations? Could you become an agent of innovation? If so, what kind? What would your trademark be? What can you do to develop your innovative potential?

(1) How do you perceive agents of innovation? Describe six of their main characteristics.
(2) Describe three initiatives or innovations in which you have played a role in the past.
(3) Describe at least two of the roles you played in these initiatives or innovations. Were you the initiator? Did you manage a group or bring people together? Were you responsible for development or for implementation or for both?
(4) Why do you want to become an agent of innovation? Describe at least three motivating factors.
(5) If you are serious about it, list at least three elements you will need to learn to achieve your goal.

Exercise 3: Identifying a Need, Creating an Opportunity, Contributing an Innovation

Agents of innovation are people who innovate – in other words, they are people who do new things that contribute added value. A first step is therefore to identify existing or emerging needs for which opportunities may be created, potentially leading to innovations. For intrapreneurs, the needs in question may be identified within their organizations or from listening to customers. For entrepreneurs, the needs will be identified by acute observation of the marketplace. For facilitators, the needs will mostly be related to their understanding of the requirements for realizing the entrepreneur's vision and projects. Once they have understood the needs they have identified, agents of innovation can then find ways to design responses. These are usually innovations that will address the needs identified.

The following exercise should help you to think about the structure you could develop to move forward in a creative way.

(1) Which sector is of most interest to you? Why? What are the main changes that have marked this sector in the last 10 years? List at least five.
(2) What changes do you think will occur in this sector in the next 10 years, and especially in the coming 2 years?
(3) Identify at least two needs generated by these future changes, along with the potential they offer for innovation.
(4) Describe an opportunity arising from one of those needs that could become an innovation compatible with your own background and/or motivations.
(5) Based on your experience and expertise, describe how you could develop and exploit this opportunity. What competitive advantage do you have that will allow you to be successful?

Exercise 4: Defining a Vision

Entrepreneurs and other agents of innovation are explorers, discoverers and conquerors. They like to occupy new territories, and they need tools to do this. One of their most powerful tools is the ability to define and imagine what they want to achieve in the future.

Defining your vision will allow you to establish clearer criteria that you can then use as reference points when choosing activities, resources and people with whom you wish to move forward and work. Your vision will also become a focal point around which you can not only organize your activities but also identify your learning needs to reach the place you wish to occupy in the market.

The following exercise was designed to help you with this process. The innovative craft consists in defining contexts. People who are new to a sector may see things that those with more experience do not see. They may be able to invent new approaches that have previously been overlooked. Be creative in your answers! You should be willing to go beyond existing boundaries!

(1) Where do you see yourself in 20 years' time? What do you want to become?
(2) Briefly describe a new element, product, service or ideal organization that you would like to create.
(3) What will you have to do to convert these dreams into a vision, and then to realize your vision?
(4) How will you use your main strengths to do this? How will you compensate for your main weaknesses?
(5) How will this change the way you organize your professional and personal life?

Exercise 5: Internal Ecosystem – Building an Internal Relations System to Support Innovation: Choosing Partners, Collaborators and Facilitators

The number of firms created by teams has increased steadily in most countries. In recent decades, team venture creation has accounted for more than 75% of SMEs and nearly 100% of technology firms. While the main creator is usually involved full-time in the project and then in the firm, this may not be the case for the other partners. Some become part-time collaborators, while others are investors.

Nevertheless, most of these financial and other partners need to understand the logic underlying the firm's activities. Many have expertise and contacts that may be useful to the firm, for example in opportunity creation, strategic positioning, vision design and, not least, implementation.

When some of the entrepreneurs interviewed for my research were asked to give reasons for their business failures, the most common response was: 'I was surrounded by incompetent people'. When they were asked to give reasons for their successes, the most common response was: 'I'm surrounded by great people and have a very competent team'. Successful entrepreneurs have defined a vision, or at least an embryo of a vision, and have then used it as a criterion for choosing people with complementary competencies with whom they can work to realize that vision.

The following exercise is designed to make you think about how you will choose and recruit the people with whom you will work. Less than 10% of firms achieve growth. It is useful to be aware that growth will not happen unless you learn to communicate and delegate.

(1) Have you been able to formulate a clear definition of your opportunity, vision and proposed innovation, so that you can use it to establish criteria for choosing and hiring people with characteristics that will help you to move forward with your project? Please list five criteria.
(2) Do you intend to spend more time working *in* the firm, managing its operations, or working *on* the firm, on its development? The way you intend to work will have an impact on how you build and manage your internal ecosystem. Please describe what you intend to do in this respect.
(3) Briefly describe the approach you have developed to recruit the people with whom you will work, starting with partners and collaborators. Indicate three elements of the psychological contract you intend to establish with them.
(4) Describe the main tasks you plan to delegate to close collaborators and other employees after starting the project, in each of the following 3 years.
(5) A firm is a social system, and two of the factors with the greatest impact on employee motivation and subsequent involvement are fair treatment and fair performance assessment. Name six performance assessment criteria that you intend to use to create a fair, merit-based social system that your collaborators will regard as being legitimate. How do you intend to reward performance? Through bonuses? Through profit-sharing? Through shareholding opportunities? In other ways?

Exercise 6: External Ecosystem – Building an External Relations System to Support Innovation

The expertise available in an external ecosystem can make all the difference in supporting the sometimes-risky decisions or actions involved in product/service development, new venture creation, venture acquisition or sale and other activities undertaken by agents of innovation. An agent of innovation's relations system plays a major supporting role. These relations usually come from the agent's external ecosystem, or the environment within which he or she works.

The synergy generated by a relations system can have some important effects. The more developed your business network is, the more contacts you have and the more antenna you use to obtain information, the easier and quicker it will be for you to achieve goals that would not otherwise be possible. However, successful agents of innovation do not always have a big or extensive external relations network. Family relations can be extremely important. Indeed, most agents of innovation, especially entrepreneurs, will admit that their success is due more to the people around them than to their business networks at large. However, mentors, coaches and advisory committee members can be very useful.

Some people tend to look to the development of weak-tie relationships – in other words, relations you do not usually develop when you work in a given sector. These relations allow them to explore new hunting territories and identify people who will contribute ideas or perspectives that are different from the norm in their sector. For example, Elmar Mock was one of the first watch makers to train in the emerging plastics sector. This led him to create the Swatch, the world's first plastic watch, a totally new and different product for the watch sector.

The following exercise should help you to become aware of the importance of your external ecosystem and the relations you can derive from it. It will encourage you to start thinking about what you can do to build a relations system more tailored to supporting your vision.

(1) List two strengths and two weaknesses of your current external relations system. Identify at least two new relationship niches that you could explore.
(2) Present and explain four major relationship needs to support the implementation of the vision you defined in the previous exercise.
(3) List two problems you face when developing relationships and three improvements you may need to make to develop a broader range of contacts and better relations.
(4) Describe at least three major characteristics that you would look for in a mentor, in a coach, in members of your advisory board.
(5) List three advantages that agents of innovation would obtain if they included you in their relations systems.

Exercise 7: Becoming Innovative – Acting as an Agent of Innovation

Many people would like to become more creative and innovative. This leads them to think about the form their innovations could take. Some want to improve their innovative skills while continuing to work within existing organizations, while others are looking for projects to create a business.

Being an entrepreneur means not only designing products or services but also negotiating, selling and implementing an innovation. That implies managing risk. Being a facilitator means understanding fits between market characteristics and the resources needed to develop the entrepreneur's projects. Being an intrapreneur means being able not only to design innovations but also to negotiate their implementation within an existing organization.

Regardless of the form your innovative skills will take, you must also develop leadership skills that will allow you to communicate, share and convince. This involves generating enthusiasm and creating movements, often forming a dynamic community around a project. In that community, people should enjoy working towards the achievement of shared goals, where they can feel involved and continue to learn and develop. The following questions should help you to start thinking about these aspects.

(1) What added value can you contribute to increase the level of innovation in a project?
(2) What motivates you? Mention at least three elements. To what extent are you able to commit? Give two examples.
(3) How big is your space? What kind of space do you leave for others? To what extent are you willing to become involved? How far are you willing to go? What are you prepared to risk when bringing your ideas to fruition? Are you a tenacious person?
(4) What are your strengths and weaknesses in terms of bringing people together and forming a team that will work to achieve innovation-focused goals?
(5) What improvements are needed in your ability to evaluate situations? To judge the right time for action? To become a transformational visionary leader?

Comments on the Exercises

You may have found these exercises difficult. You may feel the task of becoming more innovative is a demanding one. If that is the case, you are correct – it is. It can be very hard to create something from scratch. There are levels in the expression of innovation, and, in addition, the entrepreneurial craft is usually something that is superimposed onto a basic craft. As you learn more about your craft and about the innovative process, you will be better able to innovate at higher levels.

My research into agents of innovation has shown that the innovative process is incremental. People continue to learn and become more innovative as they progress within their chosen sector. If you are going to be innovative, you will need to persevere and be able to connect a lot of dots. When you have done this once, it becomes easier. The first step in this process is to become an *innovationist* – someone with a general interest in innovation. From this stepping stone, you can gradually work towards a role as an *agent of innovation*.

Index

Printed in the USA
CPSIA information can be obtained
at www.ICGtesting.com
JSHW011436030624
64243JS00004B/145

9 781837 970131